Electoral Change in Britain since 1945

Making Contemporary Britain Series

General Editor: Anthony Seldon
Consultant Editor: Peter Hennessy

* Indicates title now out of print.

The series *Making Contemporary Britain* is essential reading
for students, as well as providing masterly overviews for the
general reader. Each book in the series puts the central
themes and problems of the specific topic into clear focus.
The studies are written by leading authorities in their field,
who integrate the latest research into the text but at the same
time present the material in a clear, ordered fashion which
can be read with value by those with no prior knowledge of
the subject.

THE INSTITUTE OF CONTEMPORARY
BRITISH HISTORY

Senate House
Malet Street
London WC1H 7HU

Electoral Change in Britain since 1945

Pippa Norris

BLACKWELL
Publishers

The right of Pippa Norris to be identified as the author of this work has been asserted in accordance with the Copyright, Designs and Patents Act 1988.

First published 1997

2 4 6 8 10 9 7 5 3 1

Blackwell Publishers Ltd
108 Cowley Road
Oxford OX4 1JF
UK

Blackwell Publishers Inc.
238 Main Street
Cambridge, Massachusetts 02142
USA

British Library Cataloguing in Publication Data
A CIP catalogue record for this book is available from the British Library

Library of Congress Cataloging-in-Publication Data
Norris, Pippa
    Electoral change in Britain since 1945 / Pippa Norris.
        p.   cm. — (Making contemporary Britain series)
    Includes bibliographical references (p.   ) and index.
    ISBN 0–631–16715–3 (acid-free paper). — ISBN 0–631–16716–1 (pbk.:
    acid-free paper)
        1.   Elections—Great Britain. 2.   Voting—Great Britain. 3.   Party
affiliation—Great Britain. 4.   Great Britain—Politics and government—
1945–   I. Title. II.   Series.
JN956.N668   1997
324.941'085—dc20   96–24899
                                                                   CIP

Typeset in 10 on 12 Ehrhardt by Grahame & Grahame Editorial, Brighton, East Sussex
Printed in Great Britain by Hartnolls Limited, Bodmin, Cornwall
This book is printed on acid-free paper

Contents

Figures

Tables

General Editor's Preface

The Institute of Contemporary British History's series *Making Contemporary Britain* is aimed directly at students and at others interested in learning more about topics in post-war British history. In the series, authors are less attempting to break new ground than presenting clear and balanced overviews of the state of knowledge on each of the topics.

The ICBH was founded in October 1986 with the objective of promoting the study of British history since 1945 at every level. To that end, it publishes books and a quarterly journal, *Contemporary Record*; it organizes seminars and conferences for school students, undergraduates, researchers and teachers of post-war history; and it runs a number of research programmes and other activities.

A central theme of the ICBH's work is that post-war history is too often neglected in British schools, institutes of higher education and beyond. The ICBH acknowledges the validity of the arguments against the study of recent history, notably the problems of bias, of overly subjective teaching and writing, and the difficulties of perspective. But it believes that the values of studying post-war history outweigh the drawbacks, and that the health and future of a liberal democracy require that its citizens know more about the more recent past of their country than the limited knowledge possessed by British citizens, young and old, today. Indeed, the ICBH believes that the dangers of political indoctrination are higher where the young are *not* informed of the recent past.

Pippa Norris's book is a most welcome addition to the series, complementing most obviously David Butler's *General Elections since 1945* (now in its second edition), but also Eric Shaw's and John Stevenson's books on the Labour and Liberal Parties.

Pippa Norris in this book achieves that rare thing: a book which takes account of even the most recent academic literature yet is also accessible to those new to the subject.

The book is divided into four sections. Part I looks at the party system, and shows that whereas Conservative and Labour control of central government has remained a constant factor since 1945, nevertheless the period can be divided into two phases, from 1945 to 1970, which was the era of two-party dominance, and from 1970 to 1992, an era of two-party decline. Part II seeks to explain these developments. She overviews the different theories of voting behaviour and examines core concepts, including partisan and social alignment, and rational 'issue' voting. The arguments for the replacement of traditional class-cleavages by social identities based on gender, generation and region are explored in detail, as are phenomena such as the decline in party membership and increased volatility. This section points to the fact that in the late 1960s and early 1970s there was a decline in class voting and traditional party loyalties.

Part III explores how far these changes may be due, not to the voter, but to structural changes in the parties themselves. Was the SDP–Liberal Alliance phenomenon in the 1980s, for example, a cause or product of changing voting behaviour, i.e. top-down rather than bottom-up? Chapter 8 provides a most original analysis of the representatives the parties chose as their candidates, including women and ethnic minorities, and the effect they may have on the result of elections. Part IV discusses how far political communications have changed (enormously) and what effect they might have on the outcome of elections. A final chapter looks at the prospects for and implications of electoral reform, which has again risen up the political agenda in the mid-1990s.

Pippa Norris has provided an extraordinarily cogent overview of a fast-moving, complex yet utterly fundamental subject for all students of contemporary British politics.

Anthony Seldon

Preface

This book would not have been possible without the help of many colleagues and students who have contributed to my understanding of electoral change over the years. In particular I would like to thank all those who have commented on different conference papers which emerged from this work, or who have collaborated on related projects, including Joni Lovenduski, Ivor Crewe, Mark Franklin, Anthony Heath, John Curtice and Roger Jowell. The book draws mainly on the series of *British Election Studies*, directed by David Butler and Donald Stokes who began the surveys, by Ivor Crewe, Bo Sarlvik, James Alt and David Robertson who maintained the series at Essex University from 1974 to 1979, and Anthony Heath, Roger Jowell and John Curtice who directed the studies from 1983 to 1992. Hans-Dieter Klingemann kindly released data in advance from the Comparative Manifestos Project. The book also draws on the British Candidate Study, 1992, co-directed by myself and Joni Lovenduski, and funded by the ESRC (RR-000-23-1991). I would like to thank William Field for creating the maps for chapter 6. The general editor of the series, Anthony Seldon, is to be thanked for his patience and encouragement of this project. The book would not have been completed without the stimulus and encouragement received from all the colleagues and fellows at the Joan Shorenstein Center on the Press, Politics and Public Policy, at the Kennedy School of Government, Harvard University, particularly the support of Marvin Kalb.

Harvard University
June 1996

Introduction:
The Westminster Model
of Representative
Democracy

Elections are an essential component of representative democracy, informing the public, linking citizens and leaders, selecting decision-makers, legitimating governments, shaping the policy agenda, and framing debate about the future of the country. The outcome reflects, and in turn influences, the nation's social, economic and political life. Free, fair and competitive elections are not the sole institution for maintaining viable democracies, but they are one of the central mechanisms

The Global Context of Electoral Change

Compared with dramatic developments elsewhere, British elections might strike observers as an island of tranquillity in a sea of change. For emerging democracies, the last decade of the twentieth century has been an era of dramatic electoral transitions. The 'third wave' of democratization has been most striking in central and eastern Europe, following the downfall of the Soviet Union, but the explosion of democracy has transformed states world-wide. If democracy is measured by the criteria of public partici-pation, party competition and respect for civil liberties and political rights, Freedom House estimates that the universe of democratic states expanded globally from thirty to seventy-six during 1974–95.[1] Yet, as Huntington notes, previous expansions have encountered 'reverse' waves.[2] The transition process raises expectations and uncertainties. Democratic consolidation requires a triple transformation of the constitutional 'rules of the game', the party system and the economic system, which may prove too difficult for fragile political systems to sustain.

Many established democracies have also experienced an era of significant electoral developments, albeit less dramatic. Over the last three decades in some countries electoral alignments have weakened, and party systems have become increasingly fragmented.[3] In Italy, Canada and Japan traditional patterns of party competition have become far less stable and predictable, symbolized by the meltdown experienced in 1993 by the Canadian Progressive Conservatives, the return of the first left-wing government in Italy in 1996, under the Olive Tree coalition, and the weakening hegemony of the Japanese Liberal Democrat Party.[4] In New Zealand, fundamental reform of the electoral system has broken the old two–party grip on power, although the shape of the new party system remains in flux. In France, Austria and Belgium anti-system parties of the extreme right have been fuelled by the politics of race, immigration and nationalism.[5] Green parties have developed a niche in many countries, and become power-brokers in Germany.[6] Reformed communist parties have attempted to reinvent themselves, with success in Russia, Hungary and Poland. Neo-facists have re-emerged in Italy and extremist nationalists in Russia. Long-standing governing coalitions have been broken in Ireland and the Netherlands, producing new party alliances. In the United States, the rise of independent voters and dissatisfaction with 'all of the above' has introduced an element of unpredictability into two–party politics.

Opportunities for electoral competition have been transformed by the modernization of political communications.[7] Parties have increasingly moved from direct to mediated campaigns, combining television, professional consultants and political marketing.[8] In many countries centralized, capital-intensive, professional campaigns have replaced localized, labour-intensive, grass-roots mobilization. In response to these opportunities, new forms of party organization are evolving, relying less on mass membership for funds and volunteers, and more on state and independent resources.[9] The disintegration of old party loyalties and organizations has allowed monied entrepreneurs – like Perot, Forbes and Berlusconi – with no traditional party base, to springboard into public life through television, with mixed success.

In contrast to events elsewhere, it may appear that Big Ben struck midnight fifty years ago and Westminster party politics froze in time. Swathes of Labour and Conservative backbenchers continue to debate with each other across the floor of the Commons, just as they have since 1945. Westminster includes no parties of the radical right, equivalent to Le Pen's National Front. The British Communist party last elected a candidate in 1945 and closed up shop in 1987. The British Greens had a momentary flicker of electoral fortune in the 1989 European elections, but otherwise their share of the UK vote in general elections peaked at 0.5 per cent in 1992, and all their candidates lost deposits. The 1983 general election was the most significant attempt to 'break the mould' of post-war British politics, yet over 600 Conservative and Labour MPs were returned, out of 650 members of parliament. The most dramatic change in British party politics in recent years is the revival of 'new Labour' under the leadership of Tony Blair, but, at the time of writing (June 1996) there are striking parallels between Labour in the mid-nineties and Labour in the mid-sixties. The most appropriate adjectives to describe party politics at Westminster may be continuity and stability, perhaps even staidness. The ghost of Churchill or Attlee, transported into parliament fifty years later, would find much that was familiar.

Yet in many regards this picture is deceptive. During the last fifty years the electoral foundations of British party politics have been transformed, although not out of all recognition. Labour and Conservative control of central government has remained largely unchanged during the last half century. Westminster continues to be dominated by the conventions of adversarial two-party politics. Multi-party coalition politics may have become far more common in local government. But the most important change since the 1970s has been the significant weakening of the two-party system in the electorate, symbolized by erratic tidal waves of support for minor parties in European elections, local elections, by-elections, opinion polls, and to a lesser extent in general elections. Like 'tsunamis' – immense disturbances caused by earthquakes on the floor of oceans – these electoral waves ebb and flow, occasionally colliding on the surface of the water, while the immensity of the British political system remains relatively immutable.

Due to these developments in recent decades the power of successive Labour and Conservative governments has rested on a more fragile, rickety and narrow foundation of democratic support. The book provides an interpretative essay exploring these changes in British politics during the last half century. The opening chapters trace the tides of party fortunes since the war, and the impact of electoral trends on the British political system. Subsequent sections explore alternative explanations of these developments focusing on changes in voters, parties and the media.

The Westminster Model of Responsible Party Government

Elections are core components of representative democracy in Britain. Therefore we need to begin by understanding this broader context, and the normative assumptions which are involved in analysing and evaluating the political system. In most parliamentary democracies political representation is commonly understood to work via the 'responsible party government' model, where parties function as the critical institution linking citizens and state. Elements of this theory can be traced to the ideas of Max Weber, Moisei Ostrogorski, and Woodrow Wilson at the turn of the century.[10] Reflecting on the breakdown of democracy in Weimar Germany, strong arguments in favour of responsible party government were advocated by Joseph Schumpeter, E. E. Schattschneider, and the American Political Science Association Committee on Political Parties.[11] The widespread consensus, exemplified by textbook writers as diverse as Jennings, McKenzie, Duverger, Beer, Birch and Punnett, was that Britain exemplified the necessary conditions of responsible party government in the fifties and sixties.[12]

In the *'responsible party government'* model the electorate selects from two or more parties based on their policies and performance. This model has certain minimum conditions:

- On the supply-side disciplined parties need to provide an alternative set of programmes on the major issues facing the country and, if elected to government, they must implement their proposals. Parties may compete on other grounds: for example they may offer charismatic leadership, or clientalistic benefits. But only programmatic parties offer voters a deliberative and rational choice of policies.
- On the demand-side, voters need to choose parties based on retro-

spective evaluations of their record in government, and prospective evaluations of their policy platforms.

• And free and fair elections need to be held at regular interval to translate votes into seats, and to allow alternation of the parties in government.

If these conditions are met, citizens can hold parties in power collectively accountable for their actions, indirectly through parliament and directly through periodic elections. Citizens have the power to remove governments from office, if they want to 'kick the rascals out'. Under this system the party (or parties) in government are understood to have a democratic mandate to implement their agenda for the duration of their term of office.[13]

Comparative studies by Klingemann et al. demonstrate that the first condition of responsible party government – namely programmatic parties which implement their policy agenda – can work under different constitutional contexts.[14] Yet the full model operates most clearly in the Westminster system. In multi-party coalition governments, such as in Switzerland and the Netherlands, if voters become dissatisfied with the parties in government they may be powerless to remove them from office. Where the constitution provides for a separation of powers between president and legislature, like the United States and France, it is more difficult to assign clear praise and blame for the implementation of public policies. Responsible party government applies most clearly to majoritarian parliamentary systems, like Britain, which allow for a complete turnover of the parties in government.

The model provides an elegant and effective mechanism to shackle power with responsibility. While the government enjoys relatively unrestricted powers, it remains accountable for its actions. Yet if the necessary requirements of this model fail in Britain – notably if the two-party pendulum becomes stuck, preventing the removal of the government, or if the electoral system fails fairly to translate popular votes into seats – then there are few other effective mechanisms to safeguard representative democracy in this country. Since the Second World War successive Labour and Conservative governments have ruled unfettered by coalition partners, judicial review, a written constitution, a bill of rights, a powerful second chamber, a minority veto, an elected Head of State or President, binding initiatives and referenda, or regional authorities.

Cabinet remains accountable on a day-to-day basis to parliament, but party discipline and majoritarian governments guarantee the passage of most of its programme. In the resonant phrase of Lord Hailsham, Britain has 'an elective dictatorship'.[15] The lack of checks and balances, combined with the fusion of executive and legislature, and an unwritten constitution, produces a form of Cabinet government which is exceptionally powerful in the Western world.

In contrast, other democracies commonly limit the powers of the executive through different devices. Consociational systems, like the Netherlands and Switzerland, incorporate multiple constitutional checks and balances. Presidential systems like the United States, France and the Philippines divide power between the executive and legislature.[16] Old Commonwealth countries share the Westminster model, but Canada and Australia devolve considerable powers to the regions through federalism, while the New Zealand system has been significantly reformed. These countries also use referenda to involve the public in constitutional issues. Therefore the unrestricted concentration of power in the hands of the party controlling Cabinet government, relying on responsible party government as the main democratic mechanism of accountability, is uncommon elsewhere, and doubts about the effectiveness and legitimacy of this system in Britain have been raised in many quarters. Critics argue that in recent decades the delicate mechanism has moved out of kilter: the concentration of powers authorized to the governing party has increased, while at the same time their accountability to parliament and the public has diminished, which has fuelled demands for root-and-branch constitutional reform.

The responsible party government model is therefore the most widely understood modern conception of 'representation', particularly common in parliamentary systems with strong, competitive, programmatic parties. Yet British democracy includes several other channels of representation which are distinct, and which may be equally, or even more significant, under different conditions.[17] If responsible party government is failing in Britain, can these other channels compensate?

Functional representation

Linkages between citizens and the state may also operate via '*functional interest'* representation (which can also be termed 'pluralist' or 'neo-corporatist'). Organized interest groups and new social movements may use a variety of channels to influence government policy. This form of representation may be important if MPs see their role as spokespersons for groups such as trade unions, farmers or small business. Theories of pluralist democracy stress linkages between government and established interest groups, such as well-organized lobbies for pharmaceuticals, road transport and the tobacco industry; broader and more inchoate umbrella social movements like environmentalism and the women's movement; and single-issue groups focusing more narrowly on specific policies such as AIDS research or the export of live animals.[18] Interest groups can mobilize and articulate public demands, and provide expert advice on policy solutions. Functional representation is probably most important for the agenda-setting and agenda-building stage of the policy process. Yet functional representation is limited to those voices who are well organized, and interest group pressures may fragment the policy process. Only parties can aggregate diverse demands from pressure groups into loosely coherent policy packages with broad electoral appeal.[19]

Social representation

Alternatively, *'social representation'* is also commonly regarded as important for effective democratic bodies.[20] This concept refers to the presence of political minorities in decision-making bodies, and the demands for parliaments to reflect the social composition of the electorate as a whole whether in terms of class, gender, ethnic, linguistic, or religious minorities.[21] This concept has a long history, and it is legally embodied in electoral systems which reserve seats for specified groups, such as women or the indigenous population, in order to ensure that their voices are heard in the legislature. Social representation may be linked to organized interests, for example if trade unions sponsor working-class candidates. Nevertheless, the two concepts remain analytically distinct: women may stand for office who do not identify with the women's movement, and at the same time feminist organizations may sponsor pro-choice candidates, whether male or female. The older tradition suggested that the direct impact of the social background of members on their attitudes and behaviour was modest, at best. Nevertheless, more recent studies suggest that the social background of members – including their class, gender, generation and education – does make a difference *within* parties, at least in Germany, Sweden, Britain and the United States.[22] This suggests that social representation works primarily via, rather than instead of, party representation. Demands that legislative bodies should reflect society have increased in recent years, but parties remain the main vehicles for recruitment into political elites.

Territorial Representation

In the responsible party government model, individual MPs are elected first and foremost as *party* standard-bearers, bound by collective responsibility and constrained by the tight bonds of legislative discipline. Candidates for office appeal for support based on a national party platform and leadership, to which they will be committed if elected. Yet the link between voters and individual MPs may be closer and more direct. In the local 'delegate' conception of representation, associated with Miller and Stokes, the actions of each MP should be guided by, and consistent with, the opinions of citizens in their local constituency.[23] Populist theories of democracy envisage members as spokespersons elected to parliament to articulate the concerns of their citizens. Under the territorial conception, with medieval roots, parliaments are seen to function as a geographic forum for the nation, bringing together spokespersons from all parts of the kingdom. This understanding is reflected in the Burkean distinction between 'trustees' of the national interest and local 'delegates'. Just as lawyers are seen to 'represent' or speak for their clients, so members of parliament are seen to speak for their districts. This conception is strongest in political systems, like the United States, with parties characterized by decentralized organizational structures, low levels of discipline, minimalist programmatic platforms, and entrepreneurial candidates.

The strength of territorial representation has traditionally been measured by comparing the degree of congruence between the preferences of citizens living within a district, and the views or behaviour of their representatives.[24] Thomassen has argued that the strength of party discipline in European legislatures makes this model unrealistic in most parliamentary systems, since individual representatives have minimal freedom to 'vote the district', rather than 'vote the party'.[25] Yet the territorial basis of the

Miller and Stokes model has been extended beyond single-member districts to examine the degree of congruence between the entire parliament and the entire electorate in Sweden,[26] France[27] and the European Parliament.[28] Advocates of regional assemblies assume there will be similar views among citizens and elected members within the major regions of Britain: that Scottish MPs will reflect public opinion north of the border, while Welsh MPs will share the concerns of the people of Wales. Evidence suggests that territorial representation does matter for the attitudes and policy preferences of British MPs: with significant differences for those elected north and south of the border.[29] These differences among MPs broadly reflect differences among the public. Nevertheless party, not region, remains by far the strongest predictor of members' views and behaviour.

Service representation

The local linkage between citizens and members may operate less in terms of policy than via '*service representation*'. Service representation includes MPs' case-work on behalf of individual constituents, and their delivery of collective public goods (pork) to their district. Case-work is commonly stressed as a critical component of members' roles in parliaments as diverse as the US Congress, the Japanese Diet and the Irish Dàil, and studies have also emphasized the importance of this activity for British Members of Parliament.[30] While 'pork-barrel' politics has usually been regarded as highly undesirable in modern British politics, in some systems like Japan it can be seen as an important and legitimate way for members to act as a conduit between local districts and government services.[31] The degree of service representation varies widely in different parliaments, with case-work probably strongest for legislators returned from single-member districts, and small multi-member districts, but less well-established in legislatures elected through party-lists.[32] The time devoted to casework has expanded for British MPs in recent decades,[33] but, although useful for the redress of individual grievances, this rarely influences the overall direction of government policy.

Direct democracy

In many countries – like Switzerland, Australia and Italy – there are direct mechanisms to allow citizens to participate via referenda and plebiscites.[34] In the United States, with a strong populist tradition of direct democracy, there are frequent and multiple opportunities for political participation through candidate primaries and caucuses, local, Congressional, Gubernatorial, and Presidential elections, town-hall meetings, referenda and ballot initiatives. Yet in the British system, other than elections, citizens have limited opportunities to participate. Channels of direct democracy like referenda have been traditionally regarded as largely inappropriate in Britain, and a threat to the sovereignty of parliament.[35]

Alternative forms of representation remain important channels connecting citizens and the state. Nevertheless in Britain, in common with most parliamentary systems, responsible party government remains the central mechanism, which is a necessary if not sufficient condition for representative democracy.[36] If this is failing in Britain, there remain doubts whether other channels of democracy can compensate by providing a consistent and rational link between the preferences of citizens and the policies adopted by government. Let us turn to examining the way the British representative democracy has operated since the war, to see what has changed, and why.

Notes

1 See Adrian Karatnycky, 1995. 'The Comparative Survey of Freedom', *Freedom Review* 26(1): 5-68.
2 Samuel Huntington, 1991. *The Third Wave: Democratization in the Late Twentieth Century.* Cambridge: Cambridge University Press; Larry Diamond and Marc F. Plattner (eds), 1993. *The Global Resurgence of Democracy.* Baltimore: The Johns Hopkins University Press.
3 Mark Franklin, Tom Mackie and Henry Valen et al. (eds), 1992. *Electoral Change: Responses to Evolving Social and Attitudinal Structures in Western Countries.* Cambridge: Cambridge University Press.
4 See Lawrence LeDuc, Richard G. Niemi and Pippa Norris (eds), 1996. *Comparing Democracies.* Thousand Oaks, CA: Sage.
5 See Peter H. Merkl and Leonard Weinberg (eds), 1993. *Encounters with the Contemporary Radical Right.* Boulder, CO: Westview Press.

6 Russell Dalton, 1994. *The Green Rainbow*. New Haven, CT: Yale University Press; Ferdinand Muller-Rommel, 1989. *The New Politics: The Rise and Success of Green Parties and Alternative Lists*. Boulder, CO: Westview Press.

7 David Butler and Austin Ranney (eds), 1992. *Electioneering*. Oxford: Clarendon Press.

8 David L. Swanson and Paolo Mancini, 1996. *Politics, Media and Modern Democracy*. Oxford: Oxford University Press.

9 Richard S. Katz and Peter Mair (eds), 1994. *How Parties Organize*. London: Sage.

10 Moisei Ostrogorski, 1902. *Democracy and the Organisation of Political Parties*. London: Macmillan.

11 Joseph Schumpeter, 1942. *Capitalism, Socialism and Democracy*. New York: Harper & Row; E. E. Schattschneider. 1942. *Party Government*. New York: Holt, Reinhart and Winston; E. E. Schattschneider, 1948. *The Struggle for Party Government*. College Park, Maryland: University of Maryland; Austin Ranney, 1962. *The Doctrine of Responsible Party Government*. Urbana: University of Illinois Press.

12 Sir Ivor Jennings, 1962. *The British Constitution*. Cambridge: Cambridge University Press; R. T. McKenzie, 1955. *British Political Parties*. New York: St. Martin's Press; Samuel Beer, 1965. *Modern British Politics*. London: Faber & Faber; Maurice Duverger, 1954. *Political Parties*. New York: John Wiley; A. H. Birch, 1964. *Representative and Responsible Government*. London: George Allen and Unwin; Malcolm Punnett, 1968. *British Government and Politics*. London: Heinemann.

13 Dalton, Russell, 1985. 'Political Parties and Political Representation', *Comparative Political Studies* 17: 267-99; Hans-Dieter Klingemann, Richard I. Hofferbert and Ian Budge, 1994. *Parties, Policies and Democracy*. Boulder, CO: Westview Press; E. E. Schattschneider, 1942. *Party Government*. New York: Farrar and Rinehart.

14 Hans-Dieter Klingemann, Richard I. Hofferbert and Ian Budge. 1994. *Parties, Policies and Democracy*. Boulder, CO: Westview.

15 Lord Hailsham of St. Marylebone, Quintin Hogg, 1976. *Elective Dictatorship*. London: BBC.

16 See Arend Lijphart, 1992. *Parliamentary Versus Presidential Government*. Oxford: Oxford University Press.

17 For different concepts of representation see Jacques Thomassen, 1994. 'Empirical Research into Political Representation', in M. Kent Jennings and Thomas E. Mann (eds), *Election at Home and Abroad*. Ann Arbor, MI: University of Michigan Press; Anthony Birch, 1993. *The Concepts and Theories of Modern Democracy*. London: Routledge; Heinz Eulau and John Wahlke, 1978. *The Politics of Representation*. London: Sage.

18 See Michael Rush (ed.), 1990. *Parliament and Pressure Politics.* Oxford: Oxford University Press.

19 See Hans Dieter Klingemann, Richard I. Hofferbert and Ian Budge, 1994. *Parties, Policies and Democracy.* Boulder, CO: Westview Press.

20 Pippa Norris and Joni Lovenduski, 1995. *Political Recruitment: Gender, Race and Class in the British Parliament.* Cambridge: Cambridge University Press; Joni Lovenduski and Pippa Norris (eds), 1993. *Gender and Party Politics.* London: Sage; Joni Lovenduski and Pippa Norris (eds), 1996. *Women in Politics in Britain.* Oxford: Oxford University Press.

21 For a discussion see Anne Phillips, 1993. *Democracy and Difference.* Pennsylvania: University of Pennsylvania Press.

22 Bernhard Wessels, 1985. *Wählerschaft und Fuhrungsschicht: Probleme Politischer Repräsentation.* Berlin: Universitätsdruck der Freien Universitat Berlin; Peter Esaiasson and Søren Holmberg, 1996. *Representation from Above: Members of Parliament and Representative Democracy in Sweden.* Aldershot: Dartmouth; Sue Thomas, 1994. *How Women Legislate.* New York: Oxford University Press; Pippa Norris, 1996. 'Do Women at Westminster Make a Difference?' *Parliamentary Affairs* 49(1).

23 Warren Miller and Donald Stokes, 1963. 'Constituency Influence in Congress', *American Political Science Review* 57: 45–56.

24 Warren Miller and Donald Stokes, 1963. 'Constituency Influence in Congress', *American Political Science Review* 57: 45–56; Philip Converse and Roy Pierce, 1986. *Political Representation in France.* Cambridge, MA: Harvard University Press; Russell Dalton, 1985. 'Political Parties and Political Representation', *Comparative Political Studies* 17: 267–99.

25 Jacques Thomassen, 1994. 'Empirical Research into Political Representation: Failing Democracy or Failing Models?', in M. Kent Jennings and Thomas E. Mann (eds), *Elections at Home and Abroad.* Ann Arbor, MI: University of Michigan Press.

26 Søren Holmberg, 1989. 'Political Representation in Sweden', *Scandinavian Political Studies* 12(1): 1–36; Peter Essaiasson and Søren Holmberg, 1996. *Representation from Above: Members of Parliament and Representative Democracy in Sweden.* Aldershot: Dartmouth.

27 Philip Converse and Roy Pierce, 1986. *Political Representation in France.* Cambridge, MA: Harvard University Press.

28 Jacques Thomassen and Hermann Schmitt, 1997. 'Political Representation in the European Parliament', *European Journal of Political Research.*

29 For a detailed study of this see Pippa Norris, 'Representation in England, Scotland and Wales: Boundaries and Identities for Politicians and Voters', *Political Studies Association Annual Conference.* Glasgow, 1996.

30 Bruce Cain, John Ferejohn and Morris Fiorina, 1987. *The Personal Vote.*

Cambridge, MA: Harvard University Press; Pippa Norris, 1995. 'The Puzzle of Constituency Service', *American Political Science Association.* Chicago; Philip Norton and David Wood, 1993. *Back from Westminster: British Members of Parliament and their Constituents.* Lexington, KY: The University Press of Kentucky; Vernon Bogdanor, 1985. *Representatives of the People?* London: Gower.

31 Haruhiro Fukai, 1997. 'Japan', in Pippa Norris (ed.), *Routes to Power: Legislative Recruitment in Advanced Democracies.* Cambridge: Cambridge University Press

32 See Richard Katz, 1997. 'Roles and Representation in the European Parliament', *European Journal of Political Research;* Vernon Bogdanor (ed.), 1985. *Representatives of the People?* London: Gower.

33 Bruce Cain, John Ferejohn and Morris Fiorina, 1987. *The Personal Vote: Constituency Service and Electoral Independence.* Cambridge, MA: Harvard University Press. Pippa Norris, 1995. 'The Puzzle of Constituency Service'. Paper presented at the American Political Science Association Annual Meeting, Chicago.

34 See David Butler and Austin Ranney, 1994. *Referendums Around the World.* Washington DC: AEI Press.

35 See Vernon Bogdanor, 1981. *The People and the Party System: The Referendum and Electoral Reform in British Politics.* Cambridge: Cambridge University Press; see also David Butler and Austin Ranney, 1994. *Referendums Around the World.* Washington, DC: AEI Press.

36 For a clear discussion of the model of responsible party government see Hans-Dieter Klingemann, Richard I. Hofferbert and Ian Budge, 1994. *Parties, Policies and Democracy.* Boulder, CO: Westview Press; Cesar Cansino, 1995. 'Party Government: The Search for a Theory – Introduction', *International Political Science Review* 16(2): 123–6; Richard Katz, 1987. *Party Governments: European and American Experiences.* Berlin: De Gruyter; E. E. Schattschneider, 1948. *The Struggle for Party Government.* College Park, MD: University of Maryland.

Part I

The Nature of
Electoral Change

1 Electoral Change, 1945–1970

In analysing how the British political system has changed over time there is room for debate about the appropriate periodization of political eras. The precise dividing lines are often blurred in practice, even if demarcated by specific events. Indicators of change taken at different intervals – the results of general elections, local elections, by-elections, or opinion polls – provide different break points. Electoral seismologists detected minor rumblings in the tectonic plates of British elections throughout the mid-to-late sixties, with record levels of government unpopularity in opinion polls and by-elections, and sporadic spurts of support for minor parties symbolized by Orpington (1962), Carmarthen (1966) and Hamilton (1967). The change in general elections from 1970 to February 1974 proved critical. As a rough watershed, UK politics in the second half of the twentieth century can be divided into two major periods: *the era of two-party dominance*, which characterized UK government from 1945 to the late 1960s and early 1970s; and *the era of two-party decline* evident from 1970 to 1992. Core elements of the political system changed, and changed decisively, in the early seventies.

The Era of Two-Party Dominance: 1945–70

The British political system from 1945 to 1970 had five related features which combined to produce the 'Westminster' model (see figure 1.1), namely:

- two-party electoral competition;
- plurality elections;
- disciplined and cohesive parties;
- balanced two-party control of central and local government;
- strong majoritarian Cabinet governments.[1]

These components formed an integrated political system, which meant that change in any one component could, and did, have significant consequences for the rest.

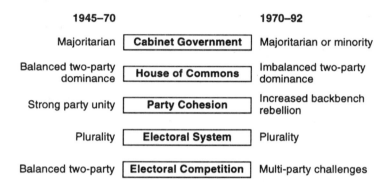

Figure 1.1   The Westminster model of government

Two-Party electoral competition

The foundation for Labour and Conservative power rested on their overwhelming electoral strength in the country at large, with minor parties confined to the wilderness in the post-war decades. In general elections from 1945–1970 the two major parties swept up 92 per cent of the vote, so their control of Westminster was legitimated by widespread popular support. In general elections the Labour and Conservative share of the vote was relatively stable and evenly balanced: in general elections during this period support for the major parties never fell below 39 per cent, or rose above 50 per cent (see figure 1.2, table 1.1).

During the early to mid-fifties the Liberals almost folded as a national party, reduced to a rump of half-a-dozen MPs. In general elections during the 1950s Liberal candidates contested one in three seats, but the electoral

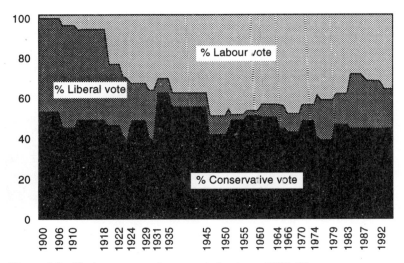

Figure 1.2   Voting support in general elections, 1900–92
Source: Table 1.1.

Table 1.1   UK vote in general elections, 1945–92

Year of General election	Percentage share of the UK vote:				Turnout
	Cons	Lab	Lib Dem.	Others	
1945	39.6	48.0	9.0	3.4	72.8
1950	43.4	46.1	9.1	1.4	83.9
1951	48.0	48.8	2.6	.6	82.6
1955	49.7	46.4	2.7	1.2	76.8
1959	49.4	43.8	5.9	.9	78.7
1964	43.4	44.1	11.2	1.3	77.1
1966	41.9	48.0	8.6	1.5	75.8
1970	46.4	43.1	7.5	3.0	72.0
1974	37.9	37.2	19.3	5.6	78.8
1974	35.8	39.2	18.3	6.7	72.8
1979	43.9	36.9	13.8	5.4	76.0
1983	42.4	27.6	25.4	4.6	72.7
1987	42.3	30.8	22.5	4.4	75.3
1992	41.8	34.2	17.9	6.1	77.7
Mean 1945–66	45.1	46.5	7.0	1.5	78.2
Mean 1970–92	41.5	35.6	17.8	5.1	75.0

Source: F. W. S. Craig, 1989. *British Electoral Facts 1832–1987*, Aldershot: Parliamentary Research Services.

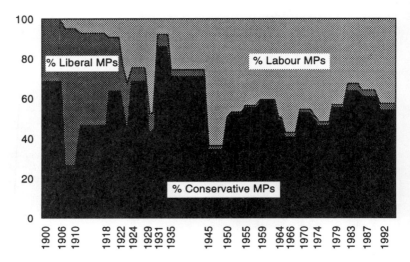

Figure 1.3   MPs in general elections, 1900–92
Source: Table 1.2.

rewards were miserable: over half lost their deposits, and in 1951 and 1955 they gained less than 3 per cent of the national vote (see table 1.1). Nor were they seriously competitive: during the fifties Liberal candidates took second place in about sixteen seats per general election. The results would have been even worse but for an electoral pact with the Conservatives. During the early fifties the Liberals were demoralized and bitterly split internally between the Radical Reform Group, representing the Beveridge tradition of social welfare liberalism, and the free trade individualists. The 1959 general election resulted in the return of six Liberals and one Independent Conservative, while all the remaining seats were filled by the major parties. There were only forty-two Liberal peers (6.4 per cent) out of 855 members of the House of Lords.[2] Faced with this gloomy record observers predicted the extinction of the party.[3]

Nationalist parties remained peripheral to parliamentary politics. The Scottish National Party, founded in 1928, split in 1942 over two opposing strategies. Under the leadership of Robert McIntyre the SNP stuck to party politics, focused on independence, but thereby confined themselves to an electoral ghetto. With a tiny membership, the Scottish National Party

Table 1.2   UK seats in general elections, 1945–92

Year of General Election	Percentage Share of UK Seats:				Overall Majority	Government
	Cons	Lab.	Lib Dems	Others		
1945	32.8	61.4	1.9	3.9	147	Lab
1950	47.7	50.4	1.4	.5	6	Lab
1951	51.3	47.2	1.0	.5	16	Con
1955	54.8	44.0	.9	.2	59	Con
1959	57.9	41.0	.9	.2	99	Con
1964	48.3	50.3	1.4		5	Lab
1966	40.1	57.8	1.9	.2	97	Lab
1970	52.3	45.7	1.0	1.0	31	Con
1974	46.8	47.4	2.2	3.6	–	Lab
1974	43.6	50.2	2.1	4.1	4	Lab
1979	53.4	42.4	1.7	2.5	44	Con
1983	61.1	32.2	3.5	3.2	144	Con
1987	57.9	35.2	3.4	3.5	102	Con
1992	51.6	41.6	3.1	3.7	21	Con
Mean 1945–66	47.6	50.3	1.3	.9	61	
Mean 1970–92	52.4	42.1	2.4	3.1	58	

Source: F. W. S. Craig, 1989. *British Electoral Facts, 1832–1987*, Aldershot: Parliamentary Research Services.

fielded only twelve Parliamentary candidates during the 1950s, achieving less than one per cent of the Scottish vote per election. The SNP was only seriously competitive (placed in second place) in two seats in general elections during the 1950s. The SNP was more of a sect than a party. Instead, nationalist energy focused on mobilizing support for a Scottish Parliament through a mass petition, the Scottish Convention, rather than party politics. While this eventually achieved over two million signatures, it failed to influence Unionist sentiment within the major parties.[4] Plaid Cymru became more ambitious by the end of the 1950s, running more candidates, but, even at their high point in this decade the party gained only 5 per cent of the Welsh vote. The Communist Party in Britain contested elections from 1922 to 1987, but their electoral peak was 100 candidates in 1950, producing 97 lost deposits and 0.3 per cent of the vote.[5]

Plurality Elections

Popular support was translated into seats via the British electoral system of 'first-past-the-post', or plurality single-member districts, which provided the foundation of the Westminster model. The basic system of simple plurality voting in general elections is widely familiar: the United Kingdom is divided into territorial single-member constituencies (659 in the next House of Commons); voters within each constituency cast a single ballot (marked by an X) for one candidate; the candidate with the most votes in each seat is returned to Westminster; and the party with an overall majority of seats forms the government.

The British electoral system has evolved through a continuous series of amendments.[6] The most significant have widened the franchise, abolished dual-member constituencies, removed corrupt practices, and standardized electoral administration. Suffrage was extended in successive Reform Acts to the middle and working class (1832, 1867, 1884, 1918), to women (1918, 1928), and to younger voters (1969). Single-member constituencies were introduced in 1707, became standard practice after 1885, and the last remaining dual member seats were abolished in 1948. Bribery was effectively eliminated through the introduction of the Secret Ballot (1872) and the Corrupt Practices Act (1883). The principle of constituencies of roughly equal population size was accepted and electoral administration was standardized (1918); regular boundary reviews were introduced following the creation of the permanent Boundary Commission in 1944; and after the Second World War certain anomalies were eliminated, such as the abolition of plural voting and university seats (1948), establishing one-person one-vote in single-member seats as the basic principle of British elections.

For admirers, this system produced the classic 'Westminster model' with the twin virtues of strong but responsive party government. The exaggerative properties of the electoral system produced a decisive *winner's bonus*: the party in first place was rewarded more handsomely than the runner-up. In the post-war period British governments have received, on the average, 45 per cent of the popular vote but 54 per cent of seats. Even a close election, with only a small lead in votes, was usually translated into a comfortable overall majority of seats for the government. In the 1955 general election, for example, the Conservatives were only 3.3 per cent ahead of Labour in the popular vote, yet Anthony Eden had an overall parliamentary majority of 59 seats. From 1945–1970 the distribution of votes to seats usually followed the principle of the 'cube law' (or rule), which translated a one per cent swing into about a 3 per cent gain in seats for the winning party.[7] The 'cube law' provided a reasonable rule of thumb to predict the outcome in five out of eight elections from 1945 to 1970.[8]

Yet, like a delicate mechanical seismograph, the electoral system remained responsive to even a minor tremor in two-party fortunes. Although governments were awarded a parliamentary majority this could easily evaporate at the next election. The system ensured a stable swing of the pendulum between the major governing and opposition parties based on a relatively small swing of votes across the country. The 'Butler' or two-party 'Swing' is measured by adding the percentage loss for one party to the percentage gains for the other, and dividing by two. In the 1950–1 period, for example, the Conservative vote rose by 4.6 per cent, while Labour's support rose by only 2.7, producing a swing of 0.9 per cent to the Conservatives.[9] This modest swing was sufficient to turn the Labour government's majority of six seats into a Conservative majority of sixteen seats, thereby ending the government of Clement Attlee and bringing Sir Winston Churchill back into power. As roughly predicted by the cube law, the 0.9 per cent swing in votes won the Conservatives twenty-three additional MPs, out of 630, a gain of 3.6 per cent of all parliamentary seats. Moreover proponents of the Westminster system stressed that at the local level the link between voters and their MP provided citizens with a voice in the nation's affairs, as well as making elected members accountable to constituency concerns.

Moreover in the post-war period the lack of regional divisions in voting behaviour meant governments could claim a national mandate. Swings in support for the major parties in the periods 1950–1 and 1951–5 were relatively uniform across the country. In McKenzie's classic 'swingometer', the two-party swing in Doncaster could be used to predict similar shifts in party fortunes from Dorset to Dunfermline.[10] Regional divisions were muted: from 1945 to 1966 the Conservatives won 39 per cent of the vote in Scotland, only 4 percentage points behind their support in England. Until February 1974 the Conservative and Unionist party contested, and won, most of the seats in Northern Ireland, as they had since 1922. With some legitimacy, governments could claim to speak for the whole of the United Kingdom.

The system penalized minor parties with dispersed support, and under-represented political minorities. Yet in the post-war decade the outcome of British elections was generally regarded as free and fair. Liberal votes, which were spatially dispersed, produced meagre parliamentary rewards but this aroused little public concern mainly because the Liberal share of the UK vote remained below 10 per cent in all but one election from 1945 to 1970. The electoral reform movement was quiescent in these years: the 1965–67 Speaker's Conference on Electoral Law overwhelmingly voted to retain the status quo.[11]

Public confidence in the British electoral system seemed to be demonstrated by reasonably high levels of electoral turnout: about 79 per cent of British citizens cast a ballot in general elections. In *The Civic Culture*, Almond and Verba reported that, compared with citizens in other countries, in the early 1960s the British public expressed considerable satisfaction, trust and pride in their own system of government.[12] Although the survey evidence is surprisingly thin, textbooks commonly stressed that the British political culture was characterized by homogeneity, consensus and moderate pragmatism, with widespread allegiance to political authority, voluntary compliance with the basic laws and acceptance of the legitimacy of government.[13]

Disciplined and Cohesive Parties

In turn the balance of seats produced by the electoral system, combined with disciplined and cohesive parliamentary parties, created the power-base for strong cabinet government. The fusion of executive and legislature enhanced party unity in the House of Commons, with few backbench rebellions.[14] MPs knew that promotion into government office, as well as readoption by their local party, required loyalty. Rebels faced the loss of endorsement by their constituency party, which meant almost certain electoral defeat. The convention of collective responsibility in Cabinet further maintained the façade of party unity, and avoided damaging factional splits in the leadership, at least in public. As a result parliamentary parties could be held jointly accountable to the electorate for their actions: ministers and backbenchers sank or swam together.

The main mechanism for accountability lay with party manifestos, which gradually evolved from Peel's original Tamworth manifesto to become detailed programmes laying out the major policies which parties promised to implement if returned to power. Once elected, governments could plan a full legislative programme in the confidence that almost all would be enacted, even at the risk of short-term unpopularity. How far manifesto promises have been implemented in practice remains a matter of continuing controversy. Studies by Richard Rose emphasize that 'secular trends' rather than government policies tended to drive most policy outputs, such as trends in government spending on defence or welfare.[15] Yet this conclusion has been disputed. The most recent examination of the comparative evidence, by Klingemann, Hofferbert and Budge, has emphasized that manifestos *do* matter for the policy-making process. The study suggests that voters who pick parties based on their programmes have good reasons to expect that these will affect the direction of government policy.[16]

Under the Westminster system the government could therefore plan to implement their full programme, while in the long term the Cabinet remained accountable to the House of Commons, and the House of Commons remained ultimately accountable to the public. Ministerial actions faced critical scrutiny by backbenchers. If governments were defeated in the House of Commons by an unambiguous vote of no confidence, or during this period if they were defeated in a division on a major item of legislation, they had to resign and either call a general election, or let the leader of the opposition try to form a government.[17] An official motion of no confidence has been rarely invoked, still less passed. In the twentieth century only two governments have resigned after losing a vote of no confidence: in 1924 and 1979, although Neville Chamberlain also stood down in 1940 after facing an unexpected fall in his majority. But the existence of this device, combined with parliamentary conventions and the fusion of personnel, meant that government ministers had to defend themselves, explain their policies, and justify their actions, on a daily basis from the floor of the House of Commons. Ministers were collectively and individually responsible to parliament. This doctrine underpinned all forms of parliamentary scrutiny in debate, parliamentary questions, and committee work. Moreover parliament remained ultimately accountable to the public. In general elections, voters had the opportunity to evaluate the governing party's record set against the platforms and leadership offered by the opposition, and exercise their choice accordingly. Individual MPs could also be held accountable for their actions by their local party, and by their constituents.

Balanced two-party control of local and central government

Party discipline reinforced two-party control of government at every level. In general elections from 1945 to 1970 the Labour and Conservative parties dominated the political landscape: contesting 98 per cent of all seats and winning 98 per cent of all seats in the House of Commons. During the 1950s most constituency contests offered voters the choice of a 'straight fight' between Labour and Conservative candidates. In over one hundred British by-elections from 1945 to 1955, Labour and the Conservatives won 95 per cent of the vote, and every seat bar one.[18] This meant, among other things, that governments did not have to fear the gradual erosion of their majority through by-elections. Independents and minor parties were slightly more successful at the grass-roots but nevertheless in local government elections from 1945 to 1970 the two major parties had outright control of 72 per cent of all borough councils. At their lowest point in 1952 the Liberals were reduced to just fifty-three borough councillors (1.5 per cent), without representatives in major cities like Birmingham and Liverpool, and without control of any significant council.[19]

At Westminster the two-parties were fairly evenly balanced in support producing fairly regular swings in the pendulum between government and opposition: six years of Labour rule after the Attlee landslide (1945–51) were followed by thirteen years of the Conservatives (1951–64), before they were replaced by six years of Labour under Wilson (1964–70). This rotation was seen to promote moderate, responsible and responsive government, since each major party was given a limited term in office. No government could afford to grow lazy, out-of-touch, and complacent, since if so they faced a realistic chance of having the red boxes, the ministerial cars, and other perks of office whisked away. Extravagant promises from the opposition benches could be tempered by the realization that they might, one day, be called to account. The system of party competition was centripetal: it encouraged the major parties to battle for the middle ground, and it discouraged minor parties on the extreme right or left. The swing of the pendulum meant the major parties had a stake in abiding by the rules of the game.

Strong majoritarian cabinet governments

In the Westminster system the general election determined the distribution of seats in the House of Commons, and the party leader commanding a majority formed the Cabinet, with members drawn from the Commons and the Lords.[20] This produced the classic fusion of the executive and legislature, with Cabinet predominance, in Bagehot's words:

> The efficient secret of the English Constitution may be described as the close union, the nearly complete fusion, of the executive and legislative powers . . . The connecting link is the Cabinet. By that word we mean a committee of the legislative body selected to be the executive body . . . a hyphen which joins, a buckle which fastens, the legislative part of the State to the executive part of the State. In origins it belongs to one, in its functions it belongs to the other . . . The committee . . . by virtue of that combination, is, while it lasts and holds together, the most powerful body in the state.[21]

Cabinet government was in marked contrast to the constitutional separation of powers under Presidential systems, such as in the United States, the Philippines and Costa Rica. Moreover, the intimate linkage at Westminster was strengthened by the overlapping membership between executive and legislature, which was banned in some other parliamentary systems like Norway. Political careers in Britain require a fairly uniform and narrow ladder of recruitment: from party to local government office, to Westminster backbenches, and finally into ministerial office. Few ambitious politicians can bypass the House of Commons.[22] Politicians who through ill-luck or ill-judgment fall at the hurdle of getting selected by one of the major parties for a winnable seat have few lateral options. In contrast members of the American Cabinet, for example, are drawn from diverse careers in public and private life, and if they have risen up through Congress, they have to resign from elected office on entering government.

From 1945 to 1970 Labour or Conservative Cabinets governed Britain and, with the exception of the 1950 and 1964 elections, they usually enjoyed comfortable parliamentary majorities. In the ideal Westminster system, the 'in' party was able to assume all responsibility for government, through a united Cabinet with a stable and disciplined parliamentary majority, while the 'out' party provided responsible opposition, critical scrutiny of government actions, and an alternative electoral choice. In the

British tradition of adversarial politics the primary goal of the major party of opposition was to become the government. Players shared a broad consensus about the basic constitutional rules of the game, and indeed many of the core policy objectives.[23] As R. T. McKenzie characterized British politics in the mid-1950s:

> Two parliamentary parties face each other in the House of Commons. Setting aside the party myths and the inter-party propaganda, it is clear that the primary function of the mass organisation of the Conservative and Labour Parties is to sustain two competing teams of parliamentary leaders between whom the electorate as a whole may periodically choose . . . The democratic process ensures that there will be a periodic opportunity for the electorate to review the record of the decision makers who currently hold office; and, if the electorate wishes, it may replace them with an alternative team.[24]

Many British observers believed multi-party coalition governments common throughout Europe offered voters less control. The process of party bargaining, not elections, determined which parties entered power. Decision-making was shared among coalition partners, diffusing responsibility and accountability. Coalition governments, exemplified by those in Italy, often proved less stable. Moreover, critics argued multi-party systems offered fewer incentives for moderate competition based on aggregating different interests into a broad-based coalition, since narrowly-based extremist parties could exercise power in coalitions out of proportion to their electoral support.[25]

Before joining the European Union, parliament was regarded as sovereign, which meant that an Act of Parliament could make or unmake any British law, a principle established by Erskine May in 1844. By convention prior to entry into Europe there was no higher court of appeal, no higher legislative or executive authority, and no codified constitution over and above parliament. Cabinet governments were maintained and discharged by the vote of the Commons.

Cabinet remained the central powerhouse of the British political system, although remaining accountable to, and ultimately dependent upon, members of parliament. As Leo Amery points out, in this regard compared with other democracies the Westminster system allows an exceptional concentration of powers in the hands of the Executive:

> It is the Cabinet which controls Parliament and governs the country. In no other country is there such a concentration of power and such a capacity for

decisive action as that possessed by a British Cabinet, provided always that it enjoys the support of a majority in the House of Commons.[26]

British governments suffered adverse votes from time to time, ministers took account of the opinions of their backbenchers through the whips office, and there were a number of cases where members clearly influenced government policy.[27] Nevertheless, the mass of the government's legislative programme was usually enacted. Governments passed well over 90 per cent of their bills through parliament, occasionally 100 per cent, depending on time constraints.[28] From 1945 to 1970 no vote was ever lost because of government supporters entering the opposition lobby.[29] The Westminster Parliament, in Peter Hennessy's words, 'has been the parade ground of the best-drilled brute votes in any advanced Western democracy'.[30] Cabinet control works through various mechanisms. Party discipline has been reinforced for government by the 'pay-roll vote', about 150 ministers, law officers, and parliamentary private secretaries who could be expected to march solidly through the government lobby. Patronage allows the prime minister to reward office to almost half the parliamentary party. The traditional rules of the game help drive government legislation forward. In the House of Commons, government business normally has precedence at every sitting, and it can invoke the closure and guillotine to ensure passage of its legislation. Three-quarters of the days when Parliament is sitting are reserved for government business. Powers of parliamentary scrutiny are concentrated in the House of Commons, although the Lords play an important role, in an arrangement which can be termed 'asymmetric bicameralism'. In the post-war period the dominance of party discipline among MPs allowed government to take parliament for granted, while party loyalties at the grassroots also allowed most members to take their constituency voters for granted.[31] Parliament continued to play a significant role in legitimating government, and serving as the principal pathway to higher office, but it had weak powers of scrutiny, and it was of marginal influence as a policy-making and law-making institution.

Conclusions: the Era of Two-Party Dominance

The Westminster model of responsible party government operated most clearly in Britain from 1945 to 1970. Once widely admired, and emulated in countries such as Canada and Australia, at the turn of the century Woodrow Wilson referred to this model as 'the world's fashion'.[32] The advantages of the Westminster model, proponents have argued, are that executives can be effective while remaining accountable. Under this system governments have full authority to implement their policies and take difficult decisions, if necessary, with the assurance of a legislative majority for a full parliament. Yet governments remain continually accountable for their actions to the House of Commons, and, at intervals, to the public. Elections provide citizens with the opportunity to evaluate government performance against the platform of the parties in opposition, and the ability to remove incumbents through the power of the ballot box. The regular swing of the pendulum between government and opposition, combined with the pressure to compete on the centre ground, are devices which make parties responsible.

To summarize, the essential components of the Westminster model include plurality single-member elections which were widely regarded as free and fair; disciplined and cohesive parties; a two-party system in government, rooted in widespread support for two-partyism in the electorate; and strong majoritarian Cabinet governments. The 'Westminster' system evolved incrementally, it was never planned. Nevertheless it was a political *system*, which meant that change in one component had the capacity to loosen the foundations for the whole mechanism. During the fifties many believed that Britain had developed the best form of representative democracy which, like cricket, was worthy of export to the Commonwealth. Parliamentary government was commonly regarded as a key precondition for the successful duration of new democracies.[33]

Yet, with the benefits of hindsight, the traditional textbook view can be seen to be guilty of considerable exaggeration, particularly the complacent assumptions common to many observers about the virtues of the Westminster system compared with coalition governments common throughout Europe. This view was heavily coloured by memories of party fragmentation, extremism and government instability during the 1920s in Weimar Germany, the Fourth French Republic and Italy. It was only in the 1980s that it was understood how smaller multicultural societies, such as Belgium, Switzerland, and the Netherlands, could enjoy stable multi-party coalition governments based on the 'consociational' or 'consensus' model of democracy. As formulated by Lijphart, the consociational model places far greater emphasis on restraining majority rule through power-sharing, the separation and devolution of power, minority veto, and proportional representation.[34] By the end of the twentieth century, few remain sanguine about the virtues of Westminster democracy, and critics have built up a head of steam in the pressures towards far-reaching constitutional reform. Many believe that in recent decades the concentration of powers authorized to the governing party inherent within this model have increased, while the mechanisms for accountability to parliament and the public have seriously weakened.

Nevertheless, stripped of its rosy glow, evidence suggests that the Westminster model remained broadly accurate as a description of Britain in the 1950s, when the two-party duopoly of government locked step with two-party support in the electorate. The critical issue to be considered in the next chapter is whether this model continues to provide an accurate description of the British political system in recent decades. If popular support for the two-party system has changed, if public confidence in the electoral system has declined, and if strong and disciplined parties have weakened, this can have significant consequences for the quality of British democracy.

Notes

1 This model is an amended version of the Westminster model of democracy developed by Arend Lijphart, 1984. *Democracies*. New Haven, CN: Yale University Press.

2 David Butler and Gareth Butler, 1994. *British Political Facts, 1900–1994*. London: Macmillan, p. 207.

3 For a discussion see Maurice Duverger, 1954. *Political Parties*. New York: John Wiley and Sons, p. 208; William Wallace, 1983. 'Survival and Revival' in Vernon Bogdanor, 1983. *Liberal Party Politics* Oxford: Oxford University Press; Chris Cook, 1993. *A Short History of the Liberal Party 1900–92*. London: Macmillan; John Stevenson, 1993. *Third Party Politics Since 1945*. Oxford: Blackwell/ Institute of Contemporary British History.

4 See Andrew Marr, 1995. *The Battle for Scotland* Harmondsworth: Penguin; Jack Brand, 1978. *The Nationalist Movement in Scotland*. London: Routledge and Kegan Paul; James Kellas, 1989. *The Scottish Political System*. Cambridge: Cambridge University Press; Michael Fry, 1987. *Patronage and Principle*. Aberdeen: Aberdeen University Press.

5 Henry Pelling, 1958. *The British Communist Party*. New York: Macmillan.

6 For a detailed examination of the legal and procedural aspects of the British

electoral system see Robert Blackburn, 1995. *The Electoral System in Britain*. New York: St. Martin's Press.

7   The 'cube law' states that if the vote cast for the two leading parties at an election is divided in the proportion A:B, the seats will be divided between them in the proportion $A^3:B^3$. This means that if the two party vote falls within the 55:45 range, about 18 seats out of 650 in Parliament would change hands for every one per cent swing of the vote. The cube law was first observed by the *Royal Commission on Electoral Systems*, 1910, Cmd. 5163, London: HMSO. It was rediscovered by M. G. Kendall and A. Stuart, 1950. 'The Law of Cubic Proportion in Election Results', *British Journal of Science*, pp. 183–96; and David Butler, 1963. *The British Electoral System Since 1918*. Oxford: Oxford University Press.

8   Pippa Norris and Ivor Crewe, 1994. 'Did the British Marginals Vanish? Proportionality and Exaggeration in the British Electoral System Revisited', *Electoral Studies* 13(3): 201–21.

9   The 'Butler swing' is calculated by the following formula:

$$\frac{(C^2-C^1) + (L^1-L^2)}{2}$$

where

C^1 = Conservative percentage share of the total vote at the first election.
C^2 = Conservative percentage share of the total vote at the second election.
L^1 = Labour percentage share of the total vote at the first election.
L^2 = Labour percentage share of the total vote at the second election.

e.g. in 1950–1

$$\frac{(48.0-43.4 = +4.6) + (46.1-48.8=-2.7) = 1.9}{2} = 0.9$$

By convention the parties are calculated in this order, so that a positive swing signifies a shift to the Conservatives, a negative swing signifies a shift to Labour.

The concept of 'swing' is a simple way to summarize changes in support for the two major parties but one which may be misleading in multiparty contests. See David Butler, 1963. *The Electoral System in Britain Since 1918*. Oxford: Oxford University Press.

10   David Butler, 1963. *The Electoral System in Britain Since 1918*. Oxford: Oxford University Press.

11   Pippa Norris, 1995. 'The Politics of Electoral Reform in Britain', *International Political Science Review* 16(1): 65–78.

12   Gabriel A. Almond and Sidney Verba, 1963. *The Civic Culture*. Princeton, NJ: Princeton University Press.

13 See, for example, Richard Rose, 1980. *Politics in England*. Boston: Little Brown, chapter IV.

14 See Philip Norton, 1975. *Dissension in the House of Commons, 1945-1974*. London: Macmillan.

15 Richard Rose, 1978. *The Problem of Party Government*. London: Macmillan; Richard Rose, 1984. *Do Parties Make a Difference?* Chatham, NJ: Chatham House; Richard Rose and Phillip L. Davies, 1994. *Inheritance in Public Policy: Change Without Choice in Britain*. New Haven: Yale University Press.

16 Hans-Dieter Klingemann, Richard I. Hofferbert and Ian Budge, 1994. *Parties, Policies and Democracy*. Boulder, CO: Westview. See also Ian Budge, David Robertson and Derek Hearl (eds), 1987. *Ideology, Strategy and Party Change*. Cambridge: Cambridge University Press; Ian Budge and Dennis Fairlie, 1983. *Explaining and Predicting Elections*. London: George Allen & Unwin; Ian Budge and Richard I. Hofferbert, 1992. 'The Party Mandate and the Westminster Model: Party Programmes and Government Spending in Britain 1949-85', *British Journal of Political Science* 22; Ian Budge and Hans Keman, 1990. *Parties and Democracy*. Oxford: Oxford University Press.

17 For a discussion of what exactly constitutes a vote of confidence in the government see Rodney Brazier, 1994. *Constitutional Practice*. Oxford: Clarendon Press.

18 Devon Torrington was won by the Liberals in 1958. See Pippa Norris, 1990. *British By-Elections: The Volatile Electorate*. Oxford: Clarendon Press.

19 Colin Rallings and Michael Thrasher, 1993 (eds). *Local Election in Britain*. Plymouth: Local Government Chronicle Elections Centre; David Butler and Gareth Butler, 1994. *British Political Facts, 1900-1994*. London: Macmillan.

20 Only very occasionally are non-members of either House appointed as ministers, and then, like Lord Young of Graffham, they are usually created peers. The only minister never to have been an MP or peer was Smuts, who sat in Lloyd George's War Cabinet. See Paul Silk and Rhodri Walters, 1995. *How Parliament Works*, 3rd edn. London: Longman.

21 Walter Bagehot, 1964. *The English Constitution*. London: C. Watt & Co., p.68.

22 Pippa Norris and Joni Lovenduski, 1995. *Political Recruitment: Gender, Race and Class in the British Parliament*. Cambridge: Cambridge University Press.

23 Dennis Kavanagh and Peter Morris, 1989. *Consensus Politics*. Oxford: Blackwell/The Institute of Contemporary History.

24 R. T. McKenzie, 1955. *British Political Parties*. New York: St. Martin's Press, p. 636

25 For studies critically examining these propositions see Michael Laver and Ken Shepsle, 1990. 'Coalitions and Cabinet Government', *American Political Science Review* 84: 873-90; Kaare Strom, 1990. *Minority Government and Majority Rule*. New York: Cambridge University Press.

26 Leo Amery, 1947. *Thoughts on the Constitution*. Oxford: Oxford University Press, p. 70.
27 Ronald Butt, 1969. *The Power of Parliament*. London: Constable.
28 Michael Rush, 1995. 'Parliamentary Scrutiny', in Robert Pyper and Lynton Robins (eds), *Governing the UK in the 1990s*. New York: St. Martin's Press.
29 Philip Norton, 1995. 'Parliament's Changing Role' in Robert Pyper and Lynton Robins (eds), *Governing the UK in the 1990s*. New York: St. Martin's Press.
30 Peter Hennessy, 1995. *The Hidden Wiring*. London: Victor Gollancz, p. 146.
31 Philip Norton, 1993. *Does Parliament Matter?* Herts.: Harvester Wheatsheaf.
32 Woodrow Wilson, 1884. 'Committee or Cabinet Government', *Overland Monthly*, January.
33 For a recent analysis of this argument see Axel Hadenius, 1994. 'The Duration of Democracy: Institutional vs. Socio-economic Factors', in David Beetham (ed.), *Defining and Measuring Democracy*. London: Sage Publications.
34 Arend Lijphart, 1984. *Democracies*. New Haven: Yale University Press.

2 Electoral Change, 1970–1992

In recent decades the Westminster model of responsible party government in Britain has been severely weakened in certain regards but has not, as yet, broken. The period from 1970 to 1992 can be regarded as the era of two-party challenge in government and two-party decline in the electorate (see figure 2.1). The shackles linking power to accountability have loosened. Britain has experienced erratic minor party tsunamis, producing sporadic underwater tidal waves which have risen to d sturb the placid surface of electoral politics. What is the evidence for this? Let us examine changes in each of the major components of the Westminster model.

Changes in Electoral Competition

During the last quarter century one of the most striking changes to the British political system, discussed in detail in subsequent chapters, has been the significant destabilization of the two-party vote. This is indicated by a variety of trends, which will be explored later,[1] including the substantial fall in two-party support as measured by voting behaviour in general elections, local elections, European elections, by-elections, and by voting intentions expressed in monthly opinion polls, producing the erratic ebb and flow in the fortunes of the minor parties since the early seventies. As a result the democratic legitimacy of one-party control of government, and two-party control of parliament, rests on a more flimsy and insecure foundation of public support.

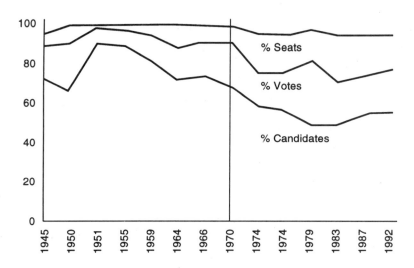

Figure 2.1 Two-party support in general elections

The most important evidence has been the substantial slump in the two-party share of the UK vote in general elections: from 91.5 per cent during the period 1945–70 to 77 per cent during the period 1970–92 (see table 2.1, figure 2.1). During the second period the two-party share of the electorate fell to only 55.5 per cent: almost as many people voted against the two major parties, or abstained, as endorsed them. In the 1945-70 period two-party support was fairly predictable, falling within the range from 39 to 50 per cent of the vote. Yet in general elections since 1970 the Conservative share of the vote has ranged from 36 to 46 per cent, while Labour's has fluctuated from 28 to 43 per cent. The two parties are also less evenly balanced: during the period from 1945 to 1970 the mean difference in the Conservative and Labour share of the vote was 3.9 per cent, whereas since February 1974 the difference has been 6.9 percentage points.

This significant erosion of support has affected both major parties. The Conservatives have won four successive elections since 1979, usually with comfortable parliamentary majorities, yet with an average share of the vote of only 42.6 per cent. In contrast from 1951 to 1964 Conservative governments were returned with a far higher share of the vote (49 per cent).

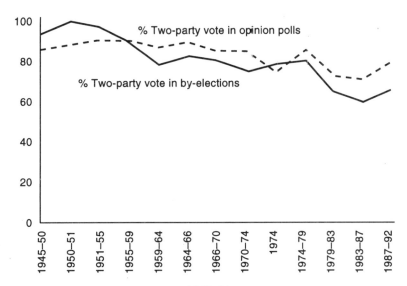

Figure 2.2   Two-party support, 1945–92

Nevertheless, as discussed in later chapters, the most consistent and significant decline has been in the Labour vote, dramatized by four successive defeats under the administrations of Mrs Thatcher and John Major, but also evident in the long-term erosion of support since their peak in 1966. Labour were returned to power (narrowly) in 1974–9 despite their shrinking share of the vote. By the 1983 election Labour stared into the abyss, with only 28 per cent of the popular vote, its lowest share since 1918. The Liberal–Social Democratic Alliance, led by Roy Jenkins and David Steel, captured 25.4 per cent of the vote, the highest third party vote for sixty years, and almost overtook Labour.[2] Nevertheless Labour won 209 seats to the Alliance's 23, enough to maintain Labour's status as the major party of opposition. In the early eighties Labour's leadership splintered but refused to self-destruct, as the Liberals had in the twenties, and the party slowly but steadily recovered support in the 1987 and 1992 general elections Under the leadership of John Smith, then under Tony Blair, Labour's performance in monthly opinion polls has been extremely strong; indeed since 1994 the party has regularly sustained their highest levels of support since Gallup began regular polling in 1945.

Yet long-term evidence of voting intentions in monthly opinion polls demonstrates lower support for the two parties, and greater willingness by the electorate to desert the party in government. Combined Labour and Conservative support in monthly Gallup polls of voting intentions was high in the post-war decade, averaging 87 per cent from 1945 to 1970. Two-party support subsequently fell to 79 per cent from 1970 to 1992, reaching its nadir in the mid-1980s (see table 2.1, figure 2.2), before recovering slightly in recent years. Similar trends over time are evident in by-elections. There is a strong correlation between support for the major parties in constituency by-elections and in national opinion polls of voting intentions, although by-elections tend to display more exaggerated swings in behaviour.[3] As a result the proportion of by-election seats which change hands has almost tripled: from 12.4 per cent of contests in the period 1945–70 to 30.4 per cent in the period 1970–92.

Moreover two-party support has become increasingly polarized regionally with the growth of the north–south divide. Since 1955, over successive elections, Labour has gradually built up invincible majorities in its areas of greatest strength: Scotland, the north-east, Yorkshire and Humberside, particularly the inner-city council estates, industrial rust-belt and unemployment blackspots. In contrast the Conservatives have strengthened their support in the prosperous south and east, especially the new towns, suburbia and small towns.[4] This pattern was slightly modified in the 1992 election, due to the recession which reversed the usual trends, producing negative equity, a deflated housing market, and greater middle-class economic insecurity through 'down-sizing' in the south and Midlands. Nevertheless the short-term reversal since 1989 has been insufficient to restore the long-term divergence in regional party strength. In 1945 the Conservatives won 40 per cent of the vote in England and 43 per cent in Scotland. In contrast in 1992 the Conservatives won 45 per cent in England but only 26 per cent in Scotland. In the same way, in 1945 Labour won 50 per cent of the vote in England and 49 per cent in Scotland. In 1992 Labour won 39 per cent in Scotland but only 34 per cent in England. As a result of regional trends over the last four decades it has become far harder for British governments to claim they were elected with a 'mandate' from the whole nation, fuelling the claims for an independent parliament in Scotland.

Table 2.1   Indicators of two-party strength, 1945–92

| | In General Elections | | | Polls | By-Elections |
	% seats	% votes	% cand	% votes	% votes
1945–50	94.2	87.6	72.5	85.9	93.4
1950–51	98.1	89.5	66.2	88.4	98.9
1951–55	98.5	96.8	89.6	90.8	96.9
1955–59	98.8	96.1	88.3	90.8	89.6
1959–64	98.9	93.2	81.1	86.6	78.2
1964–66	98.6	87.5	71.6	89.4	82.7
1966–70	97.9	89.9	73.2	85.3	80.2
1970–74	98.0	89.5	68.2	85.0	74.9
1974–74	94.2	75.1	58.4	75.0	78.3
1974–79	93.8	75.0	55.3	85.3	80.4
1979–83	95.8	80.8	48.3	73.4	64.6
1983–87	93.3	70.0	49.1	71.5	59.7
1987–92	93.1	73.1	54.4	80.2	65.8
1992	93.2	76.3	55.0		
1945–66	97.8	91.5	77.5	87.2	88.6
1970–92	94.5	77.0	55.5	78.8	70.6

Notes: In general elections the figures represent the combined Labour and Conservative share of votes, seats and candidates. With opinion polls the figures represent the mean share of voting intentions for the two major parties expressed in Gallup Polls. With by-elections the figures represent the combined mean Labour and Conservative share of the vote.

Sources: F. W. S. Craig, *British Electoral Facts, 1832–1987*; David Butler and Gareth Butler, *British Political Facts, 1900–1994*.

The centre and nationalist parties in Britain have expanded their support in recent decades, especially at local level. But the clearest pattern at Westminster has been an ebb and flow of minor party fortunes, with fluctuating waves or tsunamis, rather than a steady consolidation of their base, or advances over successive elections. The most common pattern has been a surge in protest voting during the mid-term government period, with peaks for minor parties around dramatic by-election results, which has usually failed to translate into further substantial gains in subsequent general elections.

As shown in figure 2.3, the Liberals experienced four waves of support in the national opinion polls. The first tsunami followed Orpington in 1962–3, although this spike faded before the subsequent general election. In 1972–4 the Liberals had another modest wave again during a period of

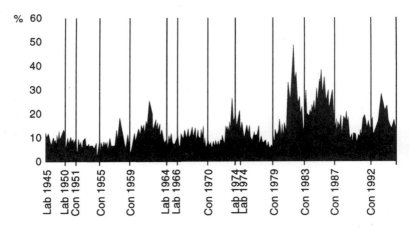

Figure 2.3   Liberal popularity, 1945–92
Source: Gallup polls of voting intentions.

deep Conservative unpopularity. The sharpest and most dramatic crest was clearly in 1981–2, peaking in polls at 50 per cent, following the creation of the SDP–Liberal Alliance, before an equally sharp fall. The Alliance showed strong and more sustained support in opinion polls in the mid-eighties, during the mid-term of the second Thatcher administration. Lastly the Liberal Democrats experienced a more modest wave in 1993–4, before support ebbed again due to the popularity of 'new Labour'.

Yet on each of these occasions it proved difficult to translate opinion poll waves, local government and by-election victories into a solid series of gains at Westminster. The tsunamis create great cataclysms on the floor of the ocean, ebbing back and forth, before colliding on the surface, while the water mass of the ocean absorbs the shock. The first significant break-through at the national level came in the February 1974 general election, when the Liberals doubled their share of the vote, from 7.5 to 19.3 per cent, and jumped from six to fourteen seats. The party was particularly successful in the south of England, where they took first or second place in the majority of constituencies. Yet rather than consolidating a steady advance in subsequent general elections, the Liberal vote fell slightly in October 1974 and May 1979, before cresting in 1983 with twenty-three members of parliament and 25.4 per cent of the vote under the banner of the SDP–Liberal Alliance. The Alliance fell back from this peak in 1987

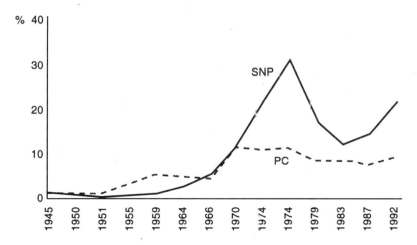

Figure 2.4   Trends in Nationalist vote, 1945–92

under the leadership of David Steel and David Owen, and then slid further
to 17.9 per cent of the vote as the merged Liberal Democrats in 1992.[5]
Standing as a candidate for the Liberals, and subsequent Liberal
Democrats, proved a triumph of hope over experience.

The Liberal performance parallels the mercurial fortunes of the nationalist parties in Scotland and Wales, with three distinct waves of revival in
by-elections, in 1966–9, in 1972–5, and, for the SNP alone, in 1988–93.
By-election performances where the party does far better than expected
usually heightens their electoral credibility, strengthens their local organization and membership, and provides the oxygen of publicity which
boosts their standing in national opinion polls.[6] Plaid Cymru increased its
share of the Welsh vote from 4.3 to 11.5 per cent in 1970, winning two seats
in heavily Welsh-speaking west and north Wales in the February 1974
general election, and the party has subsequently sustained its support at
around this level. In local elections from 1973 to 1989 the party has been
achieving about 11 per cent of the vote in Welsh county and district elections, and winning about 5.3 per cent of seats.[7]

The Scottish National party also did well in the 1970 election, before
doubling their share of the Scottish vote in February 1974. The party
reached its peak with 30.4 per cent of the Scottish vote in October 1974,

drawing support heavily from Labour and the Conservatives, returning eleven SNP members to Westminster. SNP support and representation subsequently declined from this height, mainly because of its inability to concentrate its vote, although the party recovered somewhat in 1992, and it has continued to surge in certain by-elections.[8] In district and regional elections from 1974 to 1992 on average the SNP has won 17.8 per cent of votes, and about 9.2 per cent of council seats. Other minor parties – the National Front in 1976–7, and the Greens in the June 1989 Euro-elections – have occasionally experienced similar heady, although even more evanescent, bursts of support in second-order elections.

Changes in the Electoral System

The Westminster system of adversarial rotation between government and opposition benches depended on Conservative and Labour dominance, and also the responsiveness of the electoral system to even minor tremors in the popular vote. In the early seventies increased electoral support for the minor parties, and the failure of the system to produce effective majoritarian governments, destabilized this balance, and gave new urgency to the controversy over electoral reform. From 1970 to February 1974 the two-party share of votes plummeted from 90 to 75 per cent, although Labour and the Conservative parties continued to win 94 per cent of seats. These results opened the British system to the charge of transparent unfairness to the minor parties, especially if, like the Liberals, their vote was not spatially concentrated. In the 1950s, when minor parties were almost obliterated, this raised little public concern. In recent decades these changes in party competition have highlighted serious questions of democratic legitimacy: successive Conservative administrations have held power since 1979 with the support of no more than one-third of the total electorate.

Trends over time in the exaggerative bias of the electoral system can be estimated by calculating a simple 'seats–votes' ratio.[9] This is produced by dividing each party's percentage of UK votes by the same party's percentage of UK seats, a measure which can be calculated for any party. The results (see table 2.2) indicate that in the post-war period the exaggerative qualities of the British electoral system have been influenced by two main developments.

Table 2.2   Votes:seats ratio, 1945–92

	Government			Opposition			Liberals		
	Votes %	Seats %	Ratio	Votes %	Seats %	Ratio	Votes %	Seats %	Ratio
1945	48	61	1.28	40	33	.83	9	2	.21
1950	46	50	1.09	43	48	1.10	9	1	.15
1951	48	51	1.07	49	47	.97	3	1	.38
1955	50	55	1.10	46	44	.95	3	1	.33
1959	49	58	1.17	44	41	.94	6	1	.15
1964	44	50	1.14	43	48	1.11	11	1	.13
1966	48	58	1.20	42	40	.96	9	2	.22
1970	46	52	1.13	43	46	1.06	8	1	.13
1974	37	47	1.27	38	47	1.23	19	2	.11
1974	39	50	1.28	36	44	1.22	18	2	.11
1979	44	53	1.22	37	42	1.15	14	2	.12
1983	42	61	1.44	28	32	1.17	25	4	.14
1987	42	58	1.37	31	35	1.14	23	3	.15
1992	42	52	1.23	34	42	1.22	18	3	.17
Mean 45–70	47	54	1.15	44	45	.99	7	1	.21
Mean 74–92	41	54	1.30	34	40	1.19	20	3	.14
Mean 45–92	45	54	1.21	40	43	1.07	13	2	.18

Source: Pippa Norris and Ivor Crewe, 1994. 'Did the British Marginals Vanish?', *Electoral Studies* 13(3): 201–21.

First, since 1970 the centre parties have been increasingly penalized by the system. In 1955 it took 120,400 votes to elect each Liberal member of Parliament, whereas in 1992 it took 304,183 votes. As a result the exaggerative bias of the seats-votes ratio for both main parties has increased. During the two periods under comparison the seats–votes ratio for the government increased from 1.15 to 1.30, and for the opposition from 0.99 to 1.19. To put it another way, in 1955 it took 38,582 votes to elect each Conservative MP, whereas in 1983 it took just 32,776, despite the fact that meanwhile the number of electors had increased by a fifth. The effect has been to increase the government advantage over all parties, which helps to explain how in the 1980s Conservative governments enjoyed ample parliamentary majorities although achieving historically low shares of the national vote.[10]

Second, the exaggerative bias of the electoral system has changed due to the growing disparity in the size of constituencies. The Labour party has benefited more from this than the Conservatives, hence the rise in the opposition's seats-votes ratio since 1974. When revising constituencies the Boundary Commission applies an electoral quota produced by dividing the total electorate by the number of constituencies at the time the review begins. The commissioners work to produce constituencies with an electorate close to the quota, although this is not always practical. Until 1965 the quota was calculated for Britain as a whole but since then it has been related to each part of the UK; in 1991–3 the quota was 69,000 for England but 58,500 for Wales, 54,500 for Scotland and 68,000 for Northern Ireland.

These regional quotas have benefited the Labour party, given its strength in the urban areas of central Scotland and in south Wales. Patterns of internal population migration, with the gradual depopulation of depressed inner-cities with a solid Labour vote, like Liverpool, Newcastle and Sunderland, have also disadvantaged the Conservatives, especially when the boundaries were seriously out of date. There is a significant delay between publication of the census data and the implementation of work of the commission, which means that, given the population trends, even the new boundaries fail to produce an equal number of electors in each constituency. In 1955 there were about 55,500 electors in the average British seat, with the number in Conservative and Labour seats roughly equal (indeed Labour had slightly more (700+)). By 1970, before the next major boundary revisions came into effect, the number of electors in Labour seats had gradually risen to 57,000, but in Conservative seats the number had shot up to 67,000. In 1992 the disparity had grown again, so that Conservative seats contained 71,000 electors compared with 61,600 in Labour constituencies, 58,800 in Liberal Democrat seats, and 55,700 in Nationalist seats.

The system's bias against centre parties, combined with the disparity in the size of Conservative and Labour seats, have served to close the opposition–government seats–votes ratio. The winner's bonus for the government has increased. Once we take all parties into account, we find the exaggerative bias of the British electoral system has strengthened over time. This has generated a heated debate about electoral reform, and the development of a new cleavage in party politics revolving around constitutional issues.

Cracks in Party Discipline and Unity

The responsible party government model depended not just on the ability of the electorate to 'throw the rascals out' through the workings of the electoral system, but also that parties presented cohesive and unified party platforms. One of the most striking developments to affect the Westminster model in Parliament since the early seventies has been the decline in party discipline. This has led to difficulties for the governing party in managing its own backbenchers and maintaining party unity, producing a volatile mix when combined with a small overall majority. As Philip Norton has demonstrated in a series of studies, backbenchers have become more willing to rebel against their parliamentary party.[11] Between 1945 and 1970 governments could assume that under the guidance of party whips their members would flow through the division lobbies in an orderly manner. As Samuel Beer noted: 'When one makes a statistical study of party voting, the figures are so monotonously 100 per cent or nearly 100 per cent that it is hardly worth making the count. If this is an age of cabinet government, the reason in the first instance is that it is an age of party government.'[12] Provided they had a majority, the government could always shrug off the opposition's attacks, but they were always more vulnerable to attacks from within.

The early seventies saw the rise of sporadic cross-voting by Conservative MPs, resulting in half a dozen defeats for the Conservative government under Edward Heath. Backbench rebellions continued under the 1974–9 Labour government, producing forty-two defeats on the floor of the House, and even more in committee. Some degree of independent voting has been maintained in subsequent parliaments. The size of the government's majority under Margaret Thatcher meant that cross-voting rarely changed government policy, although the Shops Bill was defeated in 1986, and the issue of student loans was modified under threat of defeat. Moreover this erosion of party unity was not confined to the Commons. Party discipline also deteriorated in the House of Lords, where Conservative peers defeated the Thatcher government on more than 150 occasions.[13]

These problems were compounded when John Major was returned in 1992 with a slim majority of twenty-one, which was rapidly whittled down in successive by-elections. The government experienced serious backbench dissent and unexpected defeats on the closure of coal pits, on MPs' allowances, on fishing policy, and above all the bill to ratify the Maastricht Treaty. The heated debate about Britain's position within the European Union has bitterly factionalized the Conservative party into Euro-fanatics and Euro-sceptics.[14] Nine anti-Brussels Conservative MPs, including William Cash, Theresa Gorman and Tony Marlow, refused to support the government over the Maastricht Treaty in July 1993, effectively creating a cabal within the party and leading to government defeat. As a result the Conservative whip was withdrawn from them for four months, until seven were subsequently readmitted. The factionalism of the party over Europe produced continued rumblings of discontent with John Major's premiership, eventually triggering the July 1995 Major–Redwood leadership contest. The long-term erosion of party discipline within the House has had major consequences, not just for the coherence of the British government's policy towards Europe, but also for the pace of unification among member states within the European Union.[15] The so-called 'beef war' has disrupted EU business and caused questions to be raised about Britain's continued membership of the Union. The need to preserve peace among both wings of the Conservative party has dominated parliamentary strategy, weakened the Cabinet, and undermined John Major's position.

Further evidence that the troops were becoming increasingly restless can be found in the strong and bitter leadership challenges within the parliamentary Conservative party which ended Edward Heath's career in 1975, Mrs Thatcher's long reign in November 1990, and which seriously challenged John Major's leadership in June 1995.[16] The party factionalism among ministers and MPs which was revealed in the full glare of television klieg lights on the Palace Green during these contests, even if patched over after the event, reinforced an image of a deeply divided government. Some previous battles for the leadership of the Labour party have proved equally, or even more, divisive, such as the 1981 deputy leadership contest between Tony Benn and Dennis Healey. But in contrast the Labour party's method of leadership selection since 1993, by ballot of the party membership, produced far greater consensus within the party.[17] The development of factions and divisions among, and between, ministers and MPs in the governing party proves problematic for the Westminster model, because if voters can no longer evaluate the performance of parties as a collectivity, this erodes the foundations of accountable government.

Yet these developments should not be exaggerated: the British House of Commons has not become the US House of Representatives, the

Russian Duma or the Italian Chamber of Deputies. We are observing a modest change in behaviour. The proportion of government bills approved by parliament was 97.5 per cent in the period 1945 to 1970 and 96.6 per cent in the period 1970 to 1987.[18] On most issues elected representatives are reduced, in Austin Mitchell's vivid phrase, to 'heckling the steamroller'.[19] Another astute observer of Westminster life, Andrew Marr, concluded that government backbenchers can very occasionally exercise leverage on the general drift of government policy. But in general, in Marr's words, 'it's more like children shouting at passing aircraft'.[20] For most of the time, British MPs continued to tow the party line, and for most MPs this continued to be the Conservative or Labour party line. From 1970 to 1992 the Commons was still dominated by Labour and Conservative members, who held 95 per cent of the seats (see table 2.1). Anyone watching the regular parliamentary question-time on television could easily suppose that the government–opposition debate was a timeless ritual, undisturbed (except for the television cameras and a female speaker) since the war, with even the shape of the chamber designed for Labour and Conservative MPs to confront each other in serried ranks.

Challenging Two-party Dominance in Government

Two-party control of parliament has come under increasing attack as other parties have contested more constituencies, producing a significant change in the nature of the electoral choice facing voters. From 1945 to 1966 voters faced a straight (Conservative–Labour) fight in half the seats. After 1974 all constituencies have been contested by at least three parties, and usually more. The two-party share of parliamentary candidates fell from 77 per cent in the period 1945–70 to 55 per cent in the period 1970–92 (see table 2.2, figure 2.2). In total 2,946 candidates fought the 1992 general election, including 645 Conservatives, 634 Labour, 633 Liberal Democrats, 250 Greens, 72 SNP, 26 Plaid Cymru, 2 SDP, and 684 others. The average number of candidates per seat increased from 2.6 in the period 1945–70 to 4.2 in the period 1970–92. In 1992 some ballot papers listed as many as ten candidates, partly due to the number of constituencies contested by the Greens, the (old) Liberals, and the Natural Law Party.[21]

Centre parties face the obvious problem of converting votes into seats,

Table 2.3   Number of parties in the House of Commons, 1945–92

	Total number
1945	8
1950	6
1951	6
1955	5
1959	5
1964	4
1966	5
1970	8
1974 (Feb.)	9
1974 (Oct.)	10
1979	11
1983	11
1987	11
1992	9
1945–66	6
1970–92	10

Note: Excludes independent and university candidates.

given the high thresholds in the British electoral system if their support is not spatially concentrated. Even so over the years more parties have gained parliamentary representation: there were on average six parties in Parliament during the period 1945-66, compared with ten during the period 1970-92 (see table 2.3). The Northern Ireland party system fragmented after the outbreak of 'the troubles' in the early seventies, and the break-up of the old Conservative and Unionist party in February 1974. The 1992 parliament included MPs standing under the banner of the Ulster Unionists (9), Democratic Unionists (3), Ulster Popular Unionists (1), Social Democratic and Labour (4), the SNP (3), Plaid Cymru (4) and the Liberal Democrats (20).

Westminster is only one arena of party competition. The strongest challenge to single-party government has come at the level of local government. Reorganization following the Local Government Act in 1972 makes it difficult to analyse post-war trends on a consistent basis. Nevertheless, election results between 1973 and 1992 show that the two major parties have continued to win about 90 per cent of London and Metropolitan Borough seats, with Labour particularly successful in these urban areas. But the Liberal Democrats, the nationalist parties, and independents win far more seats outside the main cities. From 1973 to 1992 the two major parties have held, on average, only three-quarters of English shire county seats, about two-thirds of Scottish Regional and District seats, and only half the Welsh county and district seats.[22] In the May 1996 local elections, out of 150 councils, Labour ended up controlling 86, the Conservatives 3, the Liberal Democrats 23, Independents 3, while 35 ended with no party in control.

The net effect has been dramatic: the practice of coalition government in 'hung' councils has now become widespread in Britain. After the 1985 local elections in England and Wales, no fewer than twenty-five of the forty-five county councils were left with no single party commanding an overall majority. Following the district elections in 1991, one third of all non-metropolitan councils (108 out of 333) were similarly 'hung'. In the 513 local authorities in England, Scotland and Wales, 153 (30 per cent) had no single party control.[23] This is largely a reflection of the electoral success of Liberal Democrat councillors, whose numbers quadrupled from just over 1,000 in 1979 to over 4,300 in 1993. This has produced a variety of outcomes for local government, ranging from formal coalitions, and minority administrations with the tacit support of another party, to a series of ad-hoc arrangements.[24] The net result has been the widespread growth of 'bargaining' politics, when local politicians have had to negotiate with their opposite number in other parties, as well as with their own group, to run local authorities.

Cabinet Government

In recent decades the outcome of the general election has usually continued to produce cabinets with an overall majority of seats in Parliament, with certain important exceptions. In February 1974 the general election resulted in a minority administration, the first time this had happened since 1929. Labour won the largest number of parliamentary seats (301 to 297), although coming second to the Conservatives in their share of the vote (37.2 to 37.9 per cent). Edward Heath tried to continue in government by forming a coalition with the Liberals, but when the Liberals refused, Harold Wilson returned to power heading a minority Labour government. The government was deeply divided, and faced serious economic problems, rising nationalism in Wales and Scotland, increased conflict in Northern Ireland, and the issue of Britain's membership of the EEC remained unresolved. Not surprisingly the administration proved short-lived and Wilson went to the country again nine months later.

The stronger challenge to the Westminster model came following the October 1974 general election, which returned a Labour government with a slim overall majority of only four seats. This was gradually eroded through by-elections, but the balance of power in the Commons rested with forty MPs divided into five parties, who would have had to act together to pass a vote of no confidence, so Labour was able to implement most of its radical programme despite its limited majority. This situation was challenged in March 1977 when James Callaghan's government faced a united vote of no confidence. To keep Callaghan in power the Liberals entered a formal 'pact' with Labour from March 1977 to August 1978. The 'pact' was a public agreement that the Liberals would back the Labour government on any confidence issue until the end of the summer. In return the Liberals were consulted on all major policy initiatives, and Labour agreed to proceed towards devolution and to consider a proportional representation system for European elections, although no Liberals entered the cabinet.[25] Thus despite the 'pact' there was no formal coalition government. Although coalitions are commonplace in most European systems, and were characteristic of British party politics between the wars, single-party cabinets have been maintained in UK central government throughout the last fifty years.[26]

In 1992 John Major was returned with a majority of twenty-one but this was whittled down with successive by-election defeats and defections. Gains went to all parties; the Liberal Democrats (Newbury, Christchurch, Eastleigh, Littleborough and Saddleworth), Labour (Dudley West, Staffordshire South East) and the SNP (Perth and Kinross). In addition Sir Richard Body and Peter Thurnham became 'independents' refusing the Conservative whip, Alan Howarth defected to Labour, and Emma Nicholson defected to the Liberal Democrats. Continued deep rifts over Europe within the Conservative party further undermined government stability. Reduced to a single seat majority by mid-1996, if any more Conservatives rebelled John Major would be dependent upon continued support from the Ulster Unionists to survive a vote of no-confidence.

The opposite danger was not the weakness, but the overwhelming strength, of single-party governments. Accountability is threatened if the electorate no longer has the ability to remove incumbents, and the regular swing of the pendulum between government and opposition becomes stuck. Imbalance in the two-party system allows one party to remain in power for long periods, while the other is consigned to the wilderness. Since 1979 the remarkable success of Conservative governments in maintaining their grip on power, and the remarkable weakness of the Labour party, has led to considerable speculation that Britain has developed a predominant party system, like Japan.[27] In 1992 the Conservatives experienced their fourth successive election victory, the longest period of single-party rule since the Great Reform Act of 1832. Moreover the Conservative victory in the 1992 election was unexpected, since it followed the longest depression since the thirties, and the Conservative campaign was much criticized.[28] Yet, as discussed in the next chapter, Conservative success should not disguise the fact that the last twenty-five years have continued to see a regular turnover of the major parties in central government (see table 2.4). The Conservative administration of Edward Heath (1970–4) was replaced by the Wilson/Callaghan government (1974–9), before the long-running Thatcher/Major administrations (1979–).

Table 2.4   Parties in government, 1945–92

Period	Duration	Party	Leader
1945–1951	6	Labour	Attlee
1951–1964	13	Conservative	Churchill/Eden/Macmillan
1964–1970	6	Labour	Wilson
1970–1974	4	Conservative	Heath
1974–1979	5	Labour	Wilson/Callaghan
1979–		Conservative	Thatcher/Major

In recent years there have also been significant changes in executive-legislative relations, due to entry into the European Union. The British parliament retains ultimate sovereignty, in the sense that it could pass an act withdrawing the United Kingdom from the EU, but short of this drastic step, more and more decisions affecting British citizens are being taken at European level. At present the EU Executive Commission is chosen by the member governments, legislative powers are exercised by the Council of Ministers, organized interest groups are consulted through the Economic and Social Committee, judicial powers are exercised through the independent Court of Justice, and a weak parliament is chosen in what are best characterized as second-order national elections. The most influential law-making body remains the Council of Ministers, essentially an intergovernmental negotiating forum representing member states and acting behind closed doors. The lack of transparency in negotiations between member states within Council makes normal democratic account-ability over legislation highly problematic. British Ministers attending the Council of Ministers are only one voice out of fifteen, which has reduced the independence of the British executive. Nevertheless the lack of trans-parency of discussions within the Council of Ministers has, if anything, strengthened the powers of the British cabinet over the British parliament.[29]

Concern about the weakness of the legislature *vis-à-vis* the executive has produced an extended debate about the reform of parliament, even prior to Britain's entry into Europe.[30] Recent institutional reforms like the intro-duction of departmental select committees in 1979, and improved working conditions following the Jopling Committee report in 1992, have slightly strengthened the House of Commons's powers of legislative scrutiny. Nevertheless studies have concluded that the overall impact of these reforms on the policy-making role of the legislature, while valuable, has been limited.[31] Observers like Andrew Marr are highly critical of Westminster's ability to scrutinize legislation effectively, let alone operate as an effective check on government.[32] Parliament remains a reactive insti-tution, linking citizens and government, legitimating and authorizing executive power, providing a recruitment pool for higher office, and acting as a public forum for the consent of elected representatives, but policy-making remains the prerogative of cabinet.[33]

Conclusions: the Era of Decline

Therefore the Westminster model of responsible party government has changed in many regards, although the British political system has not been transformed out of all recognition, by any means. To summarize developments: since the early seventies one-party monopoly of govern-ment, and two-party duopoly of parliament, has been maintained despite the expansion in the number of MPs from the minor parties. For the last fifty years one-party has been able to govern alone, and implement its full programme, even the minority Labour administrations in February–October 1974, and under the informal Lib–Lab pact in the mid-seventies. In government the major parties have been able to pass almost all their legislative proposals, although they have experienced a slight erosion in party discipline. The cracks in the system have become more obvious in local government where outside of metropolitan areas the 'Westminster' model has been replaced in many councils by governing coalitions, and multi-party competition has become the norm. The greatest change is evident among voters in general elections, by-elections, local elections, and opinion polls, who have demonstrated a greater willingness to desert the major parties, producing erratic and unstable tsunamis of support for the center and nationalist parties. The 'normal' party support in general elections can be calculated as the mean share of the vote for each of these periods. The 'normal' Conservative vote slipped only marginally, from 45.1 per cent in the period 1945–66 to 41.5 per cent in the period 1970–92. The normal Labour vote fell sharply during these same years, from 46.5 to 35.6 per cent. The beneficiaries were the minor parties, almost tripling their combined support, from 8.5 to 23.9 per cent.

These significant challenges to the Westminster system have undermined trust in British democracy. In the 1960s widespread confidence in the British system of government seemed to produce an exemplary 'civic culture'. In contrast many commentators believe that in recent years Britain has experienced an erosion of faith in the integrity of politicians, in the major institutions of public life, and in the fundamental political system. John Curtice and Roger Jowell note growing public disaffection with the operation of central government and its institutions during the last twenty years.[34] In mid-1995, when asked in a MORI poll to evaluate 'the present system of governing Britain', only a fifth (22 per cent) of the public felt that it worked well, down from a third (33 per cent) in 1991.[35] Patrick Dunleavy and Stuart Weir argue that the public has moved towards increased support for root-and-branch constitutional reform.[36] In evidence before the Nolan Committee, Ivor Crewe suggested that the public registered little respect for the integrity and honesty of Members of Parliament.[37] Not all evidence or measures point in the same direction,[38] and we need to distinguish the depth to which the acid of cynicism has penetrated, whether undermining faith in particular politicians and parties, or corroding more deep-rooted trust in the British political system. Nevertheless an erosion of public confidence has been widely observed.

This erosion may have been caused by a series of specific events in the mid-nineties, including front-page headlines about the marital problems of the younger Royals, the issues of parliamentary corruption investigated by the Nolan Committee, the Scott inquiry into the Matrix-Churchill affair, and tabloid revelations about the personal behaviour of ministers, leading to the string of resignations from office during the Major government. Yet confidence may also have been eroded by a broader and more systematic failure of the political system to connect citizens and the State. The debate about deep-rooted constitutional reform has widened and produced a new cleavage in British party politics, dividing the stand-patters (most in the Conservative party) from all the reformers and radicals (some of the opposition parties).

Although critics of the British political system have become increasingly vociferous in recent decades, the range of possible solutions has been narrowly defined. Few voices have been demanding the sort of populist grassroots democracy which is currently being debated in the United States. Although the '*Guardian*-reading' class may occasionally discuss the merits of term-limitations for politicians, or Putnam's plea for the restoration of social capital and civic engagement,[39] these issues do not hit a groundswell of public support in the same way as they do in the United States. Even ideas of 'deliberative' democracy, propagated by James Fishkin, or the case for 'civic journalism',[40] sit uneasily within the British culture, which distrusts populism. British reformers like Charter '88 have focused their efforts on introducing legal and constitutional fetters on executive power, or, like Lord Nolan, increasing the transparency of the rules regarding MPs relationship with lobbyists, not introducing popular mechanisms of control.[41]

Nevertheless some elements of direct democracy have been grafted onto the British system, all so far concerning constitutional questions about transferring the powers of Parliament where the major parties have been internally divided, although the use of referenda remains limited. In 1973 the Heath administration held a referendum in Northern Ireland (the border poll), in June 1975 Labour held a national referendum to ratify Britain's membership of the European Community, and in March 1979 a referendum on devolution was held in Scotland and Wales.[42] More recently, both major parties have considered holding a referendum after the 1996 Inter-Governmental Conference to test popular support for Britain's entry into the European Monetary Union. If returned to government after the next election Labour has pledged to hold a referendum on the issue of electoral reform. If a more proportional system were to be implemented for Westminster elections, this promises to have far-reaching effects on the party system. To understand the implications of these developments we need to go on to consider the nature of the British party system, and explanations for declining support for two-partyism over time.

Notes

1 Other studies have employed alternative indicators of the decline in two-party support, including changes in the level of electoral volatility and in party membership, but in this study these factors are analysed in subsequent chapters as causes of the change in two-party voting, not proxy measures.

2 For details see David Butler and Dennis Kavanagh, 1985. *The British General Election of 1983*. London: Macmillan.

3 Pippa Norris, 1990. *British By-elections*. Oxford: Oxford University Press, p. 150.

4 See J. Lewis and A. Townsend (eds), 1989. *The North–South Divide: Regional Change in Britain in the 1980s*. London: Paul Chapman; R. J. Johnston, C. J. Pattie and J. G. Allsopp, 1986. *A Nation Dividing: The Electoral Map of Great Britain 1979–87*. Harlow: Longman; R. J. Johnston and C. J. Pattie, 1993. 'Where the Tories lost and won: geographical variations in voting in the 1992 British general election', *Parliamentary Affairs* 46: 192–202.

5 See Chris Cook, 1993. *A Short History of the Liberal Party, 1900–92*. London: Macmillan; John Stevenson, 1993. *Third Party Politics since 1945*. Oxford: Blackwell/ICBH.

6 For details see Pippa Norris, 1990. *British By-elections*. Oxford: Clarendon Press, pp. 17–43.

7 Colin Rallings and Michael Thrasher, 1993. *Local Elections in Britain: A Statistical Digest*. Plymouth: Local Government Chronicle Elections Centre.

8 For details see David Butler and Denis Kavanagh, 1974. *The British General Election of February 1974*. London: Macmillan; James Kellas, 1989. *The Scottish Political System*. Cambridge: Cambridge University Press; Andrew Marr, 1995. *The Battle for Scotland*. London: Penguin; Jack Brand, 1978. *The Nationalist Movement in Scotland*. London: Routledge and Kegan Paul; Roger Levy, 1994. 'Nationalist Parties in Scotland and Wales' in Lynton Robins, Hilary Blackmore and Robert Pyper (eds), 1994, *Britain's Changing Party System*. Leicester: Leicester University Press; Alice Brown, David McCione and Lindsay Paterson, 1996. *Politics and Society in Scotland*. London: Macmillan.

9 Pippa Norris and Ivor Crewe, 1994. 'Did the British Marginals Vanish?' *Electoral Studies* 13(3): 201–21.

10 It should be noted that, as argued elsewhere, the seats–votes ratio for all parties

is the most appropriate measure to estimate electoral bias, since the government requires a working majority of seats in Parliament over all other parties, not just over the main party of opposition. In this way it is preferable to the 'cube rule' or alternative indicators based on the two-party vote.

11   See Philip Norton, 1985. 'The House of Commons: Behavioural Changes', in Philip Norton (ed.), *Parliament in the 1980s*. Oxford: Basil Blackwell; Philip Norton, 1994. 'The Parties in Parliament', in Lynton Robins, Hilary Blackmore and Robert Pyper (eds), 1994. *Britain's Changing Party System*. Leicester: Leicester University Press; Philip Norton, 1975. *Dissension in the House of Commons, 1945–74*, London: Macmillan; Philip Norton, 1980. *Dissension in the House of Commons, 1974–79*. Oxford: Clarendon Press.

12   Samuel Beer, 1990. 'The British Legislature and the Problem of Mobilizing Consent', in Philip Norton (ed.), *Legislatures*. Oxford: Oxford University Press.

13   D. Shell, and D. Beamish (eds), 1993. *The House of Lords at Work*. Oxford: Oxford University Press.

14   See Pippa Norris, 1994. 'Labour Party Factionalism and Extremism', in Anthony Heath, Roger Jowell and John Curtice, *Labour's Last Chance?* Aldershot, Hants.: Dartmouth Press.

15   See Andrew Duff, John Pinder and Roy Pryce (eds), 1994. *Maastricht and Beyond*. London: Routledge.

16   The Conservative party selects its leader by vote of the 1922 Committee, composed of all Conservative MPs, with consultation of other groups such as Conservative peers and the party outside parliament. This process was devised in 1965, and modified in 1974–5 and 1991. Under the procedure the leader must secure a majority of the votes plus 15 per cent more of the votes of those entitled to vote than his or her leading competitor. For details see Vernon Bogdanor. 'The Selection of the Party Leader', in Anthony Seldon and Stuart Ball (eds), 1996. *Conservative Century*. Oxford: Oxford University Press. Since 1993 the Labour party has selected its leadership by a ballot among all party members. For the process of leadership selection see Malcolm Punnett, 1992. *Selecting the Party Leader: Britain in Comparative Perspective*. London: Harvester Wheatsheaf.

17   For details see Keith Alderman, 'Testing Party Democracy: The British Labour Party's Leadership Election 1994', *Representation*. 33(2): 51-7.

18   Calculated from Richard Rose, 1989. *Politics in England*. London: Macmillan. Table IV.1, p. 113.

19   Quoted in John Garrett, 1992. *Does Westminster Work?* London: Hamish Hamilton, p. 16.

20   Andrew Marr, 1995. *Ruling Britannia*. London: Michael Joseph, p. 115.

21   See Pippa Norris and Joni Lovenduski, 1995. *Political Recruitment: Gender,*

Race and Class in the British Parliament. Cambridge: Cambridge University Press; *The Times Guide to the House of Commons, 1992*. 1992. London: Times Books.

22 For details of local election results see Colin Rallings and Michael Thrasher, 1994. *Local Elections in Britain: A Statistical Digest*. Plymouth: Local Government Chronicle Elections Centre.

23 John Gyford, 1994. 'Party Politics in Local Government', in Lynton Robins, Hilary Blackmore and Robert Pyper (eds), *Britain's Changing Party System*. Leicester: Leicester University Press.

24 Steve Leach and John Stewart, 1992. *The Politics of Hung Authorities*. London: Macmillan.

25 See Simon Hoggart and Alistair Michie, 1978. *The Pact*. London: Quartet Books; David Steel, 1979. *A House Divided*. London: Weidenfeld & Nicolson; Chris Cook, 1993. *A Short History of the Liberal Party, 1900–92*. London: Macmillan.

26 For the consequences of a parliament in which no party has a majority see David Butler, 1986. *Governing Without a Majority*. London: Macmillan.

27 See, for example, Helen Margetts and Gareth Smyth (eds), 1994. *Turning Japanese?* London: Lawrence & Wishart. See also T. J. Pempel (ed.), 1990. *Uncommon Democracies*. Ithaca, NY: Cornell University Press.

28 See David Butler and Dennis Kavanagh, 1992. *The British General Election of 1992*. London: Macmillan.

29 See Andrew Duff, John Pinder and Roy Pryce, 1994. *Maastricht and Beyond*. London: Routledge; Robert Keohane and Stanley Hoffman (eds), 1991. *The New European Community: Decision-making and Institutional Change*. Boulder, CO: Westview Press; W. Nicholl and Trevor Salmon, 1990. *Understanding the European Community*. Hemel Hempsted: Philip Allan; John Pinder, 1991. *European Community: The Building of a Union*. Oxford: Oxford University Press.

30 See David Judge (ed.), 1983. *The Politics of Parliamentary Reform*. London: Heinemann; John Garrett, 1992. *Westminster – Does Parliament Work?* London: Gollancz.

31 Gavin Drewry (ed.), 1989. *Commons Select Committees: Catalysts for Progress*. Oxford: Oxford University Press; Philip Norton, 1993. *Does Parliament Matter?* Herts.: Harvester Wheatsheaf; Peter Hennessy, 1995. *The Hidden Wiring*. London: Victor Gollancz.

32 Andrew Marr, 1995. *Ruling Britannia*. London: Michael Joseph.

33 David Judge, 1993. *The Parliamentary State*. London: Sage.

34 John Curtice and Roger Jowell, 1995. 'The Sceptical Electorate', in Roger Jowell et al. (eds), *British Social Attitudes: the 11th Report*, Aldershot, Hants.: Dartmouth Press.

35 MORI, May 1995. *State of the Nation, 1995*. London: Joseph Rowntree Reform Trust Ltd.

36 Patrick Dunleavy, 1995. 'Public Response and Constitutional Significance', *Parliamentary Affairs* 48(4): 602–16; Patrick Dunleavy and Stuart Weir, 1995. 'It's All Over for the Old Constitution', *Independent*, 30 May; MORI, May 1995. *State of the Nation, 1995*. London: Joseph Rowntree Reform Trust Ltd.

37 Ivor Crewe, 1995. Oral evidence before the Nolan Committee. Lord Nolan. *Standards in Public Life: First Report of the Committee on Standards in Public Life*. Vol. II: London: HMSO. Cm 2850-II.

38 See Dieter Fuchs, Giovanna Guidorossi and Palle Svensson, 1995. 'Support for the Democratic System', and Ola Listhaug and Matti Wiberg, 1995. 'Confidence in Political and Private Institutions', both in Hans-Dieter Klingemann and Dieter Fuchs, *Citizens and the State*. Oxford: Oxford University Press.

39 See Robert Putnam, 1995. 'Bowling Alone', *Journal of Democracy*; Robert Putnam, 1995. 'Tuning In, Tuning Out: The Strange Disappearance of Social Capital in America', *PS: Political Science and Politics,* December 28(4): 664–83; Robert Putnam, 1996. 'The Strange Disappearance of Civic America', *The American Prospect*. Winter.

40 See James Fishkin, 1995. *The Voice of the People: Public Opinion and Democracy*. New Haven, CT: Yale University Press; Jay Rosen, 1990. 'Politics, Vision and the Press', in *The New News and the Old News: The Press and Politics in the 1990s*. New York: Twentieth Century Fund.

41 Lord Nolan, 1995. *Standards in Public Life: First Report of the Committee on Standards in Public Life*. London: HMSO. Cm 2850. Vol. 1.

42 See Vernon Bogdanor, 1994. 'Western Europe', in David Butler and Austin Ranney, *Referendums Around the World*. Washington, DC: AEI Press.

3 The British Party System

What are the implications of all these developments for the party system? There is widespread agreement that in the fifties Britain provided the prototypical stable and balanced two-party system. Yet the few remaining examples of such systems elsewhere in the world seem threatened with extinction. Blondel defined two-party systems as those 'in which the two significant parties obtained close to 50 per cent of the votes and where any third party which might have existed was very small and politically insignificant'.[1] Based on this definition, the only democracies which Blondel classified as two-party systems in the fifties were the United States, New Zealand, Australia, Britain, Costa Rica and Austria.

Many of these countries have experienced pressures to change. The United States remains a two-party system, in part because in many states other candidates face significant legal hurdles to get on the ballot. Yet there have been periodic surges in support for third party presidential challengers, notably for Theodore Roosevelt's Bull Moose party and LaFolette's Progressives in the early twentieth century, Strom Thurmond's States Rights in 1948, Governor Wallace's American Independent in 1968, and the independent bids of John Anderson in 1980, and Ross Perot who received 19 per cent of the popular vote in 1992.[2] The last three decades have seen a steady rise in the number of American voters who identify themselves as independents, mainly at the expense of the Democrats. According to Gallup data, by 1995 independents were the largest group in the American public (36 per cent), while the rest divided evenly (32 per cent each) into the Republican or Democrat camps.[3]

Moreover, it can be argued that rather than a two-party system, the United States can better be described as having fifty states each with a two-party system.[4]

Until recently New Zealand was one of the clearest examples of a two-party system, with seats divided almost exclusively between Labour and the National party despite significant electoral support for the Alliance and the New Zealand First party. Since New Zealand decided to move towards a Mixed Member Proportional system in 1993, however, there has been a fragmentation of the party system.[5] In Austria, control by the Christian Democrats and Socialists has come under strong challenge from the far-right Freedom party, as well as the Liberal Forum and Greens. In the light of these developments, as Mair points out, it is now difficult to continue to find unequivocal examples of a pure two-party system, as traditionally defined.[6]

Following the results of the February and October 1974 general elections, many commentators like Henry Drucker suggested that Britain had become a '*moderate multi-party*' system.[7] From 1970 to 1983 observers believed they were experiencing the death knell of the two-party system, demonstrated by the formation of separate parties in Northern Ireland, the surge of nationalism in Scotland and Wales, the establishment of the Social Democratic Party in January 1981, the sudden spurt of support for the Liberal–SDP Alliance in opinion polls 1981–2, and the nadir in Labour party fortunes in 1983.[8] Although some commentators remained more cautious in their assessments of the party system, favouring a 'wait and see' approach,[9] in the early eighties there were acres of newsprint devoted to the 'breaking of the mould' of established British politics.[10] As Richard Rose recently summarized the case:

> By the majority of measures of the number of parties in a system, Britain today has a multiparty system because: three (and in Scotland and Wales, four) parties normally contest each parliamentary constituency; the electorate casts a significant share of votes for at least three different parties; a significant amount of voting change involves movement in and out of Liberal ranks rather than direct switching between the two largest parties; the second party in the House of Commons, Labour, finishes third in a large number of constituencies; and more than three parties regularly win seats in the House of Commons.[11]

The conventional wisdom for observers shifted in the late eighties, following the failure of the Liberal–Social Democratic Alliance to trounce Labour, and four successive Conservative victories. Margetts and Smyth, among others, wondered whether Britain had developed a *predominant* party system, with the UK 'turning Japanese'.[12] Since 1979 the division on the centre-left has allowed the Conservatives to retain control of government on about 42.6 per cent of the vote. Under a 'predominant party' system one party, without alternation, dominates the government, legislature, other political parties, and the public policy agenda, over a substantial period of time.[13] Examples of predominant party systems include Mexico, where the PRI has retained control for sixty years, the LDP in Japan (1955 to 1989), the Congress party in India until 1977, Labour in Israel (1948 to 1977), and the Social Democrats in Sweden (1932 to 1976). Many other established democracies have seen long periods of one-party predominance, including France, Australia, New Zealand, Austria, Norway and Canada.

In similar vein, Seldon and Ball argue that the twentieth century will be seen as the Conservative century, given their remarkable success in holding the reins of power, either alone or as the senior partner in a coalition government.[14] Andrew Heywood has expressed the case for a predominant party system even more forcefully:

Taking a longer perspective, it could be argued that Britain has had a dominant-party system through much of the twentieth century and certainly since the old Liberal–Conservative two-party system collapsed after the first World War . . . In the seventy years leading up to 1992, the Conservatives had been in government, either alone or as the dominant member of a coalition, for fifty of them. Two-party politics undoubtedly took place during this time but was largely confined to the 1964–79 period, when Labour won four out of five general elections. The important point is that Labour has only twice, in 1945 and 1966, recorded decisive election victories, and at no time has the party managed to serve two consecutive full terms in office. With hindsight the Labour governments . . . merely punctuated Conservative dominance but did not succeed in breaking the mould of twentieth-century British politics.[15]

There have been considerable changes in party fortunes since 1970, notably the long-term erosion in Labour's share of the vote, the extended period of Conservative government, oscillating waves of support for the Liberals, nationalist and unionist parties, and short-lived bursts of votes for new parties such as the National Front and the Greens. As a result, party politics in the mid-1990s is different, and significantly different, to the 1950s.

Yet Britain has not become a multi-party or predominant system. Rather Britain has evolved from a *dominant* two-party system to a *declining* two-party system during the last fifty years. The Labour and Conservative duopoly of parliamentary seats, and single-party monopoly of central government, remains almost unaltered, although the democratic foundation of this hegemony has been undermined at the electoral level. Despite successive Conservative victories, Labour continues to operate on the assumption that it has a reasonable expectation of securing an absolute majority of seats. Labour has been unwilling to countenance a cross-party coalition, involving a formal electoral pact with the Liberal Democrats or the nationalist parties, to displace the Conservative government.[16] In Bogdanor's words: 'Since 1931, Labour has been dominated by the ghost of Ramsay MacDonald, and has seen any form of power-sharing with another party in peacetime as a species of betrayal.[17] As such party behaviour remains within the two-party model.

This is not to deny that the two-party system could break down in future, indeed fairly rapidly under certain conditions. As discussed in subsequent chapters, party systems fragment for different reasons. Major reform of the electoral system, currently advocated by all parties except the Conservatives, has the potential to strengthen greatly the representation of minor parties, depending upon the system finally adopted, and whether reforms are introduced to local, regional, European and Westminster elections.[18] As shown by the move from plurality to the 'Mixed Member Proportional' system introduced in New Zealand in 1993, electoral reform can dramatically fragment long-standing two-party systems.[19] Moreover a serious fissure in party leadership, such as the rift between the Euro-sceptics and Euro-fanatics within the Conservative party, has the potential to fragment the party system.[20] When Sir Robert Peel repealed the Corn Laws in 1846 the resulting split consigned the Conservatives to opposition for thirty years. In 1885 the issue of the union ruptured the Liberal Party from the Irish Nationalists, fragmenting the duopoly of seats. Lastly partisan realignment in the mass basis of party support, such as the Labour party mobilization of working-class voters in the early twentieth century, or the creation of Roosevelt's New Deal coalition in 1932, has the ability to restructure established systems. Yet no matter the speculation about the potential for change, from 1970 to 1992 Britain retained a recognizable two-party system, albeit one in decline.

Classifying Party Systems

The concept of a 'party system' refers to the durable structure of party competition, in government and the electorate. Party politics are in constant flux, but the party system represents the relatively enduring features of British politics which persist across a series of elections. Systems involve patterned, stable and predictable interactions between the parties in the competition for seats and votes.[21]

When applied to discussions of British politics the concept of a 'two-party' system is often used very loosely. If defined as a system in which two, and only two, parties stand for election, then no country has a pure two-party system. Multiple parties have always competed in Britain: in the 1945 general election there were candidates standing under the banners of the Conservatives, Labour, Liberals, National Liberals, Democratic Party, Communists, Common Wealth Movement, Commonwealth Land Party, the Independent Labour, Irish Nationalists, Plaid Cymru and Scottish National Party, as well as numerous independents.[22] In the same way the United States, New Zealand and Australia have been commonly cited as exemplary two-party systems, but in all these countries minor parties and independent candidates have usually stood, and sometimes been successful.

Alternatively, if a party system is defined by the number of 'relevant' parties which achieve more than a minimum threshold of votes or seats, conventionally defined as about 3 per cent, again British politics during the post-war decade can be defined as a multi-party system. Since 1970 about ten parties have usually been returned with some seats to Parliament. The Liberals, and subsequently Liberal Democrats, have qualified as a 'relevant' party above the minimum threshold of seats, since 1983. Based on this sort of evidence, some argue there are no real two-party systems. Instead, Peter Merkl suggests, we should categorize systems as one party, moderate multi-party, or extreme multi-party.[23] Yet classifications based solely on the number of parties are inherently unsatisfactory since they inevitably involve fairly arbitrary distinctions. For instance, we may draw a line between moderate pluralism (say, four or five parties) and extreme pluralism (say, more than five parties), but there is no theoretical justification for this division. If a new party enters Parliament with one or two seats, this does not necessarily change the nature of the party system by itself.

Others, dissatisfied with conventional classifications, have suggested that we need to move from nominal labels towards continuous measures, such as Rae's fractionalization index,[24] which measures the number and size of parties in parliaments (with seats) and the electorate (with votes). An alternative is the Laakso and Taagpera measure of the 'effective' number of parties.[25] The 'effective number of parliamentary parties' (ENPP) can be compared using this measure based on seat shares in the lower house. Two-party systems can be defined as those democracies with an ENPP score ranging from 2.0 to 2.3, with an alternation of parties in government within the last two decades. If we compare election results in forty-three democracies world-wide, the only two-party systems which meet these criteria in the mid-nineties are Costa Rica, Greece, Australia, New Zealand, the United States and the United Kingdom.[26] These measures are useful for comparative purposes, but they also have certain shortcomings: they take no account of the political position of parties, and therefore cannot differentiate theoretically between types of ideological competition, for example the distinction between segmented and polarized fragmentation.[27] The indexes are one-dimensional (about party strength) thereby excluding the other dimension of party systems (concerning party competition on the ideological spectrum).

Classifications based on counting the number of parties cannot measure their political significance. Early attempts by Duverger distinguished between two-party systems and multi-party systems based on the number of parties.[28] Jean Blondel developed a typology which distinguished four types: two-party systems, two-and-a-half party systems, multi-party systems with a dominant party, and multi-party systems without a dominant party.[29] In an influential study, Giovanni Sartori took this a step further, by taking account of two principle dimensions: the *strength* of parties, conventionally measured by votes in the electorate and seats in Parliament, and the *position* of parties across the ideological spectrum.[30] This combination of criteria yielded four principle types of party system: *two-party* systems, characterized by few parties and a small ideological distance; *moderate pluralism* characterized by multi-parties and a small ideological distance; *polarized pluralism* characterized by extreme multi-partyism and a large ideological distance; and *predominant-party* systems where one party consistently wins a majority of parliamentary seats.

If we adopt Sartori's criteria it is apparent that during the 1950s Britain provided the prototypical model for a two-party system, namely:

1 The two major parties were in a position to compete for an absolute majority of parliamentary seats;
2 One of these parties succeeded in winning a workable parliamentary majority;
3 The winning party was able to govern alone;
4 Alternation or rotation in power remained a credible expectation.

Moreover, in considering the political system in Britain, Sartori suggests that we need to distinguish between minor parties relevant, and irrelevant, to the governing process. According to this understanding what matters is not whether minor parties pass a certain minimum threshold of votes or seats, but whether they are capable of influencing the policy agenda or electoral strategies of the governing parties. Sartori's criteria of relevance are based on the two dimensions of the 'coalition' potential or 'blackmail' potential of the minor parties.[31]

'*Coalition potential*' refers to whether minor parties have entered, or seem likely to have the potential to enter, a working collaboration with the government. This is the stronger of the two criteria, easier to identify. In Sartori's words:

> We have a two–party format whenever the existence of third parties does not prevent the two major parties from governing alone, i.e. whenever coalitions are unnecessary. This is the same as saying that alternation in power is the distinguishing mark of the mechanics of two–partyism. One may say that 'two' differs from 'three' whenever third parties do not affect, in the long run, and at the national level, the alteration in power of the two major powers.[32]

In other countries there are long-standing governing alliances between two parties, like the Liberal and National parties in Australia, the Christian Democratic Union and Christian Social Union in Germany, (until recently) Fine Gael and the Labour party in Ireland, and in Belgium the Christian People's and Christian Social parties. Coalition government is common in most established democracies. Gallagher, Laver and Mair compared fifteen European and Scandinavian countries, with 430 post-war administrations from 1945 to 1992. They found that only 11 per cent of these were single-party majoritarian governments, and nearly all these cases came from the UK and Finland.[33] The Social Democratic–Liberal Alliance is the only post-war example of a formal nationwide electoral pact among separate parties in Britain, but this never affected governing coalitions, and soon merged into a single-party organization as the Liberal Democrats.[34]

In contrast, by the criteria of coalition governments, Britain can be characterized as a multi-party system for much of the late nineteenth and early twentieth centuries. From 1885 to 1910 the Conservatives worked with the support of the Liberal Unionists, while the Liberals depended upon a coalition with the Irish Nationalists. Formal coalition governments, with more than one party holding cabinet office, existed under the leadership of Herbert Asquith (1915–16), David Lloyd George (1916–22), Ramsay Macdonald (1931–35), Stanley Baldwin (1935–37), Neville Chamberlain (1937–40), and Winston Churchill (1940–5).

Yet by this same yardstick post-war Britain can be classified as a continuous two-party system in central government since minor parties have never held cabinet office. Since 1945 Labour and the Conservatives have normally been able to form governments based on an absolute parliamentary majority, without coalition partners. As discussed earlier the only exceptions were the minority Labour administration from February to October 1974, and the Lib–Lab pact from March 1977 to May 1979, although even here there was no formal coalition in government. The Liberals agreed to sustain the Callaghan government, but in return they were offered 'regular consultations', not access to Cabinet. In retrospect, Liberal influence on the Callaghan government seems minimal.[35] At other times the government has been sustained by only a slim majority, notably the 1950–1 Attlee administration, the first Wilson administration in 1964–6, and the Major government after 1995. By the mid-nineties the Major administration's majority was eroded through defections and successive by-election losses, threatening its ability to govern. Nevertheless one-party government has been maintained until dissolution rather than formal coalitions.

Coalition government is only one criterion for multi-party systems. Using Sartori's conceptualization minor parties may also be relevant to the configuration of power outside government by '*blackmail potential*', that is, by influencing the electoral strategies, ideological position or policy agenda of the governing parties. Blackmail potential is the weaker criterion of relevance, and one far more difficult to assess by any objective standards. If we accept this criterion, one interpretation suggests that Britain had a two-party system during the 1950s since the minor parties were unable to influence the direction of public policy. But since the mid-seventies it could be argued that the centripetal minor parties (the Liberals, Social Democrats and Liberal Democrats, the Greens), and the centrifugal minor parties (the Unionist and Nationalist parties), have greater leverage to alter the policy agendas of the governing parties.

This interpretation could stress the significant Labour party shift towards the centre ground since 1983, under the leadership of Neil Kinnock, John Smith and Tony Blair. Successive electoral defeats may have forced Labour to steal many of the minor parties' clothes. This includes Labour's hesitant and somewhat uncertain move towards constitutional and electoral reform, which has long been the defining cornerstone of Liberal Democrat policy. An even clearer case could be Labour's pledge to introduce parliaments in Scotland and Wales within the first year of office, following cross-party talks within the Scottish Convention. Moreover, the 'blackmail potential' of minor parties may have influenced the Conservatives as well. In the mid-nineties official talks with Sinn Fein as part of the Northern Ireland peace process signified a significant shift in the stance of the Conservative government, and the voice of the Ulster Unionists became more influential following the gradual erosion of the government's majority through defections and by-election losses.

One problem with this argument is that a wide range of factors may affect the development of party policy, including the influence of the leadership, internal party bodies, political advisors, the grassroots membership, international agencies, and affiliated groups. Without careful historical research, and access to political memoirs, correspondence and official archives well after the events, it is not possible to determine how far the influence of any of these factors, or the role of minor parties, led to a specific policy shift. Crewe and King's exhaustive study of the rise and fall of the SDP concludes that the party had virtually no long-term impact: 'The Conservatives under Margaret Thatcher would have won their massive victories that finally led Labour to reform itself. Similarly new Labour's policies today owe far more to the Zeitgeist of the Nineties and traditional Labour values than they do to original Social Democratic thinking.'[36] The 'blackmail potential' of minor parties may have been one of the influences, among many others, on the development of Labour and Conservative party policy, but this has to remain an open question.

Conclusions

During the 1950s the two-party system in the electorate meant that Labour and the Conservatives provided balanced and stable party competition, at all levels: national, regional and constituency. This reflected the governing two-party system, characterized by majoritarian governments, Labour and Conservative alternation in office, adversarial parliamentary politics and electoral stability. In short, the Westminster model provided a coherent normative standard of responsible party government, and a fairly accurate empirical description of how the British political system operated.

Since the 1970s the two-party duopoly has continued largely unchanged at Westminster, preserved by the workings of the electoral system. Nevertheless, the influence of minor parties on certain policies of the two major parties may have increased in recent decades. The practice of multi-party politics and coalition governments has become widespread at local level. Most importantly, the two-party system has persisted but declined at the electoral level: changing patterns of party competition, the increased national and regional imbalance in electoral support for the two major parties, and irregular waves of support for the minor parties, has on occasion given the minor parties increased leverage power to influence the strategies, tactics and policies of Labour and the Conservatives. Explaining these developments is the task of subsequent chapters.

Notes

1   Jean Blondel, 1995. *Comparative Government*, 2nd edn. Herts.: Harvester Wheatsheaf, p. 170.
2   See Pippa Norris, 1992. 'The 1992 Election: Voting Behavior and Legitimacy', in Gillian Peele et al., *Developments in American Politics*. London: Macmillan.
3   Gallup poll, April 1995. See Harold W. Stanley and Richard G. Niemi, 1995. *Vital Statistics on American Politics*. Washington, DC: CQ Press, pp. 148–9. It should be noted that National Election Studies data which include 'leaners' who consider themselves closer to one party reduce the proportion of self-identified independents in the electorate. The NES measure which excludes 'leaners' produces similar results to the Gallup poll. See also Bruce E. Keith et al., 1992. *The Myth of the Independent Voter*. Berkeley: University of California Press.
4   Richard Katz and Robin Kolodny, 1994. 'Party Organization as an Empty

Vessel: Parties in American Politics', in Richard Katz and Peter Mair (eds), *How Parties Organize*. London: Sage.

5 See Stephen Levine and Nigel S. Roberts, 1994. 'The New Zealand Electoral Referendum and the General Election of 1993', *Electoral Studies* 13(3): 240–53.

6 Peter Mair, 'Party Systems', in Lawrence LeDuc, Richard Niemi and Pippa Norris (eds), 1996. *Comparing Democracies*. Thousand Oaks, CA: Sage.

7 Henry M. Drucker (ed.), 1979. *Multi-Party Britain*. London: Macmillan. See also Richard Rose, 1989. *Politics in England*. London: Macmillan.

8 For contemporary discussions of developments see Ivor Crewe, 1982. 'Is Britain's Two-Party System Really About to Crumble?' *Electoral Studies* 1(3): 275–313; John Curtice, 1983. 'The Alliance's First National Test', *Electoral Studies* 2(1); David Denver, 1983. 'The SDP–Liberal Alliance: The End of the Two-Party System?', *West European Politics* 6(4); Donley Studlar and Ian McAllister, 1987. 'Protest and Survive? Alliance Support in the 1983 British General Election', *Political Studies*; Paul Whiteley, 1984. 'Can the Alliance Replace Labour as the Main Party of Opposition?', *Politics* 4(1).

9 See, for example, Ivor Crewe, 1995. 'How to Win a Landslide Without Really Trying', in Austin Ranney (ed.), *Britain at the Polls, 1983*. Washington, DC: AEI/Duke University Press; Ivor Crewe, 1984. 'The Electorate: Partisan dealignment ten years on', in Hugh Berrington (ed.), *Change in British Politics*. London: Frank Cass.

10 See Ian Bradley, 1981. *Breaking the Mould? The Birth and Prospects of the Social Democratic Party*. Oxford: Martin Robertson.

11 Richard Rose, 1995. 'A Crisis of Confidence in British Party Leaders?', *Contemporary Record* 9(2): 273–93, p. 285.

12 Helen Margetts and Gareth Smyth (eds), 1994. *Turning Japanese? Britain with a Permanent Party of Government*. London: Lawrence & Wishart; Dennis Kavanagh, 1994. 'Changes in Electoral Behaviour and the Party System', *Parliamentary Affairs* 47(4): 596–612; Geoffrey Alderman, 1989. *Britain: A One Party State?* London: Christopher Helm; Robert Garner and Richard Kelly, 1993. *British Political Parties Today* Manchester: Manchester University Press.

13 See T. J. Pempel (ed.), 1990. *Uncommon Democracies*. Ithaca, NY: Cornell University Press.

14 Anthony Seldon and Stuart Ball (eds), 1994. *Conservative Century*. Oxford: Oxford University Press.

15 Andrew Heywood, 1994. 'Britain's Dominant-party System', in Lynton Robins, Hilary Blackmore and Robert Pyper (eds), *Britain's Changing Party System*. Leicester: Leicester University Press.

16 See Vernon Bogdanor, 1994. 'Electoral Pacts: The Lessons of History', in

Helen Margetts and Gareth Smyth, *Turning Japanese?* London: Lawrence & Wishart; Vernon Bogdanor, 1992. 'Electoral Pacts in Britain Since 1886', in Dennis Kavanagh (ed.), *Electioneering*. Oxford: Oxford University Press.

17   Vernon Bogdanor, 1992. 'The 1992 General Election and the British Party System', *Government and Opposition* 27(3): 287.

18   Pippa Norris (ed.), 1995. 'The Politics of Electoral Reform', *International Political Science Review* 16(1). For estimates of the effects of different systems in the 1992 election see Patrick Dunleavy, Helen Margetts and Stuart Weir, 1992. *Replaying the 1992 General Election*. LSE Public Policy Paper No. 3. London: LSE; See also Gareth Smyth (ed.), 1992. *Refreshing the Parts*. London: Lawrence & Wishart.

19   Jack Vowles, 1995. 'The Politics of Electoral Reform in New Zealand', *International Political Science Review* 16(1): 95-116; James Lamare and Jack Vowles, 1994. *Changing an Electoral System: The Case of New Zealand*. Paper at the Annual Meeting of the American Political Science Association, New York.

20   See Vernon Bogdanor, 1992. 'The 1992 General Election and the British Party System', *Government and Opposition* 27(3): 283–98.

21   For a useful discussion see Alan Ware, 1996. *Political Parties and Party Systems*. Oxford: Oxford University Press.

22   For the history of some of the minor parties in Britain see G. Thayer, 1965. *The British Political Fringe*. London: A. Blond.

23   Peter H. Merkl, 1980. *Western European Party Systems*. New York: Free Press, p. 6.

24   Douglas Rae, 1967. *The Political Consequences of Electoral Laws*. New Haven, CN: Yale University Press.

25   See Arend Lijphart, 1994. *Electoral Systems and Party Systems*. Oxford: Oxford University Press.

26   Calculated from Lawrence LeDuc, Richard Niemi and Pippa Norris, 1996. *Comparing Democracies*. Thousand Oaks, CA: Sage. Table X; for a discussion see Alan Ware, 1996. *Political Parties and Party Systems*. Oxford: Oxford University Press.

27   Giovanni Sartori, 1976. *Parties and Party Systems*. Cambridge: Cambridge University Press. p.314.

28   Maurice Duverger, 1954. *Political Parties*. London: Methuen.

29   Jean Blondel, 1968. 'Party Systems and Patterns of Government in Western Democracies', *Canadian Journal of Political Science* 1(2): 180-203.

30   Giovanni Sartori, 1976. *Parties and Party Systems*. Cambridge: Cambridge University Press.

31   Ibid.

32   Ibid.

33 Michael Gallagher, Michael Laver and Peter Mair (eds), 1995. *Representative Government in Modern Europe*, 2nd edn. New York: McGraw Hill.

34 See Ivor Crewe and Anthony King, 1995. *The Birth, Life and Death of the Social Democratic Party*. Oxford: Oxford University Press.

35 For details see David Coates, 1980. *Labour in Power?* London: Longman, pp. 152–4

36 Ivor Crewe and Anthony King, 1995. *The Birth, Life and Death of the Social Democratic Party*. Oxford: Oxford University Press; Anthony King, 1995. 'The end of the Mad Hatters', *The Independent*, 16 November, p. 4.

Part II

Changes in the Electorate

4 Changes in the Electorate

If we accept that Britain has shifted from the era of two-party dominance over the period 1945–70, to the era of the declining two-party system from 1970 to 1995, the central question is how we explain this development. This chapter focuses on voter-led explanations, the most common approach within the literature, which suggest that the decline in two-party politics can be attributed primarily to psychological changes in the character of the individual voting decision. This overview aims to review these theories and clarify the core concepts before critically considering the evidence for them in subsequent chapters.

The debate at the heart of this chapter is how far voters remain affective party loyalists, steadfast Conservative and Labour supporters out of long-standing and habitual attachments, and how far voters are now influenced more strongly by the policies and performance of parties. During the 1950s and early 1960s, in the orthodox theory, most voters were believed to be stable in their voting choice due to enduring party loyalties, which shaped their attitudes towards issues, leaders and party images, and ultimately their electoral behaviour. In turn party identification was thought to be based on a cohesive socialization process within the family, work group and social milieu. The predominant class cleavage in British society was seen as the primary divide in party politics. Theories of dealignment suggest that from the mid-sixties onwards the strength of party and class attachments weakened. As a result, it has been argued, electoral volatility increased and short-term factors became more important in determining individual voter choice: whether policy issues, party leadership, the government record or events during the campaign. Let us consider the assumptions behind these theories.

Theories of Party Alignment

The American voter

Social psychological accounts became widely accepted in electoral studies following research in the United States by Angus Campbell, Philip Converse, Warren Miller and Donald Stokes, published in *The American Voter* (1960).[1] This seminal work was based on surveys of the American electorate from 1948 to 1956 carried out by the Survey Research Center at Michigan University, hence it became known as the 'Michigan' model. The study suggested that, contrary to assumptions about voters in theories of responsible party government, or more populist beliefs about direct democracy, most American citizens were largely uninvolved, uninterested and ill-informed about political life. Campbell et al. argued that the typical American voter lacked information about politics, opinions on major issues and political sophistication. For 'issue voting' to occur Campbell et al. set fairly strict hurdles, namely (1) people had to be familiar with the issue, (2) the issue had to arouse some feelings, and (3) people had to perceive a party difference on the issue.[2] The study reported most Americans lacked familiarity with government policy and programmes. For example, in 1956 about a third of all Americans could not offer an opinion, or did not know what the government was doing, regarding policies on education, medical care, racial equality or overseas aid. Even where individuals had opinions about an issue, many could not distinguish where the parties stood on domestic and foreign affairs.

Nor did people organize their attitudes in a consistent manner, or think in structured, ideological terms. Although observers commonly refer to 'liberals' and 'conservatives' in the electorate, *The American Voter* argued that most voters lacked a coherent set of beliefs, or an ideology, to order their political attitudes. The study analysed the content of unstructured comments when asked what they liked or disliked about the parties and candidates. The study reported that in the mid-fifties about 12 per cent of the electorate could be classified as 'ideologues' or 'near-ideologues' who could express fairly consistent responses across policy issues, and who were familiar with the abstract distinction between 'liberal' and 'conservative'. About 42 per cent of the electorate viewed parties largely in terms of group benefits. One-quarter saw politics in terms of the 'goodness' or 'badness' of the times, such as associating the government with war or peace, recession or prosperity. The remaining fifth of the electorate failed to comment upon any issues in response to unstructured questions.[3] The authors concluded that a large segment of the public lacked the ability, knowledge and educational background to manipulate the abstract political concepts which give order and consistency to political debates.

Nevertheless even without knowledge of specific issues, or a general ideological orientation, faced with a range of complex electoral choices for candidates at presidential, congressional, gubernatorial, state and local levels, American voters could choose, and did choose, on a fairly consistent and stable basis. The central discovery of *The American Voter* was that most citizens had a general political orientation – a cognitive and affective map – which guided their electoral choice. For Campbell et al. partisan identification was the key to understanding the structure of voter's cogitive maps, and hence the stability of their voting choice. People structured their perceptions of complex issues, candidates and campaign events through the prism of party loyalties.

The concept of party identification has two main dimensions: *direction* (for which party) and *strength*. Based on the standard survey measure, party identification in America could be arrayed along a continuum extending from strong Republicans, weak Republicans, via Independents, to weak Democrats and strong Democrat voters.[4] Partisan identification was seen as *affective*, relating to an individual's feelings of self-identity; *stable*, persisting across successive elections; *durable*, not readily disturbed by passing issues, events and personalities; and *pervasive*, most Americans had this sense of attachment to one party or another. Party loyalties were seen to endure across different elections, even when people temporarily changed their voting choice, to provide the 'normal' base of support for the Republicans and Democrats. People could therefore temporarily defect, for example, voting against their normal party to express dissatisfaction with the government or the choice of presidential nominee, then return to their 'home' vote in subsequent elections. Party loyalties ('voting the ticket') provided voters with simplified decisions and information shortcuts when confronted with the diverse and complex array of presidential, congressional, state and local candidates.

In turn, party identification was seen to be derived from a voter's social milieu, particularly their early family and group socialization. In the United States during the 1950s groups such as the labour unions in Chicago, Jewish city-dwellers in New York, Irish-American Catholics in Boston, and Swedish Lutheran farmers in Minnesota, acted as reference points for political attitudes. These groups were seen to generate a sense of identity or group membership (a 'we' feeling), so that they represented more than simple demographic aggregates. Where cohesive and for-malized for example, organized labour), group standards acted as reference points in political life. Age effects were also important: party loyalties were found to strengthen over a citizen's lifetime. New voters were least likely to have developed stable party attachments, and were therefore the most open to prevailing political moods. But the longer voters saw themselves as belonging to a party, the stronger their sense of loyalty.[5] The argument was clear and powerful:

> Evidently no single datum can tell us more about the attitude and behaviour of the individual as presidential elector than his location on a dimension of psychological identification extending between the two great parties.[6]

Yet if enduring and stable social structures led to partisan alignments which stabilized voting choice for most Americans, this could not explain dramatic changes in party fortunes, such as Roosevelt's Democratic land-slide in 1932. Campbell et al. therefore proposed a dynamic element to the theory, following the work of V. O. Key,[7] classifying elections into three basic types: maintaining, deviating and realigning. In *maintaining* elections there are no strong issues or candidates to deflect the electorate from voting in accordance with its standing partisan allegiances. Each side mobilizes its natural base of support. In *deviating* elections the basic division of party loyalties are not seriously disturbed, but particular personalities, issues, or events produce a temporary reversal for the majority party. In *realigning* elections, associated with a decisive national crisis such as the Civil War or the Great Depression, significant groups of voters change their partisan loyalties and political attitudes on a long-term basis.

Walter Dean Burnham, among others, has extended this further by considering the essential historical preconditions for 'realigning' or 'crit-ical' elections, and whether the process of partisan change has been essentially cyclical, with major realignments in the social basis of party support occurring at roughly thirty-year intervals in America.[8] The theory of partisan realignment has subsequently developed an extensive literature in the United States, debating the essential causes and consequences of this process.[9] Recent years have also seen a body of work in cognitive psychology critically re-examining the concept of party identification, and supporting or challenging fundamental notions about the ill-informed nature of the American electorate.[10]

Nevertheless throughout the sixties the 'Michigan' model represented the orthodox view. Democratic and Republican support was seen as rooted in long-standing and complex historical alignments based on successive waves of external and internal immigration, regional polarization over the Civil War, racial divisions over civil rights, the urban–rural split, and to a lesser extent the cleavage between unionized workers and employers. Once established, party loyalties were thought to be maintained for decades, rooted in group socialization processes. The theory suggested that at periodic intervals major realignments provided opportunities to re-establish the social basis of party politics, notably the New Deal coalition which Roosevelt created in 1932. But during periods of 'normal' politics, party identification anchored most groups as predictable Democratic or Republican voters for successive elections, perhaps throughout their life-times.

Political Change in Britain

This social psychological framework became widely influential in Britain following publication of *Political Change in Britain* (1969, 2nd edn, 1974) by David Butler and Donald Stokes, which shared many of the same concepts and theoretical assumptions developed by the Michigan school. The seminal study became widely accepted as the most authoritative account of British voting behaviour, decisively reshaping the established research agenda. Drawing on the British Election Study from 1963 to 1970, Butler and Stokes suggested that politics remained peripheral to most people's lives: the British electorate rarely participated politically and had minimal involvement in civic life. 'Only one in two voted in local elections and only one in ten went to an election meeting. Only one in fifty took an active part in the campaign and the number engaged in party activities between campaigns was altogether negligible.[11]

The typical British voter was seen as fairly uninformed about politics, falling far short of the expectations of citizenship in liberal theories of representative democracy. In the sixties parliament was concerned with complex and technical issues revolving around the effectiveness of the British nuclear deterrent, the repercussions of the Cuban missile crisis, the problems of African decolonization, entry into the European Economic Community, and Britain's balance of payments difficulties. Most voters, Butler and Stokes argued, lacked sufficient knowledge to understand these problems. Issue voting can only occur in this theory if three conditions are met, namely if voters are concerned about the problem (*saliency*); if public opinion is divided (*skewness*); and if parties offer alternative policy solutions (*differentiation*). Butler and Stokes believed that most issues failed to meet these requirements.

British Election Study (BES) panel surveys were used to examine the same voters over successive elections. Butler and Stokes concluded that few people had consistent and stable opinions about well-known issues which divided the parties, such as Britain's entry into Europe, the nationalization of industry, or the use of nuclear weapons. Many seemed to alter their opinions from one survey to the next which suggested, Butler and Stokes argued, that they lacked stable and deep-rooted attitudes. In the mid-sixties, only the welfare state (social services, pensions and housing), strikes and immigration were issues of widespread public concern, which divided the public and the parties, and therefore met the strict conditions necessary for issue voting.[12] The typical British voter was found to display fairly mixed-up attitudes, adopting left-wing and right-wing stances on different issues. For most people political attitudes were not organized on a consistent basis, let alone structured into a sophisticated, abstract 'conservative' or 'socialist' ideology.

Yet despite widespread ignorance about politics, and minimal interest, in general elections, about three-quarters of the electorate cast their vote. When faced with the choice of parties at the ballot box, Butler and Stokes concluded that British voters sought cognitive short-cuts, or 'standing decisions', to guide them through elections. As in the United States, during periods of stable partisan alignment, voters in Britain were seen as being rooted for many years, even for their lifetime, to one or other of the major parties.

> It is clear that millions of British electors remain anchored to one of the parties for very long periods of time. Indeed many electors have had the

same party loyalties from the dawn of their political consciousness and have
reinforced these loyalties by participating in successive elections.[13]

The concept of partisan 'self-image' (rather than identification) was
used to describe how voters saw themselves as party supporters on an
enduring basis. Social identities represent how we describe ourselves,
perhaps as Geordies, Glaswegians or Londoners due to our local roots, as
Church of England or Catholics, or by our occupation, or generation. In
the same way people derived their political identity from their usual
allegiance to the Labour or Conservative parties. For Butler and Stokes
partisan self-image had three characteristics: it was *pervasive*, 90 per cent
of the British electorate described themselves as generally Conservative,
Labour or Liberal; *stable*, four-fifths of the electorate reported always
voting for the same party; and *strengthened with age*, in 1970 only one-
quarter of younger voters (18–24) described themselves as strongly
attached to a party compared with two-thirds of pensioner age. To this
extent it fulfilled the Michigan model. Party attachments provided a frame
of references which allowed voters to slot unfamiliar problems or new
information into an established pattern. Instead of trying to understand
technical foreign policy or economic issues, such as Rhodesia or the balance
of payments crisis, voters used party identity as a prism to filter their
political opinions. Most citizens expressed positive feelings about parties,
and these attachments helped to mobilize citizens into civic life.
Nevertheless in contrast with the American evidence, where party loyalties remained stable whilst voting behaviour changed, Butler and Stokes
reported that in Britain the two moved in tandem to a greater degree.[14]

Social Alignments

If we can accept the assumption that party loyalties are critical, how are
they acquired? Butler and Stokes emphasized two sources: when young,
voters were influenced through the socialization process by the party loyalties of their family. This was seen as particularly important among
first-time voters, in the impressionable years, when political attitudes were
relatively plastic, but this inheritance gradually weakened as other factors
came into play during their lifetimes. The socialization process within the
family could also be expected to be particularly strong where both parents

shared the same Labour or Conservative party loyalties. In the words of Butler and Stokes:

> A child is very likely indeed to share the parents' party preference. Partisanship over the individual's lifetime has some of the quality of a photographic reproduction that deteriorates with time: it is a fairly sharp copy of the parent's original at the beginning of political awareness, but over the years it becomes somewhat blurred, although remaining easily recognisable.[15]

In later years voters were more strongly influenced by groups within their social milieu including the neighbourhood, workplace and community. Political attitudes would be reinforced by discussions with friends, colleagues and family who shared party attachments. Religion provided the primary cleavage in British party politics prior to the First World War, dividing Liberal non-conformists from the Conservative Church of England supporters, with regional and class differences as secondary influences. From the mid-twenties onwards, after the major realignment when Labour displaced the Liberal party, class became the dominant cleavage of British party politics.[16] For Butler and Stokes, modern party loyalties were founded on the rock of class identities: 'The individual, identifying with a particular class, forms a positive bond to the party which looks after the interests of the class.'[17] Class was seen to provide the major reference group voters used to define themselves (class self-image), and the main parties (the party for 'working people' or 'good for business'). Butler and Stokes noted there was evidence this relationship was weakening even during the late 1960s, nevertheless class cleavages continued to be more closely associated with party loyalties than other social divisions, such as region, housing tenure, religion, age or gender. In this model, social group identities could be expected to have a direct effect on voting choice, as well as an indirect effect via party attachment (see figure 4.1). The Labour and Conservative parties were widely regarded as representing the major

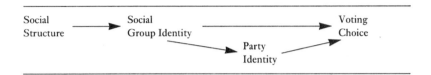

Figure 4.1   The Michigan model of voting choice

cleavage in post-war British society, based on divisions of social class, competing in balanced equilibrium.

Party Systems and Voter Alignments

This account of British voting behaviour was given powerful reinforcement by the widely influential study of European *Party Systems and Voter Alignments* (1967) by Seymour Martin Lipset and Stein Rokkan. This explained how party competition and voting choices stabilized around the dominant structural cleavages within European nation-states.[18] For Lipset and Rokkan 'cleavages' may prove politically salient if they have three characteristics: if they divide nations based on social characteristics such as occupation, religion or language; if the groups involved in the division were conscious of their collective identity; and if the cleavage was expressed in organizational terms. Contemporary political alignments in western Europe were seen to reflect the imprint of four major cleavages based on the historical divisions of centre–periphery, church–state, urban–rural and worker–employer.[19]

The first divided the dominant culture in the centre of the political arena (London, Paris, Rome) from subject cultures at the periphery (Glasgow, Marseilles, Sicily). Linguistic or national cultural minorities developed parties reflecting their interests such as the Basque separatists and Plaid Cymru. The second cleavage divided church from state, with Catholic churches closely related to Christian Democratic parties such as those in France, Spain, Belgium, Italy and Austria. The third cleavage divided those working in rural areas from the commercial and industrial classes in the cities, resulting in agrarian parties in Scandinavia and in parts of Central and Eastern Europe. The last cleavage – based on social class divisions between the landed aristocracy and the rising bourgeoisie, and later between employers and their workers – proved the critical source of political conflict in twentieth century Britain. The class conflict became ingrained throughout European party politics. It divided the 'insiders' favouring the established Church, the monarchy, and the old social order of privilege from the radical challenge of the 'outsiders' who represented the non-conformist churches, peripheral regions and the less privileged. With the expansion of the franchise, European parties needed extra-parliamentary organizations to mobilize the new voters. In order to develop grassroots membership, expand electoral support, raise resources, and stabilize their base, parties forged long-standing alliances with groups representing the major cleavages in society. Parties could gain temporary support without such a base, due to the appeal of particular popular leaders, or a temporary surge of protest voting against the incumbents, but such support could melt as fast as spring snow.

For Lipset and Rokkan, party-group linkages, founded on the dominant cleavage in each society, permeated all aspects of electoral politics, stabilizing and 'freezing' the party system in European countries in the 1920s. Some organizations were mobilized into politics, and once well-entrenched, it proved difficult for new parties to challenge the status quo. The rules of the game – especially electoral laws – favoured the established parties. Mass parties insulated and captured their supporters, developing political sub-cultures which gave supporters a psychological sense of belonging. Hence this seemed to explain why electoral behaviour in the fifties and sixties, in Britain and elsewhere, proved so stable. Rose and Urwin's study of nineteen western nations from 1945 to 1969 showed that, except in countries with a regime-change, 'the electoral strength of most parties had changed very little from election to election, from decade to decade, or within the lifespan of a generation'.[20]

Lipset and Rokkan's theory reflected a long tradition of the structural analysis of voting behaviour in Britain, linking class and party, which became the widely accepted orthodoxy in British textbooks. The earliest British studies of voting behaviour during the 1950s and 1960s – drawing on evidence from Gallup polls of the electorate, constituency surveys and aggregate constituency data – emphasized class cleavages as the pre-eminent division in party choice.[21] In an influential early study, Robert Alford compared working-class support for the left party in Britain, America, Australia and Canada, using Gallup data, and found that Britain had the highest and most stable level of class voting.[22] Alternative social cleavages which divided voters in other countries – such as religion, region, generation and gender – while influencing British voters, had less significant impact on party choice. Moreover, as Guttsman demonstrated, class politics in the electorate were reflected, to a lesser degree, in class divisions in the background of Labour and Conservative MPs.[23] Many of the issues which divided the post-war British policy agenda – the nationalization of industry, the growth of the welfare state and the management of the economy – reflected classic divisions between capital and labour.[24] Not surprisingly, as a result, the public's image of the major parties was also commonly seen in class terms. The remaining puzzles, spawning a series of studies, seemed to be how to explain the anomalies of this model, notably the phenomenon of cross-class voting and the working-class Tories, the 'floating' voter and the non-voters.[25]

Theories of Partisan Dealignment

The strength of Labour and Conservative loyalties seemed to provide a convincing explanation for the stability of two-party politics during the 1950s and early 1960s. But, just as the new orthodoxy became widely accepted, voting studies seemed to be overtaken by political events. If voters were so stable, how could theories of voting behaviour explain sudden bursts of support for the Liberals, Plaid Cymru, and the Scottish National parties in the 1974 general elections? If voters were so loyal, why did Wilson's 1966-70 administration, then the 1970-4 Heath government, start to experience unprecedented electoral turbulence as indicated by monthly opinion polls, by-elections and local elections?

Moreover patterns in Britain seemed to reflect trends experienced elsewhere. In Belgium the three major parties split into Flemish and Walloon divisions; in Norway the traditional parties fragmented over Europe; in Italy the Communists almost overtook the ruling Christian Democrats; in the 1973 Danish election the number of parties in the parliament doubled overnight from five to ten, and a new radical group emerged as the second largest party. Systematic studies of electoral volatility, by Morgens Pedersen and by Maria Maguire, compared support for European parties from 1948 and reported increased electoral instability in the seventies.[26]

The major challenge to the old orthodoxy was provided in the mid-seventies by theories of dealignment. Partisan and social dealignment should be treated as analytically distinct, since these phenomena may be independent, although in many accounts the two are closely linked. Theories of dealignment remain within the social psychological tradition, locating the explanation for the weakening two-party grip over the electorate in the changing character of the voting decision among individual electors. The concept of partisan dealignment is often used rather loosely, indeed sometimes as a synonym for the electoral volatility it seeks to explain. Here the concept of partisan dealignment will be understood to refer to the weakening of affective, habitual and stable party loyalties among the electorate. Without such ties, the electorate is potentially more fluid and dynamic, open to the appeal of new parties, leaders or issues, and short-term influences on their vote, although this does not necessarily mean that electors will actually change their voting behaviour, or indeed that there will be any difference in aggregate levels of party support. The theory of partisan dealignment suggests people may continue to vote Labour or Conservative, in this sense the thesis is perfectly compatible with two-party politics, but it suggests that their reasons for so doing have changed. Without the ballast of traditional loyalists Labour and Conservative party support is more open to sudden shifts in the winds of electoral fortunes. Dealignment theory suggests that we need to distinguish between enduring partisanship and short-term voting choice; between a party's long-term level of support and its actual vote at a specific election; and between the basis of the former and the influences upon the latter.

The Changing American Voter

Why should party loyalties have weakened? In the United States, the argument was most fully developed in *The Changing American Voter* by Norman Nie, Sidney Verba and John Petrocik in the United States.[27] Nie et al. found that in the early seventies party identification remained a long-term commitment, established early in life, and usually maintained after that. But, they argued, the blandness of party politics during the Eisenhower years misled Campbell et al. into assuming that issues were consistently unimportant in structuring voting choice. In contrast, Nie et al. suggested, in the sixties consensual issues faded from the policy agenda, replaced by deeply divisive conflict over race, Vietnam, crime and drugs. These issues were particularly salient for the younger generation, protesting over the war, civil rights and sexual politics. The Democratic party, a diverse amalgam of conservative Dixiecrats, civil rights blacks, Italian, Irish and Jewish voters, organized labour in northern cities, and younger, liberal McGovernites, proved unable to accommodate these issues without fragmenting its New Deal coalitional base. In the early seventies the Republicans became deeply divided and demoralized by

Watergate. These developments led to the erosion of traditional party commitments, and the swelling of the pool of independent voters. As Nie et al. summarized their findings:

> (1) Fewer citizens have steady and strong psychological identification with a party. (2) Party affiliation is less a guide to electoral choice. (3) Parties are less frequently used as standards of evaluation. (4) Parties are less frequently objects of positive feelings on the part of citizens. (5) Partisanship is less likely to be transferred from generation to generation.[28]

Decade of Dealignment

During the late sixties and early seventies, theorists suggested that many European countries experienced similar trends.[29] As Ivor Crewe summarized the British evidence:

> Partisan dealignment in all its manifestations – a plummeting of party membership, a weakening of party identification, a wavering and prevarication among major party supporters, negative voting, and a growing instability and unevenness of electoral change – have all occurred, indeed, accelerated, over the past three decades.[30]

The dealignment argument rests on three major premises: that citizens are no longer so strongly attached to political parties; as traditional affective loyalties have weakened, short-term influences have become more salient in voting choice; and as a result voters have become more willing to desert the major parties, producing the sporadic waves of temporary support for the Liberals, SDP, Nationalists and Greens.

Many dealignment commentators have suggested that party identities have become more fluid and less clear-cut, producing a major change in the social psychology of the individual voting decision. As long-term party loyalties have weakened and fragmented, this thesis suggests voters are more open to the effects of short-term factors, including particular campaign events, the appeal of party leaders, the government's record in office, and the marketing of party images.[31] Looser class identities and party loyalties should increase the willingness of voters to consider different parties, and hence the chances that minor parties can mobilize support, especially in second-order contests such as local, European and by-elections.

Theories of Social Dealignment

In Britain the literature has emphasized that partisan dealignment has been accompanied by, and can be primarily attributed to, class dealignment. Butler and Stokes noted that the class–vote relationship was declining at the time they were writing, in the late sixties, with greater volatility of support notable particularly amongst the younger generation.[32] Subsequent studies by Ivor Crewe, Mark Franklin and others have argued that the link between social class and voting choice has diminished further over the years.[33] As Rose and McAllister summarized the situation by the mid-eighties:

> The electorate today is wide open to change; three quarters of voters are no longer anchored by a stable party loyalty determined by family and class. More voters float between parties – or are wobbling in their commitment to one party – than show a lifetime loyalty to a particular party.[34]

The most comprehensive examination of the evidence, based on national election surveys in fourteen countries, by Franklin, Mackie and Valen, found that many advanced industrialized democracies experienced social dealignments during the seventies and early eighties. 'Almost all of the countries we have studied show a decline during our period in the ability of social cleavages to structure individual voting choice.'[35]

Yet social and party dealignment, which are frequently assumed to go hand-in-hand, could involve separate processes. The developments which we have described can be envisaged to produce four possible results (see figure 4.2). If traditional social and partisan alignments remain strong then we would expect the continuation of a stable two-party system in Britain.

	Partisan Alignment	Partisan Dealignment
Social Alignment	Stable two-party system	Declining two-party system
Social Dealignment	Declining two-party system	Multi-party system

Figure 4.2   Partisan and social alignments

If partisan and social attachments to the Labour and Conservative parties progressively weaken, this could potentially lead to a multi-party system, within the constraints of the institutional context set by the electoral system. Lastly, if either social or party alignments weaken, this may undermine the foundations of the established two-party system, without necessarily replacing it.

There is little doubt that the social structure of Britain has been transformed in the post-war era due to demographic, economic and cultural trends common to most post-industrial societies – the rise of the service sector, the 'new' working class, the growth of the underclass, patterns of immigration, changes in the public/private employment divide, increased social and geographic mobility, the expansion of educational opportunities, the decline in the traditional family, technological innovation, the information age, and the growth and subsequent contraction of the welfare state.[36] Yet there remains considerable debate about the effects of these structural changes on voting behaviour in Britain, as discussed in subsequent chapters. Theories fall into four distinct categories:

- *orthodox* structural theories which suggest that class is the basis of British party politics;
- the *revision* of traditional concepts and measures of social class;
- the *restructuring* of social identities; and lastly,
- the *replacement* of affective group loyalties by more rational 'issue' voting.

Revising concepts of social class

Revisionists have suggested that traditional measures of social class, based on divisions between blue-collar and white-collar occupations, need to be modified to take account of the complexity of inequalities in modern society. Structural arguments suggest that social class was the critical political cleavage in post-war Britain since it determined so much else about social identity. Working-class communities based on traditional industries such as steel, shipbuilding or coal-mining, where families worked and lived in close proximity, provided a common life-style and homogeneous culture. The traditional division between factory and office workers could be used to predict household income and wealth, levels of education, health and standards of housing, networks of friends and neighbours, even language and accent, and therefore cultural attitudes and values.[37]

As discussed in later chapters, Heath, Jowell and Curtice have strongly advocated the most significant revision to the traditional occupational classification of the middle and working classes, based on the work of the sociologist, John Goldthorp. These authors argue that given the appropriate classification and measurement, the relationship between social class and party vote has not weakened.[38] Heath et al. acknowledge that there has been a shift in the size of the working-class, which has slowly produced a shrinkage in the natural base of Labour's support, but they argue that the relative strength of the linkage between class and party has not diminished.

In a variant of this theme, Dunleavy and Husbands argue that following the growth of the welfare state the division between public-sector and private-sector workers has become increasingly important in determining voting behaviour, along with alternative proxies for socioeconomic inequalities such as households in council housing or owner-occupiers.[39] Crewe has argued that the working class has become fragmented into the 'old' working class, the factory workers living in council housing estates in Scotland and the north, and the 'new' affluent working class in skilled and semi-skilled jobs in light industry, living in owner-occupied households in the Midlands and the south.[40] What these accounts share in common is the notion that voters continue to acquire their political attitudes and party loyalties through the socialization process within their social milieu, but the nature of class inequalities has become more complex in post-industrial societies.

The restructuring of social identities

Yet others have argued that new social identities and structural cleavages have replaced old ones. Modernization theory suggests that occupational class has become less relevant in post-industrial societies, which are characterized by social fragmentation and differentiation, increasing geographic and social mobility, rising levels of education, and the expansion of mass communications.[41] In recent decades the Lancashire mill-towns, the Welsh valley pit-communities, and the Staffordshire potteries have been swept away. As a result modernization theories suggest that Britain has experienced a fragmentation of simple social identities. In

Robertson's words, 'the old classes have ceased to be cultural communities' as multiple influences have come to shape political socialization.[42] Post-industrial trends towards a more fragmented, polycultural, and pluralistic society, with diverse groups and social movements, may have eradicated older social and political identities.

What may have replaced class? *Regional* divisions were once thought likely to fade with the development of the modern national state. Yet since the mid-fifties, as mentioned earlier, Britain has experienced a growing north–south divide, generating an extensive literature.[43] Regional identities have also fragmented party cleavages in Belgium and Italy, the Basque nationalists have used terrorist violence in Spain, and Quebec separatism has almost broken up Canada. Rose and Urwin noted regionalism as one of the most important influences on political behaviour during the twentieth century.[44] Bogdanor and Field have argued that the traditional core–periphery cleavage, which existed in Britain at the turn of the century, has reopened due to the decline of class divisions.[45] Far from fading, regional identities and nationalist sentiment may have strengthened over time.

Moreover, *generational* differences may have become more important. Post-materialist theory developed by Ronald Inglehart suggests that a new cleavage has developed among younger, well-educated voters, centred around issues of the quality of life and protection of the environment, bolstering support for new social movements and Green parties. Post-materialist values have become more popular in the post-war era, Ronald Inglehart has argued, because the younger generation have grown up during a period of widespread affluence, without economic insecurities under the welfare state. In a comparison of value-trends from 1970 to 1993, Abramson and Inglehart reported a clear trend towards post-materialism in seven out of eight European countries, with the proportion of post-materialists doubling in Britain, from 7 to 15 per cent,[46] reflecting trends throughout West European publics.

In a related development, *gender* may have become more politically salient. Post-war developments have seen the increased participation of women in the paid labour force, the decline of the traditional family, and the growth of the women's movement. These events have heightened the salience of gender politics, revolving around economic issues including demands for equal opportunities, affirmative action, and equal pay; social issues including reproductive rights, child-care and care of the elderly; and criminal justice issues including protection against domestic violence, rape and child-abuse.[47] The gender-gap where women are more liberal than men, which emerged in American elections in the early-eighties, has become evident in some other advanced democracies.[48] In Britain there has been a long-standing 'gender-generation gap', which has attracted increasing attention as the major parties have tried to mobilize 'the women's vote'.[49] Lastly, patterns of immigration have transformed British society, producing ethnic and religious diversity. This has brought new issues onto the political agenda, including race relations and equal opportunities, and changed the composition of many inner-city constituencies in London, the Midlands and the north-west. From this perspective, the social identities of voters continue to structure party choice, but simple inequalities of occupational class have been replaced by more diverse and complex cleavages based on differences of region, generation, gender and race. For Rose and McAllister, party choices continue to be affected by a 'lifetime learning' process of socialization within the home, workplace and community. What has altered, they argue, is less *dealignment* than a *restructuring* of the components contributing to the vote.[50]

The rise of rational 'issue voting'

The last school of thought has argued that as old class and party loyalties waned, party policies and performance count for more. Theories of 'issue voting', which became common in the eighties, suggested voters had become more open to rational argument, more willing to switch parties, more influenced by the election campaign and assessments of prospective policy issues, or retrospective evaluations of the government's performance. In Britain, Hilde Himmelweit and her colleagues argue, voters act like rational consumers in the political marketplace.[51] In the United States, Samuel Popkin has developed the thesis that voters use 'low-information' rationality, or gut reasoning, to assess candidates, parties and issues, drawing on information from past experiences and daily life, from the media and from political campaigns.[52] Therefore, although there is considerable agreement (although not total consensus) that the old order of strong party attachments is passing, the form of the new order of voting behaviour is not yet apparent. Commentators have disputed the relative influence of different short-term components of voting choice.

One view has focused on the rise of 'issue voting'. Mark Franklin emphasized how issue voting arose to fill the vacuum left by the decline of class-structured voting:[53]

> The British electorate has moved to a more sophisticated basis for voting choice. No longer constrained to the same extent by characteristics largely established during childhood, British voters are now more open to rational argument than they were in the past.[54]

Others, like Jim Alt, David Sanders, and Helmut Norpoth, have focused attention on prospective and retrospective evaluations of the government's record on the economy, using econometric techniques to trace the relationship between economic indicators and party popularity.[55] Richard Rose and Ian McAllister have argued that 'political values' have become more strongly associated with voting choice, particularly those associated with trade unions and privatization.[56] Others have stressed the increased importance of judgements about leadership character and personality, suggesting that there has been a 'presidentialization' of British elections parallel to the focus on candidates in the United States.[57] The newest school of thought has emphasized the influence of political communications during the campaign, including increased penetration of the mass media, the explosion of opinion polls, and adoption of professional political marketing.[58]

Conclusions

To summarize the arguments: the two-party dominance of the electorate in the fifties and sixties was attributed by Butler and Stokes to long-term patterns of stable party loyalties, which in turn rested on a profound structural stability in post-war British society. This explanation appeared to be undermined in the early seventies by the decline of two-party support among the electorate – as demonstrated in earlier chapters by erratic waves of support for third parties in general elections, by-elections and opinion polls.

These developments generated a large theoretical literature. Revisionist theories suggest that the conceptualization, classification and measurement of social class need to be modified to take account of more complex social inequalities. Once revised, it is argued, the relationship between class and party remains as strong as ever. In contrast, restructuring theories suggest that traditional class cleavages have been displaced in post-industrial societies by social identities based on divisions of region, generation, and gender. Lastly, issue-based theories suggest that today voters have become more rational, less habitual Conservative and Labour loyalists, and more open to support other parties depending upon the nature of the electoral contest. Let us go on to consider evidence for these accounts of electoral change.

Notes

1 Angus Campbell, Philip Converse , Warren E. Miller and Donald E. Stokes, 1960. *The American Voter*. New York: John Wiley and Sons.
2 Ibid. p. 170.
3 Ibid. pp. 216–65. For a critique of these measures see Eric R. A. N. Smith, 1989. *The Unchanging American Voter*. Berkeley, CA: University of California Press.
4 The standard SRC items were as follows: 'Generally speaking, do you usually think of yourself as a Republican, a Democrat, an Independent, or what?' and 'Would you call yourself a strong (Republican, Democrat) or not very strong (Republican, Democrat)?' For a discussion see Philip E. Converse and Roy Pierce, 1986. 'Measuring Partisanship'; *Political Methodology* 11: 143–66.
5 See Campbell et al., 1960. *The American Voter*. New York: John Wiley and Sons, pp. 146–67
6 Ibid., pp. 142–3
7 V. O. Key, 1955. 'A Theory of Critical Elections', *Journal of Politics* 17: 3–18; Angus Campbell et al., 1960. *The American Voter*. New York: John Wiley & Sons, pp. 531–8.
8 Walter Dean Burnham, 1970. *Critical Elections and the Mainsprings of American Politics*. New York: W. W. Norton.
9 For a good review of the debate see Byron Shafer (ed.), 1991. *The End of Realignment*. Wisconsin: The University of Wisconsin Press.
10 For a thorough recent defence see, for example, Eric Smith, 1989. *The Unchanging American Voter*. Berkeley: University of California Press. For an extensive critique see Samuel L. Popkin, 1994. *The Reasoning Voter*. Chicago: University of Chicago Press.
11 David Butler and Donald Stokes, 1974. *Political Change in Britain*, 2nd edn. London: Macmillan, p. 21.
12 Ibid., pp. 276–313.
13 Ibid., p. 47

14 Ibid., pp. 43–7
15 Ibid., p. 51.
16 Kenneth D. Wald, 1983. *Crosses on the Ballot: Patterns of British Voter Alignment Since 1885*. Princeton, NJ: Princeton University Press.
17 David Butler and Donald Stokes, 1974. *Political Change in Britain*, 2nd edn. London: Macmillan, p. 88.
18 Seymour Martin Lipset and Stein Rokkan, 1967. *Party Systems and Voter Alignments*. New York: Free Press.
19 Stefano Bartolini and Peter Mair, 1990. *Identity, Competition and Electoral Availability: The Stabilization of European Electorates, 1885–1985*. Cambridge: Cambridge University Press.
20 Richard Rose and Derek Urwin, 1970. 'Persistence and Change in Western Party Systems Since 1945', *Political Studies* 18: 287–319.
21 See Jean Blondel, 1963. *Votes, Parties and Leaders*. Harmondsworth: Penguin; Frank Bealey, Jean Blondel, and W. P. McCain, 1965. *Constituency Politics: A Study of Newcastle-under-Lyme*. London: Faber and Faber, pp. 168–86; Peter G. J. Pulzer, 1967. *Political Representation and Elections in Britain*. London: George Allen & Unwin; Henry Durant, 1969. 'Voting Behaviour in Britain, 1945–1966', in Richard Rose, *Studies in British Politics*. London: Macmillan.
22 Robert Alford, 1964. *Party and Society*. London: Murray.
23 W. L. Guttsman, 1963. *The British Political Elite*. London: MacGibbon & Kee; see also J. F. S. Ross, 1955. *Elections and Electors*. London: Eyre & Spottiswoode.
24 Samuel H. Beer, 1969. *Modern British Politics*. London: Faber and Faber.
25 R. T. McKenzie and Allan Silver, 1968. *Angels in Marble*. London: Heinemann; E. A. Nordlinger, 1967. *The Working Class Tories*. London: MacGibbon & Kee; W. G. Runciman, 1966. *Relative Deprivation and Social Justice*. London: Routledge & Kegan Paul.
26 Morgens N. Pedersen, 1985. 'Changing Patterns of Electoral Volatility in European Party Systems: 1948–1977', and Maria Maguire, 1985. 'Is There Still Persistence? Electoral Change in Western Europe, 1948–1979', both in Hans Daalder and Peter Mair (eds), *Western European Party Systems*. London: Sage.
27 Norman Nie, Sidney Verba and John Petrocik, 1979. *The Changing American Voter*. Cambridge, MA: Harvard University Press.
28 Ibid., p. 48.
29 Ivor Crewe, Bo Sarlvik and Jim Alt, 1977. 'Partisan Dealignment in Britain 1964–1974', *British Journal of Political Science* 7: 129–90; Ian Budge, Ivor Crewe and D. Fairlie (eds), 1976. *Party Identification and Beyond*. New York: Wiley; Bo Sarlvik and Ivor Crewe, 1983. *Decade of Dealignment*. Cambridge: Cambridge University Press; David Robertson, 1984. *Class and the British*

96 Changes in the Electorate

Electorate. Oxford: Basil Blackwell; Mark Franklin, 1985. The Decline of Class Voting in Britain. Oxford: Clarendon Press; Ivor Crewe and David Denver, 1985. Electoral Change in Western Democracies. London: Croom Helm; James Alt, 1984. 'Dealignment and the Dynamics of Partisanship in Britain', in Russell Dalton, Scott Flanagan and Paul Allen Beck (eds), Electoral Change in Advanced Industrial Democracies. Princeton, NJ: Princeton University Press.

30 Ivor Crewe, 1982. 'Is Britain's Two-Party System Really About to Crumble?', Electoral Studies 1(3): 275–313, p. 279.

31 Ivor Crewe and David Denver, 1985 (ed.). Electoral Change in Western Democracies. New York: St. Martin's Press; Russell Dalton, Scott Flanagan and Paul Beck (eds), 1984. Electoral Change in Advanced Industrial Democracies. Princeton, NJ: Princeton University Press.

32 David Butler and Donald Stokes, 1974. Political Change in Britain. London: Macmillan. pp. 204–8.

33 See Bo Sarlvik and Ivor Crewe, 1983. Decade of Dealignment. Cambridge: Cambridge University Press; David Robertson, 1984. Class and the British Electorate. Oxford: Basil Blackwell; Mark Franklin, 1985. The Decline of Class Voting in Britain. Oxford: Clarendon Press; Anthony Heath, Roger Jowell and John Curtice. How Britain Votes. Oxford: Pergamon; Ivor Crewe 1986. 'On the Death and Resurrection of Class Voting: Some comments on How Britain votes', Political Studies 34(4): 620–38; Patrick Dunleavy, 1987. 'Class Dealignment in Britain Revisited', West European Politics 10(3); Anthony Heath, Roger Jowell and John Curtice, 1987. 'Trendless Fluctuations: A Reply to Crewe', Political Studies 35(2): 256–77.

34 Richard Rose and Ian McAllister, 1986. Voters Begin to Choose. London: Sage, p.1.

35 Mark Franklin, Tom Mackie and Henry Valen et al., 1992. Electoral Change. Cambridge: Cambridge University Press, p. 385.

36 Alaine Touraine, 1969. La Société Post-industrielle. Paris: Denoel; Daniel Bell, 1973. The Coming of Post-Industrial Society. New York: Basic Books.

37 For a summary of the evidence on social stratification in Britain see Ivan Reid, 1989. Social Class Differences in Britain, 3rd edn. London: Fontana Press.

38 Anthony Heath, Roger Jowell and John Curtice, 1985. How Britain Votes. Oxford: Pergamon.

39 Patrick Dunleavy and Christopher T. Husbands, 1985. British Democracy at the Crossroads. London: George Allen & Unwin.

40 Ivor Crewe, 1984. 'The Electorate: Partisan Dealignment Ten Years On', in Hugh Berrington (ed.), Change in British Politics. London: Frank Cass; Ivor Crewe, 1985. 'Great Britain', in Ivor Crewe and David Denver (eds), Electoral Change in Western Democracies. London: Croom Helm.

41 Ronald Inglehart, 1990. Culture Shift in Advanced Industrialised Society. Princeton, NJ: Princeton University Press; Ronald Inglehart, 1977. The

Silent Revolution. Princeton, NJ: Princeton University Press.

42 David Robertson, 1984. *Class and the British Electorate*. Oxford: Basil Blackwell, p. 86.

43 See, for example, R. J. Johnston, C. J. Pattie and J. G. Allsopp, 1988. *A Nation Dividing?* London: Longman; David Smith, 1989. *North and South*. Harmondsworth: Penguin.

44 Richard Rose and Derek Urwin, 1975. *Regional Differentiation and Political Unity in Western Nations*. Beverly Hills, CA: Sage.

45 Vernon Bogdanor and William Field, 1993. 'Lessons of History: Core and Periphery in British Electoral Behaviour, 1910–1992', *Electoral Studies* 12(3): 203–24.

46 Paul R. Abramson and Ronald Inglehart, 1995. *Value Change in Global Perspective*. Ann Arbor, MI: University of Michigan Press, p. 14; Ronald Inglehart, 1990. *Culture Shift in Advanced Industrial Society*. Princeton: Princeton University Press.

47 See Joni Lovenduski and Vicky Randall, 1993. *Contemporary Feminist Politics*. Oxford: Oxford University Press; see also Joni Lovenduski and Pippa Norris (eds), 1996. *Women and Politics in Britain*. Oxford: Oxford University Press.

48 Pippa Norris, 1996. 'Gender Realignment in Comparative Perspective', in Marian Simms (ed.), *The Future of the Australian Party System*. Melbourne: Allen and Unwin.

49 Pippa Norris, 1996. 'The Gender-generation Gap in British Politics', in *Parliamentary Affairs* 49(2): 333–42.

50 Richard Rose and Ian McAllister, 1990. *The Loyalties of Voters*. London: Sage, p. 162.

51 Hilde Himmelweit et al., 1981. *How Voters Decide*. London: Academic Press.

52 Samuel Popkin, 1994. *The Reasoning Voter*. Chicago: University of Chicago Press; Mark Franklin, 1985. *The Decline of Class Voting*. Oxford: Oxford University Press.

53 Mark Franklin, 1985. *The Decline of Class Voting in Britain*. Oxford: Oxford University Press.

54 Ibid., p. 152.

55 For a review of the extensive body of literature on economic voting see Michael Lewis-Beck, 1991. *Economics and Elections: The Major Western Democracies*. Ann Arbor, MI: University of Michigan Press. For recent British studies see David Sanders and Simon Price, 1994. 'Party Support and Economic Perceptions in the UK, 1979–87', in David Broughton et al., *British Elections and Parties Yearbook, 1994*. London: Frank Cass; David Sanders, Hugh Ward and David Marsh, 1991. 'Macroeconomics, the Falklands War, and the Popularity of the Thatcher Government: A Contrary View', in Helmut Norpoth, Michael Lewis-Beck and Jean-Dominique Lafay (eds), *Economics*

and Politics. Ann Arbor, MI: University of Michigan Press; Helmut Norpoth, 1992. *Confidence Regained: Economics, Mrs. Thatcher and the British Voter*. Ann Arbor, MI: University of Michigan Press; Helmut Norpoth, 1987. 'The Falklands War and Government Popularity in Britain: Rally without Consequence or Surge without Decline?', *Electoral Studies* 6(1): 3–16.

56 Richard Rose and Ian McAllister, 1990. *The Loyalties of Voters*. London: Sage, pp. 106–8.

57 Clive Bean and Anthony Mughan, 1989. 'Leadership Effects in Parliamentary Elections in Australia and Britain', *American Political Science Review* 83: 1165–79; see also Richard Nadeau and Matthew Mendelsohn, 1994. 'Short-term Popularity Boost Following Leadership Change in Great Britain', *Electoral Studies* 13(3): 222–8; Richard Rose, 1995. 'A Crisis of Confidence in British Party Leaders?', *Contemporary Record* 9(2): 273–93.

58 See Margaret Scammell, 1995. *Designer Politics: How Elections are Won*. London: Macmillan; Dennis Kavanagh, 1995. *Election Campaigning*. Oxford: Blackwell; Bob Franklin, 1993. *Packaging Politics*. London: Edward Arnold.

5 The Partisan Identity of Voters

The partisan dealignment argument rests on three major premises: (1) many voters no longer have a strong and stable commitment to anchor them to political parties; (2) as a result voters have become more volatile in their electoral behaviour, more willing to desert Labour and the Conservatives, thereby producing erratic waves of support for the minor parties; and that (3) as party loyalties have weakened, short-term factors have become more influential in voting choice. In Ivor Crewe's words:

> As partisan and class ardour cooled, however, considerations other than habitual party and class loyalties began to influence the voting decision of more and more electors. In particular campaign-specific factors – the outgoing government's record, the major issues of the day, the party leader's personal qualities, specific and perhaps quite trivial incidents – took on greater significance . . . The committed electorate has begun to make way for the hesitant electorate.[1]

The focus of psychological theories of dealignment is essentially 'bottom-up': they emphasize continuity or change in how individual citizens make up their mind when confronted by electoral choices.

The first academic surveys in Britain analysing the basis of party support were carried out in constituencies in the fifties and sixties.[2] The field was transformed by the series of British Election Study (BES) surveys in every general election. The series was created by David Butler and Donald Stokes (1963, 1964, 1966, 1969, and 1970), continued by Ivor Crewe, Bo Sarlvik, James Alt and David Robertson at the University of

Essex (February 1974, October 1974, and 1979), while the most recent series was co-directed by Anthony Heath, Roger Jowell and John Curtice (1983, 1987, and 1992).[3] Most of the controversy in Britain based on this data has revolved around the relative importance of long-term factors influencing voting behaviour, including the role of class and regional cleavages, and the strength of partisan identification.[4]

In considering evidence for partisan and class dealignment due to structural development we are searching for a pattern of continuous secular trends, with a smooth linear or cyclical pattern, which glacially transforms the electorate over decades. One major difficulty with interpreting trends based on the BES is that the series is limited to nine general elections from 1964 to 1992. This makes it difficult to assess whether an apparent change represents the start of a long-term trend, a temporary shift, or merely random measurement error. 'Noise', such as even minor changes in sampling, fieldwork, the phrasing of questions, or the categories of responses, may produce spurious blips. Moreover, surveys taken at the intervals of general elections underestimate intra-electoral flux, indicated by opinion polls or by-elections. These limitations reinforce the importance of comparing developments in Britain, not only across time, but also cross-nationally. Comparative analysis has been facilitated by the growing availability of international surveys including, among others, the annual EuroBarometer series, the International Social Science Programme, the European and World Values Surveys, and the Manifesto Research Group.[5] If we find similar trends across modern democracies, such as partisan or class dealignment, or the rise of post-materialism and issue voting, this strengthens the argument that these developments are due to common structural factors. What is the evidence from these sources for the weakening of party attachments and increased electoral volatility?

The Decline in Party Identification

The first claim is that citizens have become less committed to political parties. The dealignment thesis should not be over-stated: commentators suggest that in Britain party loyalties remain important and pervasive, but there has been an overall decline, particularly in the proportion of strong loyalists, in the post-war period. No British surveys measured party identification prior to the early sixties, so any assumptions about the strength of such loyalties in the post-war decade have to remain speculative. Since 1964 two standard questions have been used, with only minor wording change, throughout the BES series to measure the direction and strength of party identification:

'Generally speaking, do you usually think of yourself as Conservative, Labour, Liberal, or what?'
[If accepts party affiliation] 'How strongly (chosen party) do you generally feel – very strongly, fairly strongly, or not very strongly?' (BES 1964).

The evidence supporting the theory of partisan dealignment is familiar: the proportion of respondents with a general sense of party identification has dwindled very modestly over the years, from 91.7 per cent in the period 1964–70 to 87.9 per cent in the period 1974–92 (see table 5.1, figure 5.1). More significantly, the proportion of the electorate with a *strong* party identification halved from 43.4 per cent in the period 1964–70 to 22.8 per cent in the period 1974–92. One of the most striking features of this development, however, is that this decline is not linear. The fall was steep in one period, during the decade of dealignment of the seventies, before stabilizing at the lower rate.[6] Moreover this decline in strong loyalists cannot be attributed simply to the weakness of the Labour party, since it has affected both major parties. The most notable change is in the strength, not direction, of party attachments.

David Denver has suggested that party habits may have been weakened by rising levels of education and the impact of non-partisan television,

Table 5.1   Trends in partisan identification, 1964–92

	1964	1966	1970	1974	1974	1979	1983	1987	1992
With party id	92	90	89	88	85	85	86	86	86
With Cons/Lab id	81	80	81	75	74	74	67	67	74
V strong id	43	43	41	29	26	21	20	19	18
V strong Cons/Lab id	40	39	40	27	22	19	18	16	17

Note: The question, with some minor wording changes over the years, is as follows: 'Generally speaking, do you usually think of yourself as Conservative, Labour, Liberal, or what?'
[If accepts party affiliation] 'How strongly (chosen party) do you generally feel – very strongly, fairly strongly, or not very strongly?'
Source: *British Election Studies, 1964–92.*

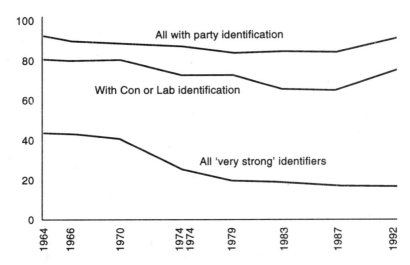

Figure 5.1   Trends in party identification, 1964–92
Source: Table 5.1.

producing a more sophisticated electorate, in other words, by secular trends in post-industrial society.[7] If so, we would expect to find British patterns to be broadly replicated in similar societies. Hermann Schmitt and Søren Holmberg conducted the most thorough recent comparison, based on a linear regression analysis of partisan identification with data from national election studies and the EuroBarometers for fifteen European countries and the United States.[8] Schmitt and Holmberg concluded that there has been a general decline of partisanship but nevertheless the depth and spread of this development varied for different countries and for different periods of time. The evidence from the seven countries with a long-standing tradition of national election studies showed that the United States, Sweden and Britain exhibited significant, steep declines in strong party identifiers. Yet the study found that irrespective of short-term movements, party attachments remained stable in Norway, Denmark and the Netherlands, and trends proved insignificant in Germany. Evidence from the annual series of EuroBarometer surveys confirmed similar results. This data indicated weakening party attachments in Britain, Ireland, Italy, France and Luxembourg, but, in contrast, a pattern of insignificant and trendless fluctuations in Germany, the Netherlands, Denmark and Belgium. In contrast, in recent years Greece, Spain and Portugal may even have experienced slightly stronger attachments to parties following the consolidation of new democracies. Most importantly, rather than a secular trend, Schmitt and Holmberg argue that the loosening of party loyalties occurs in period-specific phases in different countries, which strongly suggests the root cause is political not structural. The authors conclude:

> What we find, however, is anything but a smooth and uniform decline across Western Europe. Sweeping macro-level explanations which, for example, talk of the importance of rising educational levels, increased penetration by the mass media, and the coming of the post-industrial age, cannot do justice to all these differing trends. Political factors like the extent of party competition and the content of ideological conflicts, the evolution of new parties, changes in political leadership, and the scope of politics are the key considerations to understanding shifts in mass partisan ties.[9]

The decline in party membership

Evidence that British voters are less committed to parties is further supported by the decline in party membership. Again some argue that this may be due to the modernization of post-industrial societies. Russell Dalton has suggested that stable links with parties have become less widespread in modern democracies because of new avenues of civic participation, through new social movements and single-issue political organizations, especially for younger, better-educated and more politically skilful 'new citizens'.[10] Becoming active in campaigns to protest against the export of live animals, to block motorway road-building plans through forests, or to develop a battered women's shelter in the local community, may seem a more attractive and effective form of engagement than attending humdrum ward meetings about party fundraising and electioneering.

Yet cross-cultural trends suggest that again the most appropriate explanation may be political rather than structural. Based on a comparison of official party records, Katz and Mair report that many European countries have experienced a slight erosion in the relative size of party membership (compared with the size of the electorate) during the last thirty years, but the fall has been most dramatic in Denmark, and more significant in

Finland, the Netherlands and Britain than elsewhere. The proportion of the British electorate belonging to a party dropped from 9.4 per cent in the early sixties down to 3.3 per cent by the end of the eighties. In contrast Katz and Mair found that some countries maintained stable figures, while parties in Sweden, Belgium and Germany attracted growing memberships.[11] If we compare membership in the eleven European countries for which we have party records, Britain emerges at the low end of the spectrum. By the end of the eighties the proportion of the electorate who belonged to a party ranged from 21.8 per cent in Austria and 21.2 per cent in Sweden, down to 3.3 per cent in the UK and 2.9 per cent in the Netherlands.[12] Widfeldt compares these official records with trends over time in party membership based on survey data in fifteen west European countries. He confirms the modest decline of membership in some countries, and the lack of a uniform or steep cross-national fall.[13]

In Britain, how does membership vary by party? Figures based on the official records of individual party membership are not wholly reliable for various reasons: the criteria of membership are often loose and vary by party; all parties have some ancillary categories of membership where little information is available; Liberal and Conservative party headquarters do not keep track of membership levels, and centralized records are hampered by a federal structure and decentralized organization. Nevertheless, the available records suggest the fall in membership noted earlier has affected all British parties, although not at the same pace or level (see figure 5.2).

Estimates suggest that Labour's individual membership expanded rapidly in the mid-1940s, and peaked at just over one million (1,015,000) in 1952, after which it gradually declined. The number of individual Labour party members fell by two-thirds in the periods under comparison, from 908,000 in the period 1945–70 down to 294,000 in the period 1970–92. Yet an analysis of trends over time, in figure 5.2, shows membership was held fairly steady throughout the 1970s. The precipitate plunge occurred in 1980, at the time of the deep battles between left and right within the party, the bitter deputy leadership contest between Benn and Healey, and the defection of the Gang of Four. After this point membership stabilized throughout the 1980s. As part of the reorganization process Labour introduced a more effective membership drive in the early 1990s, and this, combined with the surge in Labour popularity in the opinion polls, boosted membership to 376,000 in mid-1996. Therefore, far from a long-term secular slide, the Labour party has demonstrated the capacity to

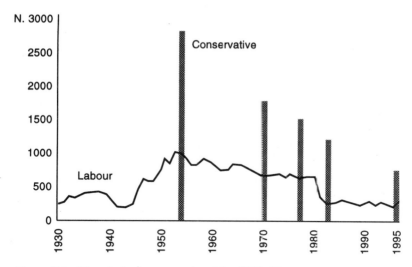

Figure 5.2   Trends in party membership, 1930–95
Source: D. Butler and G. Butler, *British Political Facts, 1900–1994.*

staunch the flow of members, and even expand its grassroots base, within a fairly short period.

The Conservatives have been the largest mass membership party in Britain. The party claimed 2.8 million members in 1953, but the Houghton Committee estimated this had fallen to 1.5 million in 1974, or an average membership in each constituency association of about 2,400.[14] In 1984 internal estimates suggested membership was down to 1.2 million,[15] and the most recent study suggests that membership had fallen to about 780,000 in 1992.[16] This would mean that the Conservatives remain the largest party in Britain, although Seyd et al. suggest that many members are relatively or wholly inactive. There are considerable variations between local Conservative Associations, ranging from about 1,853 members in safe seats down to 277 in unwinnable constituencies.[17] Membership in the Liberal party was just under 250,000 in 1960, falling to about 100,000 as the merged Liberal Democratic party in 1992.[18] Although estimates have to remain approximate, the SNP claims around 20,000 members, Plaid Cymru about 9,000 and the Green Party around 4,600.[19]

Does this decline matter? In the past, party members have provided the volunteer labour in grassroots campaigns, including campaigning, fund-raising, propaganda and recruitment. Political functions, such as the discussion and formulation of policy, does occur in constituency meetings, but policy debate normally takes a back-seat to routine organizational business and campaigning. Since the early eighties, centralized, capital-intensive, professional organizations, drawing on the techniques of television advertising, political marketing and opinion polls, have replaced much of the work of local constituency parties, particularly in Labour and Conservative general election campaigns.[20] Katz and Mair have argued that new forms of party organization have evolved in some countries which do not need a mass base to raise revenue or to campaign. Nevertheless, as discussed later, in Britain a well-managed campaign by local volunteers may help boost national efforts, although there is dispute about the precise electoral rewards of such efforts.

To summarize these trends, the Michigan model suggests that in the fifties and sixties the two–party duopoly in government was based on the foundation of stable and habitual attachments to political parties among the British electorate. People saw themselves as Labour or Conservative, much as they saw themselves as Protestants or Catholics, factory or office workers, Scots or English, men or women. Elections were less about brand new choices of policies and leaders than about familiar standing decisions. Approximately four million people were party members, or about one in ten of the electorate. Moreover almost all voters acknowledged a general sense of partisan identification, and many had a strong attachments to one of the major parties.

In contrast by the early nineties total party membership had fallen to less than a million, and less than a fifth of the British electorate (17.8 per cent) expressed strong party loyalties. To this extent the theory of partisan dealignment is correct. But overall the common structural explanations for this development seem largely unconvincing. The evidence indicates that citizens' links with parties have declined more sharply in Britain than in many comparable post-industrial societies in Europe. This, combined with the pattern of trends over time, strongly suggests political reasons lie at the root of these developments.

Political explanations fall into two major categories. The *organizational* approach emphasizes how parties build and maintain their links with citizens, how they target, organize and recruit grassroots support, and how they shape their policy platforms strategically to appeal to different groups in the electorate. Along these lines Peter Mair has argued that as parties move towards a 'catch-all' model, targeting their appeal more broadly rather than to distinctive sub-groups, this may encourage voters to switch more easily between closely-related parties.[21] In the same vein, Herbert Kitschelt carried out one of the most comprehensive examinations of the electoral fortunes of European social democratic parties in the post-war period. Kitschelt develops a powerful argument that changes in the socio-economic class structure have less influence over the success or failure of particular social democratic parties than their strategic appeals. Deterministic arguments which suggest that the shrinkage of the industrial working class inevitably weakens parties on the left are strongly rejected on the basis of this study:

> External social, economic and institutional settings within which parties operate are less important for determining a party's fortunes than its own choice of objectives and strategies in the arena of party competition.[22]

Parties like the Austrian Social Democrats end up with fourteen times the mass membership achieved by the British Labour party,[23] which suggests no inexorable slide in the mass appeal of the parties of the left.

Alternatively, *performance* based accounts emphasize the need to reinterpret the concept of partisan identification. In Downsian theory, the concept can be interpreted less as an affective psychological attachment, and more as an instrumental running tally which depends upon evaluations of past and future benefits from government. Morris Fiorina developed this case most fully in the United States.[24] The study re-analysed American National Election panel survey data over the period 1956–58–60, and over the period 1972–74–76. Fiorina concluded that American party identification was less stable than expected on the basis of *The American Voter*. Rather than affective loyalties, Fiorina concluded that party identification was shaped by evaluations of economic and political conditions, and retrospective evaluations of the performance of the government. If this account is correct, the decline in party identification in Britain can be attributed to the 'crisis of governability' and 'government overload' which many observers noted followed the economic recession generated by the oil shock in the early seventies. Anthony King noted that in this decade governments could not deliver what voters expected, and the disappointment this generated may have led to dissatisfaction with the established parties.[25] Average government approval in Gallup polls was around 40 per cent in the

1945–70 era, but approval plummeted to 25 per cent in the period from 1970 to 1995. Low economic growth, U-turns, and the series of policy failures which plagued the Callaghan and Heath governments in the seventies may have undermined voter's habitual faith in parties.[26]

The Rise of a More Volatile Electorate?

One way to help resolve debates about the meaning and continued influence of party identification is to consider its expected consequences. The most important proposition of the Michigan theory is that party identification is one of the strongest anchors of voting choice. In the original formulation by Campbell et al., party identification was regarded as pervasive, affective and durable. If voters inherited habitual party identities from their parents, or from their social milieu, then it would be relatively immune to change. Party identification was believed to anchor voters over a series of contests even when they temporarily defected or split their ticket at the ballot box. Commentators commonly referred to groups like the 'Reagan Democrats', cross-over voters who still saw themselves as long-standing Democrats despite supporting the policies and leadership of President Reagan at the ballot box. For dealignment theorists the decline in partisan identification which we have noted was thought to produce less stability among the electorate.

In Europe, however, the durability of party identification has been questioned. In the Netherlands Jacques Thomassen found that party identification was *less* stable than vote preference over successive elections, suggesting that surveys may be measuring one and the same phenomenon: the preference for a particular party at a certain moment in time.[27] In the same way in Britain, as Butler and Stokes acknowledged, if we compare changes in party identification and voting choice we find that the trend lines move in parallel with each other over time (see table 5.2). The Conservatives consistently win more votes than could be expected from their party identification, while fewer people identify with the Liberals than vote for them, and Labour's vote share and party identification run almost parallel. This undermines the utility of the concept, since party identification loses its predictive power.

If party attachments have declined, then theories of partisan dealignment predict that electoral volatility should increase. In Miller's words:

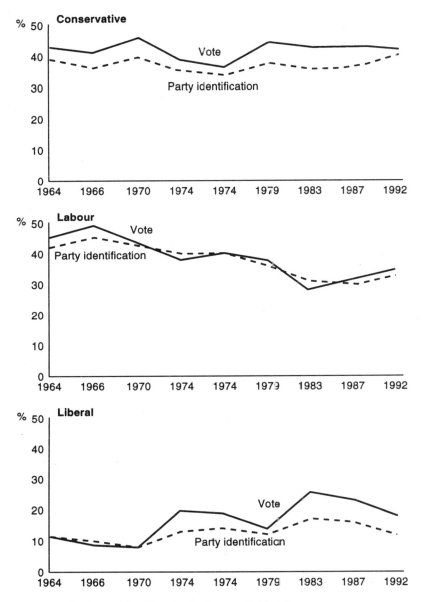

Figure 5.3 Party identification and vote, 1964–92

Table 5.2   Party identification and the vote, 1964–92

	Cons Vote	Cons Id	Lab Vote	Lab Id	Lib Vote	Lib Id
1964	43	39	45	42	11	12
1966	41	36	49	45	9	10
1970	46	40	44	43	8	8
1974	39	35	38	40	20	13
1974	37	34	40	40	19	14
1979	45	38	38	36	14	12
1983	44	36	28	31	26	17
1987	43	37	32	30	23	16
1992	43	41	35	33	18	12

Source: *British Election Studies, 1964–92.*

By the mid-eighties we have evidence that the British electorate was dealigned and volatile. Its tendency to vote along class lines and, more directly important, its psychological commitment to parties was only half as strong as it had been twenty years earlier . . . Net volatility, as measured by swings in general elections, by-elections and opinion polls was much higher than in the stable fifties; and gross volatility, measured in panel surveys was high.[28]

Electoral volatility can be measured in different ways. Crewe draws an important distinction between 'net' and 'gross' volatility.[29] '*Net*' volatility refers to the change in the distribution of the vote between two elections. This is commonly measured by the 'Butler swing' of the vote, already described, or the Pederson Index of dissimilarity which can be calculated to summarize change in the share of the vote for all parties.[30] In contrast '*gross*' volatility refers to the total amount of change which takes place between two points in time, as measured by panel surveys or recalled vote. The important point is that many people may change their vote, but often these changes may cancel each other out. If many Labour voters switch to the Liberal Democrats, and vice versa, this may produce considerable electoral flux and yet little flow of the vote.

Net volatility

If we first look at trends in net volatility, the 'Butler swing' calculated for successive pairs of elections reveals an erratic pattern (see figure 5.4). The

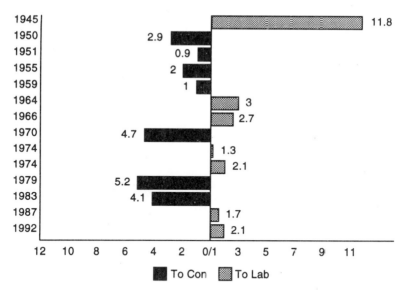

Figure 5.4   Butler swing, 1945–92

largest swing recorded (11.8 per cent) followed the Labour victory in 1945, producing a landslide almost off the scale. The following swings in the fifties and sixties proved more modest, under 3 per cent. In the era of decline of two-party strength general elections produced three major swings, in 1970 (4.7 per cent), 1979 (5.2 per cent), and 1983 (4.1 per cent). Yet the pattern over time does not reveal a secular trend towards ever increasing volatility, since the general elections in February and October 1974, 1987 and 1992 proved rather stable by this measure. Indeed, in part because of 1945, the average swing was slightly higher from 1945 to 1970 (3.6 per cent), than from February 1974 to 1992 (2.7 per cent).

Nor is this simply a result of the measure, since the 'Pederson' index shows no linear increase (figure 5.5). The largest volatility in this index is recorded for the period 1970–4, with the rise of the minor parties. Another major shift is evident under the first two Thatcher victories. Yet the overall pattern from 1945 to 1992 is one of trendless fluctuations rather than a glacial and consistent rise in volatility. As Heath et al. suggest, this points more strongly towards political than structural explanations.[31]

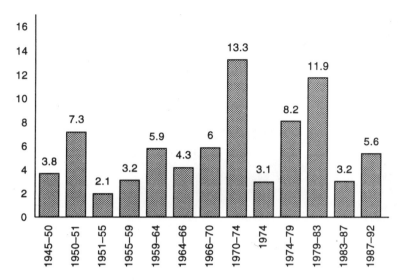

Figure 5.5   Pederson index, 1945–92

Gross Volatility

Yet there could still be a great deal of electoral flux which could cancel itself out in party fortunes. Gross volatility can be estimated by using BES panel surveys to calculate the proportion of those eligible to vote in both elections who changed their electoral choice (see table 5.3). The results show a decline in the proportion of stable voters from 1966 to February 1974, but far from producing a secular or linear trend, stability subsequently recovered. About a third of the electorate changed from one election to the next, and the largest category of switchers are those who move between abstention and voting participation. Conversions across the major parties were rare, and slightly more voters switched between the major parties and the Liberals.

We would expect consistency to decline with panels stretching over more than two elections. The most extensive study was carried out by Himmelweit et al. who used a longitudinal study which traced a group of young voters over two decades. The study found that over six successive

Table 5.3 Vote change between pairs of elections, 1964–92

	1964	1966	1970	1974ᵃ	1979ᵇ	1983	1987	1992
STABLE VOTERS:								
Con–Con: Lab–Lab	51	55	47	43	42	52	54	52
Lib–Lib	2	4	3	4	7	7	10	6
Abstain–Abstain	11	15	16	11	3	5	5	4
Stable	64	74	66	58	62	64	69	62
Con–Lab: Lab–Con	5	3	5	5	4	4	3	3
Lib–Con: Lib–Lab	7	4	4	8	9	14	13	15
Abstain–Vote	24	19	25	29	25	18	15	20
Switchers	36	26	34	42	28	36	31	38

Note: 1983 and 1987 are recalled vote; (a) 1970–Feb. 1974, (b) Oct. 1974–79.
Source: British Election Studies, 1964–92.

elections, the majority of their panel proved to be floating voters who had a preferred party to which they returned, but they often switched in or out of the voting population, or between parties. In particular, as with the BES data, the study found the most common switching was between voting and abstention, or to and from the Liberals: 'the Liberals (are) a turn-around station rather than a halfway house in the journey from right to left or from left to right.'[32]

Lastly, we also have evidence of potential volatility, by looking at the proportion of waverers and late deciders. The BES has regularly asked the following:

> *Waverers:*
> 'Was there any time during the general election campaign when you seriously thought you might vote for another party?'
> *Late Deciders:*
> 'How long ago did you decide that you would definitely vote the way you did: was it . . . a long time ago, sometime last year, sometime this year, or during the election campaign?'

The results, presented in figure 5.6, show an increase in waverers and late deciders in successive elections during the seventies, but this trend declined somewhat in the early eighties, and then plateaued at this slightly higher level.

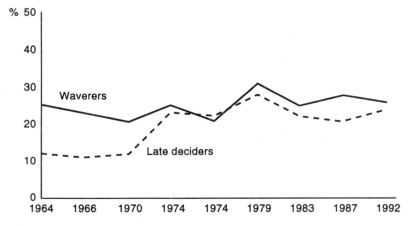

Figure 5.6   Waverers and late deciders, 1964–92
Source: British Election Studies, 1964–94.

Conclusions

Weighing all this evidence together we can conclude that party identification has declined in strength from the earliest BES surveys, accompanied by a growth in waverers and late deciders, leading contemporary observers to predict the steady growth of the dealigned electorate. This loosening of party attachments occurred during successive elections in the seventies, which did indeed prove, in Sarlvik and Crewe's prescient phrase, the 'decade of dealignment'.

Yet with the benefit of hindsight it appears that rather than an inexorable secular or linear trend, Britain experienced a period-specific shift during the seventies. The eighties and early nineties saw no further glacial decline in patterns of strong partisan identification, party membership, waverers and late deciders, and most importantly vote switchers. Moreover indicators of net volatility show periodic waves of change, rather than linear trends. As noted earlier, Schmitt and Holmberg found similar patterns in other European countries. Far from party attachments providing a stable anchor for voting behaviour, changes in voting choice and party identification tend to move in tandem. Overall this evidence tends to throw doubt on explanations of growing voter instability based on structural trends in post-industrial society, such as demographic, cultural or economic shifts. Rather the pattern of the trends lead us more strongly towards political explanations, such as the performance of successive British governments during the seventies, or the strategies which parties used to mobilize and organize their electoral base. Before examining the evidence for these arguments let us consider whether social dealignment has followed similar, or divergent, patterns.

Notes

1   Ivor Crewe, 1984. 'The electorate: partisan dealignment ten years on', in Hugh Berrington (ed.), *Change in British Politics*. London: Frank Cass.
2   See S. B. Chrimes (ed.), 1950. *The General Election in Glasgow, February 1950*. Glasgow: Jackson, Son and Company, Glasgow University Publications; R. S. Milne and H. C. Mackenzie, 1954. *Straight Fight*. London: Hansard Society; R. S. Milne and H. C. Mackenzie, 1958. *Marginal Seat*. London: Hansard Society; A. H. Birch, 1959. *Small Town Politics*. Oxford: Oxford University Press; Frank Bealey, Jean Blondel and W. P. McCann, 1965. *Constituency Politics: A Study of Newcastle-Under-Lyme*. London: Faber and Faber; Joseph Trenaman and Denis McQuail, 1961. *Television and the Political Image*. London: Methuen; Jay Blumler and Denis McQuail, 1968. *Television in Politics*. London: Faber and Faber.
3   For details of the research design and main contents of these surveys see Ivor Crewe, Anthony Fox and Neil Day, 1995. *The British Electorate, 1963-1992*. Cambridge: Cambridge University Press.
4   For a review of the mainstream debates see, for example, the articles included in David Denver and Gordon Hands (eds), 1992. *Issues and Controversies in British Electoral Behaviour*. Herts.: Harvester Wheatsheaf; also successive volumes of the *British Elections and Parties Yearbook* (seq. 1991–5). Herts.: Harvester Wheatsheaf/ London: Frank Cass.
5   To see how these sources have become integrated in the Beliefs in Government research programme see Hans-Dieter Klingemann and Dieter Fuchs (eds), 1995. *Citizens and the State*. Oxford: Oxford University Press.
6   It should be noted that W. L. Miller, S. Tagg and K. Britto, 1986, using surveys for the Conservative party, noted that party identification had already started to decline in the mid-sixties. See 'Partisanship and Party Preference in Government and Opposition: the mid-term perspective', *Electoral Studies* 5: 31–46.
7   David Denver, 1994. *Elections and Voting Behaviour*. Herts.: Harvester Wheatsheaf, pp. 55–6.

8   Hermann Schmitt and Søren Holmberg, 1995. 'Political Parties in Decline?', in Hans-Dieter Klingemann and Dieter Fuchs, *Citizens and the State*. Oxford: Oxford University Press.

9   Ibid., p. 110.

10   Russell Dalton, 1996. *Citizen Politics*, 2nd edn. Chatham, NJ: Chatham House.

11   Richard Katz and Peter Mair, 1994. *How Parties Organize*. London: Sage; Richard Katz and Peter Mair, 1992. *Party Organizations: A Data Handbook on Party Organizations in Western Democracies 1960-90*. London: Sage.

12   Richard Katz and Peter Mair, 1994. *How Parties Organize*. London: Sage, Table 1.1. It should be noted that there is some dispute about the Swedish figures in this table and Anders Widfeldt suggests the data need to be adjusted downward to 8 per cent of the electorate to exclude collectively enrolled members. See Anders Widfeldt, 1995. 'Party Membership and Party Representativeness', in Hans-Dieter Klingemann and Dieter Fuchs (eds), *Citizens and the State*. Oxford: Oxford University Press.

13   Anders Widfeldt, 1995. 'Party Membership and Party Representativeness', in Hans-Dieter Klingemann and Dieter Fuchs (eds), *Citizens and the State*. Oxford: Oxford University Press.

14   Lord Houghton, 1976. *Report of the Committee on Financial Aid to Political Parties*. London: HMSO.

15   David Butler and Gareth Butler, 1994. *British Political Facts 1900–1994*. London: Macmillan, p. 152; Labour Party, 1990. *NEC Report*. London: Labour Party.

16   Paul Whiteley, Patrick Seyd and Jeremy Richardson, 1994. *True Blues*. Oxford: Oxford University Press.

17   Philip Tether, 1991. 'Recruiting Conservative Party Members: A Changing Role for Central Office', *Parliamentary Affairs* 44(1).

18   Paul Webb, 1994. 'Party Organisational Change in Britain', in Richard Katz and Peter Mair, *How Parties Organize*. London: Sage.

19   Peter Hennessy, 1995. *The Hidden Wiring*. London: Victor Gollancz; Andrew Pierce, 'Greens in attempt to recapture past glory', *The Times,* 12 April 1996.

20   See David Swanson and Paolo Mancini, 1996. *Politics, Media and Modern Democracy*. New York: Praeger.

21   See, for example, Richard Katz and Peter Mair, 1994. *How Parties Organize*. London: Sage; Peter Mair, 1989. 'Continuity, Change and the Vulnerability of Party', *Western Political Quarterly* 12: 170–85; Stefano Bartolini and Peter Mair, 1990. *Identity, Competition and Electoral Availability*. Cambridge: Cambridge University Press.

22   Herbert Kitschelt, 1994. *The Transformation of European Social Democracy*. Cambridge: Cambridge University Press.

23 Richard Katz and Peter Mair, 1994. *How Parties Organize*. London: Sage.
24 Morris Fiorina, 1979. *Retrospective Voting in American National Elections*. New Haven, CT: Yale University Press.
25 Anthony King, 1975. 'Overload: Problems of Governing in the 1970s', *Political Studies* 23(2–3): 284–96.
26 James E. Alt, 1984. 'Dealignment and the Dynamics of Partisanship in Britain', in Russell J. Dalton, Scott C. Flanagan and Paul Allen Beck (eds), *Electoral Change in Advanced Industrial Democracies*. Princeton, NJ: Princeton University Press.
27 Jacques Thomassen, 1976. 'Party Identification as a Cross-National Concept: Its Meaning in the Netherlands', in Ian Budge, Ivor Crewe and Dennis Farlie (eds), *Party Identification and Beyond*. London: John Wiley & Sons.
28 William Miller et al., 1990. *How Voters Change*. Oxford: Clarendon Press, p. 11
29 Ivor Crewe, 1985. 'Great Britain', in Ivor Crewe and David Denver (eds), *Electoral Change in Western Democracies*. London: Croom Helm.
30 The 'Pederson' index sums the proportion of voters who change their votes for each party between each pair of elections, divided by 2. See Morgens Pedersen, 1979. 'The Dynamics of European Party Systems: Changing Patterns of Electoral Volatility', *European Journal of Political Research* 7:1-27.
31 Anthony Heath, Roger Jowell and John Curtice, 1991. *Understanding Political Change*. Oxford: Pergamon, p. 17.
32 Hilde Himmelweit, Patrick Humphreys and Marianne Jaeger, 1985. *How Voters Decide*, 2nd edn. Milton Keynes: Open University Press, pp. 37–9.

6 The Social Identity of Voters

As discussed in earlier chapters, from the mid-seventies onwards theories of structural change challenged the old orthodoxy of class voting. Advanced post-industrial societies have been transformed in recent decades by a complex range of economic and technological trends – the decline of manufacturing industry and the rise of services, the contraction of the industrial working class, de-unionization, the growth of the 'enterprise' society, secularization, the spread of education, the white blouse revolution, the rise and fall of the public sector and the information age.[1] Moreover these shifts have been reinforced by demographic trends, including in Britain the drift from north to south, the ageing society, the baby-boom generation, the decline of the traditional family and patterns of ethnicity. What is less clear are the electoral implications of these developments. Accounts of class voting fall into four distinct categories:

- Orthodox *structural* theories, notably the seminal historical sociology of Stein Rokkan and Seymour Martin Lipset, suggest that social cleavages provide the basis for party politics;
- *Revisionist* theories, advocated most strongly by Anthony Heath and his colleagues, suggest that class remains the bedrock of British voting choice, but we need to alter traditional classifications and measures of social class to take account of the complexities of modern social inequalities;
- *Restructuring* theories suggest that occupational class has been replaced over time by more complex social and political cleavages, including

those based on regional, gender, generational and ethnic divisions in the electorate;

- *Rational voter* theories argue that affective group loyalties have been replaced by retrospective evaluations of government performance and prospective assessments of party policies.

The aim of this chapter is to consider the evidence for the changing relationship between social cleavages and party support.

Structural Theories of Electoral Stability

As summarized earlier, the structural model became the widely accepted orthodoxy based on the classic theory of Seymour Lipset and Stein Rokkan.[2] In this account, social class, region and religion formed the bedrock political cleavages in most European countries. The reason, Lipset and Rokkan suggest, is that these were the broadly-based and long-standing social and economic divisions within Europe when parties were mobilizing voters just before and after the final expansion of the franchise. For Lipset and Rokkan social cleavages were produced by complex historical processes, notably the national and industrial revolutions experienced by societies from the seventeenth century onwards. In Catholic Europe the division between Church and nation-state produced a religious cleavage which led to the formation of Christian Democrat parties; the division between landowners and industrialists helped generate agrarian parties; while the division between employers and workers provided the foundation for the formation of Social Democratic, Labour and Communist parties.

Social cleavages in different countries became the primary building blocks for the party system. Parties organized and mobilized coalitions of groups to forge a stable mass base of electoral support. For Lipset and Rokkan, the varying pattern of social cleavages across Europe in the nineteenth and early twentieth centuries established the essential framework for contemporary party systems. After the systems were established, Lipset and Rokkan suggest they 'froze', as parties strengthened links with their supporters, absorbed new social cleavages, and developed long-standing party images. The expansion of the mass franchise provided a unique opportunity for party mobilization and organization.

In the same way, during the last decade the first free elections in emerging democracies in eastern and central Europe, Latin America, and Asia were contested by a wide range of parties. In countries like Russia, the Ukraine and Bulgaria it proved difficult for most parties to develop a stable base of popular support which could tide them through bad times as well as good.[3] Yet if the system of party competition manages gradually to consolidate over successive elections, it may become progressively harder for new parties to mobilize groups of voters, to achieve parliamentary representation, and to become credible contenders for government. Equally importantly, it may also become more difficult for established parties to change their coalitional bases and ideological identities. The freezing process may be expected to affect voters, but also members, leaders and organizations. Given this 'freezing' process, theories of realignment suggest that fundamental changes in the mass basis of party systems are most likely to come during periods of crisis which puncture the equilibrium of the status quo.[4] Such crises force parties to adapt to new issues on the political agenda (like environmentalism), new groups in the electorate (such as second-generation immigrants), or new forms of party competition (for example, if old Communist parties contest elections as reconstructed Social Democrats).

Based on the evidence reviewed in *Political Man* (1959), Lipset concluded that in the 1950s the class cleavage was one of the most pervasive in western politics:

> Even though many parties renounce the principle of class conflict or loyalty, an analysis of their appeals and their support suggest that they do represent the interests of different classes. On a world scale, the principle generalisation which can be made is that parties are primarily based on either the lower classes or the middle and upper classes.[5]

Richard Rose's comparison of the empirical data, and Arend Lijphart's analysis of party systems, also identified the class cleavage as one of the most widespread in virtually all Western democracies.[6]

Class came to dominate British electoral politics in the early twentieth century. Based on the analysis of constituency results, Wald demonstrates that the major social and ideological divisions which demarcated party politics in the nineteenth century were between Anglicans and the nonconformists, and to a lesser extent between land and manufacturing interests, as well as between core and periphery regions. Looking at variations in party support at constituency level, Wald found that the class cleavage emerged more strongly in Britain after 1918, overlaying earlier divisions, and providing the basis for partisan realignment.[7]

The working class became organized politically when trade unions and socialist societies came together to form the Labour Representation Committee in 1900, which became the Labour Party in 1906. The mass base was provided by the trade unions, whose membership surged from three-quarters of a million in 1888 to over two million in 1899. The unions provided the party with general election expenses, grassroots volunteers, and an organizational basis necessary for mobilizing mass politics.[8] It was only in 1918 that Labour recognized individual members as it established constituency organizations. At the same time the 'one-nation' Conservative party of Disraeli became increasingly associated with the interests of business and commerce. The party relied upon informed social links with the families of prominent merchant bankers like the Rothschilds and Barings, and industrialists like the Baldwins and Weirs, for much of its revenues. Conservative party links with business, industry and the city became formalized during the inter-war years, relying upon larger economic organizations and interest groups.[9]

The first systematic evidence of class voting came from Gallup polls published just after the Second World War. In monitoring trends over time in voting behaviour we can use several measures of social class. The earliest studies relied upon the distinction between social classes used by the Market Research Society, based on the Registrar-General's Classification of Occupations. This produced six categories:

A   Higher professional, managerial and administrative
e.g. barristers, company directors, physicians

B   Intermediate professional, managerial and administrative
e.g. teachers, junior executives

C1   Supervisor, clerical and other non-manual
e.g. secretaries, bank tellers, police sergeants

C2   Skilled manual
e.g. electricians, machinists

D   Semi- and un-skilled manual
e.g. factory fitters, bus conductors

E   *Residual, casual workers, people on state benefits*
   e.g. pensioners, the unemployed

These categories were grouped into non-manual workers (A, B, C1), who formed 40 per cent of the occupied population in 1961, and manual workers (C2, D, E), 60 per cent.[10] The class–vote relationship has been summarized conventionally by the Alford Index, which measures the relative strength of the left-wing party in two classes. This is calculated by subtracting Labour's percentage share of the vote among non-manual workers from its share among manual workers. Based on this definition, the earliest surveys of the British electorate confirmed that class was the strongest demographic predictor of party choice. As noted earlier, Robert Alford used Gallup data to compare Britain, America, Australia and Canada, and concluded that Britain had the highest and most stable level of class voting.[11] Figure 6.1 presents comparative trends in the Alford Index for Britain, Sweden, Germany and the United States in the post-war period.

This evidence confirms, as many have observed, a process of class dealignment during the last half-century, but the pattern is not a steady,

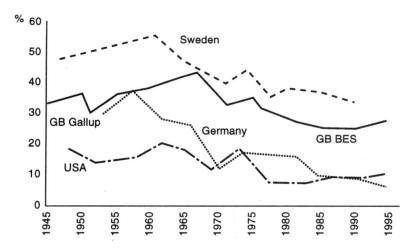

Figure 6.1   Cross-national trends in class voting, 1945–92
Source: GB Gallup/*British Election Studies*; Dalton 1996.

secular decline, as some accounts have suggested. The strength of the association between class and the vote did weaken from 1960 to 1970 in Sweden, Germany and the United States, and in Britain from 1966 to 1970. The strength of the Alford Index almost halved in Sweden and Britain. Nevertheless trends became somewhat erratic after this point, with a slight recovery of class voting in the early 1970s, followed by a pattern of broad stability during the 1980s.[12] If we turn from trends over time to the comparison between countries, it is apparent that class voting has been strongest in Sweden and weakest in the United States, with Britain in a middle position. In the United States this may reflect the strength of other cleavages, based on divisions of race and ethnicity, region, religion and gender.

The decline of class voting has also become evident in many other democracies, although, most importantly, not necessarily at the same pace or level.[13] Dalton compared eighteen advanced industrialized democracies, based on the World Values Survey 1990–1, and found that the strongest class voting was found in (respectively) Norway, Denmark, Austria, Iceland and Britain, while the weakest relationship was in the United States, Canada, Portugal and Japan.[14] We can conclude that class has become a less useful predictor of left-wing voting in many countries, but accounts which focus on two points in time (say the early 1960s and the late 1980s)[15] fail to notice the shape of the longitudinal trends. The pattern, like that of the weakening of partisan attachments, is one which can attributed more to period-specific phases than to a glacial, long-term decline.

The Revision of Class Definitions

Yet is the Alford Index, based on the simple distinction between manual and non-manual workers, an appropriate measure of class voting? There is little doubt that the structure of British society has changed fundamentally during the last half-century due to major economic and demographic developments.[16] As a result there have been dramatic shifts in the workforce, and in the size of the voting groups which form the building blocks of party support. In 1945 Britain's economy was based on heavy industry – the world of steel mills, shipbuilding yards and coal mines. The size of the male labour force working in manufacturing and construction fell from half in 1971 to one-third in 1994.[17] In common with other post-industrial societies, at the end of the twentieth century Britain's economy is increasingly based on the high-tech, communication-age, service-sector, symbolized by high streets crowded with building societies, banks and fast-food chains. The traditional industrial working-class constituted three-quarters of the British labour force in 1911, two-thirds in 1951, but only half the labour force in 1991, according to census occupational classifications.[18]

These trends, combined with higher unemployment, and the growth of less secure career-paths and part-time work, have transformed the labour force.[19] The growth of the post-industrial economy has been characterized by a revolution in the working lives of women and men: in 1951 a third of all adult women (32.7 per cent) were in the paid labour force, compared with just over half (52.6 per cent) by 1992. During the same period the proportion of men in paid work dropped from 87.6 per cent to under three-quarters (71.9 per cent). Trade union membership steadily grew in the post-war years until the peak of 13.3 million individual members in 1979. These decades also experienced an increase in the density of union membership (that is, the number of trade unionists relative to the size of the workforce), up from about a third (36 per cent) in 1941 to almost one-half (49 per cent) in 1981. In contrast, from the early 1980s onwards the contraction of the manufacturing sector, the rise in long-term unemployment, and legal changes in employment practices, combined to produce a steady decline in union membership which fell to just over 9 million in 1992, or 36 per cent of the labour force.[20]

As a result of post-industrial trends it can be argued that the black–white market research simplicities of dividing people into factory-workers or office-workers, based on the occupation of the (usually male) head of household, which once seemed to fit so neatly, no longer seems adequate to encapsulate the grey complexities of our lives. The most appropriate classification of social class remains a matter of continuing dispute.[21] In the 1970s John Goldthorpe developed a new categorization of social stratification incorporating an occupation's degree of economic security, authority in the workplace, prospects of economic advancement, and sources, as well as levels, of income.[22] This schema is designed to distinguish groups based on shared economic interests, not just income inequalities or occupational status per se. This produced a five-fold classification of social class which has been applied to electoral behaviour in a series of studies by Heath, Jowell and Curtice.[23] The revised categories are:

1   The *salariat*, including managers, administrators, supervisors, professionals, with a high level of income, security, autonomy and authority;

2   *Routine non-manual*, including clerks, salesworkers, secretaries, with lower income and autonomy;

3   The *petty bourgeoisie*, including farmers, small proprietors and self-employed manual workers like own-account plumbers, who are directly exposed to market forces;

4   *Foremen and technicians*, the blue-collar elite with supervisory functions; and,

5   The *working class*, the residual rank and file manual employees.

The schema has been applied to women and men based on their own occupations, if economically active. Based on this analysis, Heath et al. have argued that two major trends have become evident. First, due to post-industrial trends, the size of the working class has shrunk as a proportion of the electorate. According to the Goldthorpe measure, in 1964 the working class (47 per cent) was three times the size of the salariat (18 per cent). In contrast, by 1992 the working class (36 per cent) was almost the same size as the salariat (28 per cent). Heath et al. suggest this trend has reduced the pool of working-class support, and hence the potential Labour base. Yet Heath et al. also argue, more controversially, that once class is measured by the Goldthorpe schema to reflect the complexities of modern social inequalities, it is apparent that the strength of the class–voting relationship has not gradually and steadily fallen over time. Based on log-linear modelling, which controls for the size of social groups and the share of the vote going to each party, Heath et al. conclude that the pattern of class voting can best be characterized as a sharp fall from 1966 to 1970, followed by a pattern of trendless fluctuations, rather than a steady, secular decline. Moreover, they argue, social identities based on subjective class consciousness remain an important predictor of voting choice.

This work sparked a heated debate in British political science. Analysts such as Patrick Dunleavy and Ivor Crewe criticized the odds ratio used by Heath, Jowell and Curtice in their study of the 1983 election to summarize the strength of class–voting.[24] The more technical arguments about the pros and cons of odds ratios, and the class schema employed, has gradually

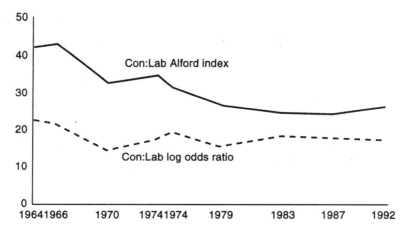

Figure 6.2   Trends in class voting, UK, 1964–92
Source: British Election Studies, 1964–92; Heath et al., 1991.

faded in intensity in recent years, with the recognition that much of the dispute revolved more around semantics than substance. Yet the debate has served to disguise one of the most striking observations, namely that there are similar trends in the manual:non-manual Alford Index favoured by traditional accounts of voting behaviour, and the salariat:working class log odds ratios favoured by Heath, Jowell and Curtice (see figure 6.2). Those on both sides of the debate share more in common than has been assumed. As figure 6.2 reveals, trends in the Alford Index and the log odds ratio both show a parallel steep decline in class voting for the major parties between 1966 to 1970. Both measures show class voting recovered slightly in 1974, before slipping modestly in 1979. During the 1980s there is a modest divergence in the trend lines, but both indicate a broadly stable pattern. As noted earlier, this pattern in both measures is more consistent with class dealignment, most notably during periods of Labour government,[25] rather than a long-term secular slide based on structural trends in society and the economy.

Other revisionist theories suggest that alternative measures of social inequality have become stronger predictors of party support. In the mid-eighties commentators noted a growing cleavage between the expanding

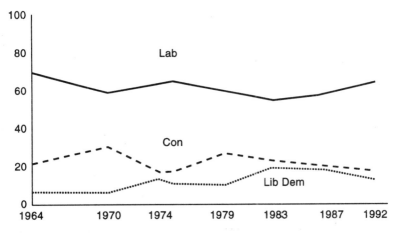

Figure 6.3   Vote by council tenants, 1964–92
Source: British Election Studies, 1964–92.

group of more affluent owner-occupiers, and the residual pool of poorer and more elderly residents living in council estates.[26] During the Thatcher years the sale of council housing was concentrated among the socially mobile groups, leaving behind a residual core of tenants, notably the elderly, the long-term unemployed, and those with young families. The pool of local authority housing shrivelled from about a third of all households (31.5 per cent) when Mrs Thatcher was first elected in 1979 down to about a fifth (21 per cent) in 1991. Yet if we look at trends in the vote among council tenants (see figure 6.3) it is apparent that housing tenure has been a good predictor of party support since the mid-sixties. The proportion of council tenants voting Labour has remained relatively high, as has the proportion of owner-occupiers voting Conservative, although there are some trendless fluctuations over time.

Dunleavy and Husbands also stressed that another important distinction, cutting across the manual and non-manual divide, could be drawn between those working in the public sector, whether teachers, lawyers or civil engineers, and those in comparable skilled-manual or administrative jobs employed in the private sector. Dunleavy and Husbands argued that the growth of the state produced an expansion in public-sector workers,

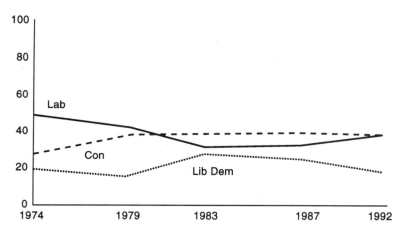

Figure 6.4   Vote by public sector, 1974–92
Source: British Election Studies, 1974–92.

especially those employed in health care and local government. In turn this produced a new fault line around which people could define the interests of their social location.[27] Unfortunately we do not have a breakdown of vote by employment sector for the whole of the BES time-series but nevertheless the trends from October 1974 onwards (see figure 6.4) show that working for the public sector did not prove a particularly strong predictor of party support, indeed in the period 1983–7 more public sector workers voted Conservative than Labour.

The restructuring of social identities

Restructuring approaches suggest that new social identities may have gradually replaced older ones based on economic inequalities. According to Butler and Stokes, post-war Britain was characterized by stable social groups living within tight communities which reinforced class identities.[28] The British electorate formed life-long party loyalties due to the transmission of party identification from parents to children, and from a stable class environment. At the end of the twentieth century, restructuring arguments suggest that Britain has become a multicultural, post-industrial

European society, characterized by more fluid and constructed social identities based on the multiple and overlapping cleavages of generation, ethnicity, gender and nationality. As these alternative identities have become more important the imprint of traditional occupational class divisions may have faded.

During the post-war era socialization processes within the family have become more complex as the traditional two-parent, two-children family has turned into disparate sorts of families, perhaps with responsibility for elderly parents or unemployed sons, perhaps lone-parent. Patterns of marriage and divorce, combined with greater longevity, mean that in 1961 one-eighth of all households in Britain were one-person, compared with over one-quarter in 1995. Increased spatial mobility produced the population drift from north to south, and the middle-class migration from inner cities to suburbs, and then to gentrified country villages. This pattern has broken up traditional communities, where people lived and worked in the same place, perhaps for their lifetimes. The demands of new technology and the expansion of higher education have created an expanded pool of highly-specialized professionals, but also a prospectless underclass who fall through the qualification safety-net. Since the 1960s Britain has experienced a significant expansion in higher education, with the growth of the 'plate glass' universities and the old polytechnic/new university sector.[29] Despite this growth, the census reports that in 1991 only 7.1 per cent of the adult population in Britain held a degree (or higher degree) as their highest qualification.[30] Restructuring theories suggest that these demographic trends may have produced more cross–cutting social cleavages, which fragment occupational class identities, and heighten the salience of the new politics of identities based on nationality, gender, generation and ethnicity. What is the evidence for this thesis?

Region

Regional divisions were once thought likely to fade over time, given the growth of the modern nation state. Since the mid-fifties one of the most striking trends has been the growth of the 'north–south' divide in British politics. The causes and consequences of geographical variations in voting behaviour have generated an extensive literature.[31] The United Kingdom has become increasingly polarized regionally, making it more difficult for governments to claim a national mandate. As shown in table 6.1, in the mid-fifties the Conservatives were strongest in the suburban and affluent south-east, in outer London, East Anglia and the south-west, but they also won a majority of votes across vast swathes of the north-west of England and Scotland. The 1955 general election saw a fairly uniform swing (of 1.8 per cent) to the Conservatives throughout the country: over three-quarters of all seats had a swing within 2.5 per cent of the national average. In contrast by 1992 the Conservatives had experienced a long-term haemorrhage of votes in Scotland, the north and north-west of England. A comparison of the bastions of strongest Conservative support in 1951 and 1992, shown in figure 6.5, reveals the extent to which they have retreated into the south. During the last four decades the Scottish Conservative vote halved, reducing the number of Conservative MPs from thirty-six to eleven.[32] At the same time over successive elections Labour has gradually been piling up more substantial two-party majorities in the industrial inner-city seats in its heartland regions of Scotland and the north, while experiencing a long-term erosion of support in the south-west, the south-east, East Anglia and greater London. The two-party swing in the 1992 election was far from uniform: variations between one constituency and another produced a standard deviation in the swing of 4.1 per cent.[33]

Table 6.1   Regional distribution of the GB vote, 1955–92

	1955 Con	1992 Con	Change	1955 Lab	1992 Lab	Change	1955 Lib	1992 LibDem	Change
South-west	52	47	−5	39	20	−19	9	31	22
South-east	58	54	−4	39	21	−18	2	23	21
East Anglia	52	51	−1	47	29	−18	1	19	18
Greater London	54	44	−10	51	38	−13	2	15	13
West Midlands	50	44	−7	48	40	−8	2	15	13
East Midlands	47	46	−1	51	38	−13	1	15	14
Wales	31	28	−3	60	49	−11	4	13	9
Yorkshire and Humberside	45	36	−9	53	46	−6	2	16	14
North	43	33	−10	56	51	−5	4	16	12
North-west	53	37	−16	46	46	1	1	16	15
Scotland	51	24	−27	46	40	−6	1	13	12
Britain	51	41	−10	48	37	−11	2	18	15

Table 6.2 Regional distribution of seats

	1955 Con	1992 Con	Chg	1955 Lab	1992 Lab	Chg	1955 Lib	1992 Lib Dem	Chg
London	15	48	33	27	35	8	0	1	1
Rest of South	163	161	-2	42	10	-32	0	6	6
Midlands	39	57	18	57	43	-14	0	0	0
Wales	6	6	0	27	27	0	3	1	-2
North	75	53	-22	88	107	19	2	3	1
Scotland	36	11	-25	34	49	15	1	9	8
Great Britain	344	336	-8	277	271	-6	6	18	12

There is little disagreement about the nature of the north–south cleavage, although there is considerable dispute about the causes. Among restructuring theorists, one school of thought is that class dealignment opened the way for regional diversity.[34] Bogdanor and Field have argued that the traditional core–periphery cleavage, which existed in Britain at the turn of the century, has reopened due to the decline of class divisions.[35] Others commonly attribute these changes to variations in economic prosperity between the regions.[36] During the seventies and eighties the areas most distant from London were characterized by economic recession and deprivation, while southern areas enjoyed unprecedented economic growth. As a result McAllister and Studlar argue that the social structure of different regions account for much of what is interpreted as regional polarization.[37] But the evidence suggests that the social characteristics of Scotland and the north, that is the greater proportion of manual workers and council tenants in these areas, are insufficient by themselves to explain the north–south divergence.[38] Lastly cultural explanations focus on regional differences in attitudes and values, including subjective evaluations of the state of the economy, and ideological differences in beliefs about the market. Curtice concluded that in both regards there are important regional differences in social attitudes in Britain, which continued even after controlling for differences in social class, housing and unemployment.[39] Moreover in Scotland in particular there are complex issues of identity and nationality which influence voting behaviour.[40] Far from fading, distinct regional and national cultures may therefore have strengthened over time.

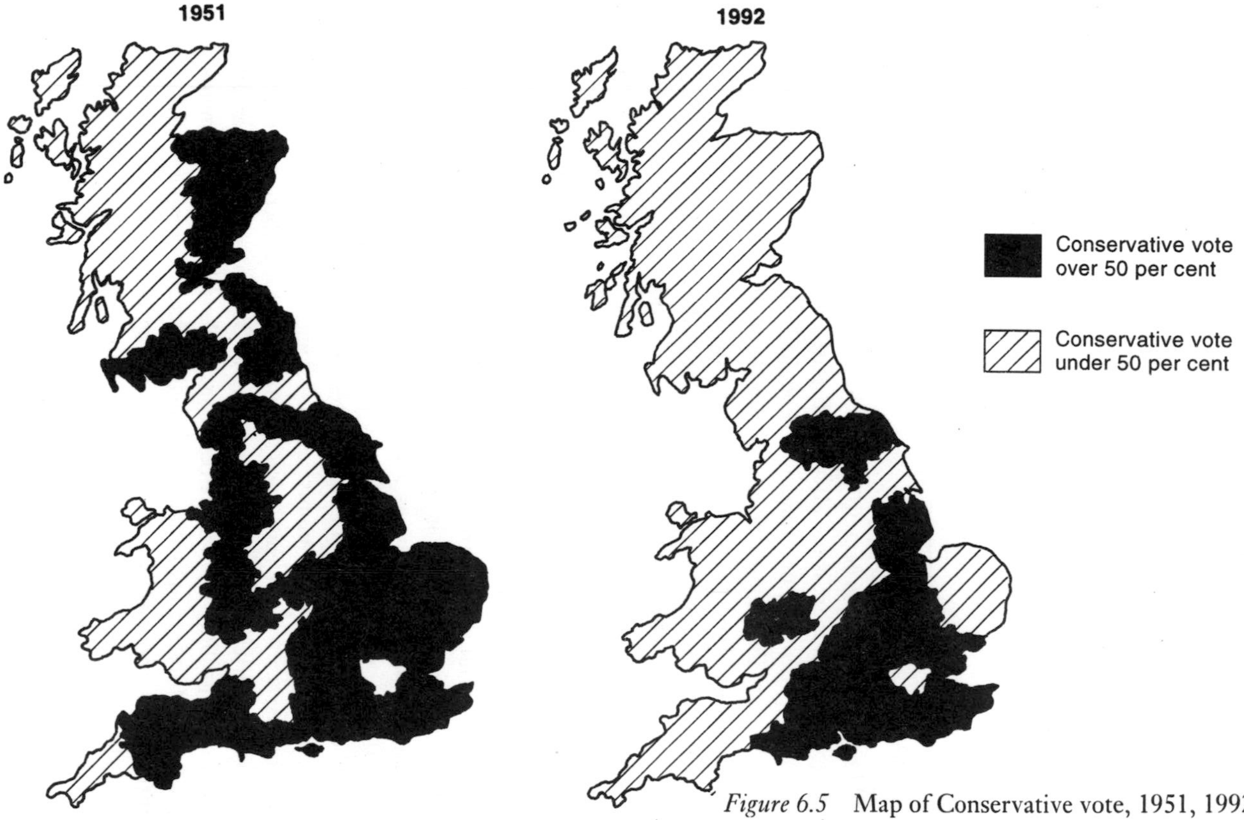

1992

1951

Conservative vote
over 50 per cent

Conservative vote
under 50 per cent

Figure 6.5 Map of Conservative vote, 1951, 1992

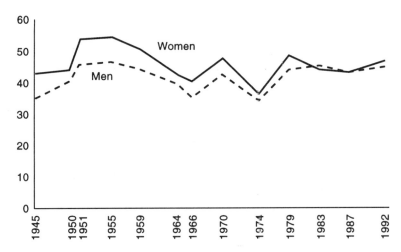

Figure 6.6   Conservative vote by gender, 1945–92
Source: Gallup 1945–59; *British Election Studies, 1964–92.*

Gender

In recent years more attention has also been paid to issues of gender politics, as the rise of the second-wave women's movement has brought new demands into the political system.[41] In 1918, when the female franchise was first granted, it was widely expected that women would favour the Conservatives, given the party's traditional emphasis on Church and family, while more men were expected to support Labour due to the party's links with trade unions in traditional heavy industries like mining, steel manufacturing and the shipyards.

The evidence in Gallup polls from 1945 to 1959 confirms the conventional wisdom.[42] If we compare women and men voters in the Gallup series we find the Conservatives consistently did better among women while Labour proved stronger among men (see figure 6.6). Indeed if Britain had continued with an all-male franchise, all other things being equal, there would have been an unbroken period of Labour government from 1945 to 1979. The Conservative lead among women was significant throughout the fifties, when the gender gap ranged from 11 to 17 points. In 1964 Wilson entered Number 10 in part due to a stronger pro-Labour swing among women than men. In 1970 men favoured Labour while women gave a greater lead to the Conservatives, producing a gender gap of 11 points and victory for Heath. As a result the political science literature in the sixties focused on explaining why women were more conservative, noting that the pattern in Britain was also evident in early voting studies in the United States, Italy, France and West Germany.[43] Indeed this became the accepted view in political science, as Randall notes:

> Up to the 1970s, women were apparently more inclined than men to vote for conservative parties in every country for which information is available including not only Greece, Belgium, Switzerland and the Netherlands but also Sweden and Finland.[44]

During the eighties the Conservative edge among women became statistically insignificant, but the 1992 general election saw the return of a small but significant gender gap (in the region of 4–8 points), confirmed in the final campaign polls by all the major companies. In the 1992 BES the Conservative lead over Labour was 8.6 per cent among all men, but 14.4 per cent among all women, producing a gender gap of 6 points.

One of the most striking aspects of this phenomenon is the fact that the gender gap *reverses* by generation. In the 1992 general election, among the younger group (those aged under thirty) women gave a lead to Labour, while men shifted sharply towards the Conservatives, producing a –14 point gender gap. Among older voters, the pattern reverses, with women more Conservative than men, creating a substantial gender gap of 18 points. Moreover, this is not a new development. This reflects patterns from 1964 where younger women have proved the least Conservative in successive elections, except for the period from 1970 to October 1974.[45] Older women have usually been the most Conservative, except for the 1987 election. The consistency of this trend indicates that there is a well-established 'gender-generation' gap.

This pattern has had a significant impact on party fortunes. The overall gender gap among all women has been small in percentage terms, compared with class or housing cleavages, but it has been statistically significant, it has been replicated in all the final polls, and it has been sizable in delivering ballot box votes since women are the majority of the population, with slightly higher rates of voter participation. There were 3.6 million older women voters in the 1992 election, compared with 2.6 million men in the equivalent age group (over 65). The Conservatives received 14 million votes in the 1992 general election. Of these 1.9 million were from older women. Given the narrowness of the government's parliamentary majority, it could be claimed that Mr Major was returned to Number 10 in part due to the older 'woman's vote'.

Generation

Moreover, generational differences may have become more important in recent decades. The theory of post-materialism, developed most extensively by Ronald Inglehart, suggests that as the class cleavage has faded in European politics so a new political division has developed between younger, well-educated voters and the older generation. This cleavage has centred around value priorities, in particular a shift away from 'materialist' concerns focused upon economic and physical security, towards a greater emphasis on post-materialist values concerning the quality of life, freedom, self-expression and protection of the environment.[46] The growth of post-materialism, Inglehart claims, has far-reaching implications since it has created the underlying conditions favourable to the development of

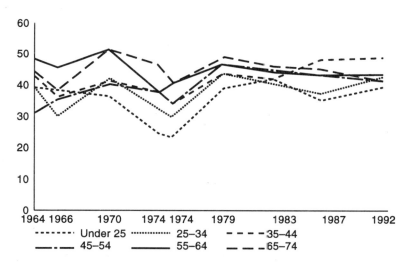

Figure 6.7   Conservative vote by age group, 1964–92
Source: British Election Studies, 1964–92.

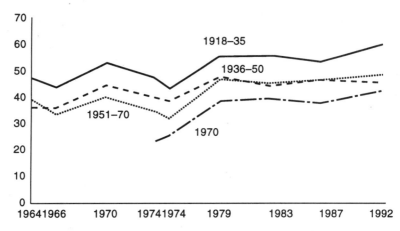

Figure 6.8   Conservative vote by generation, 1964–92
Source: British Election Studies, 1964–92.

new social movements, such as organized feminism and the environmental movement, as well as bolstering support for Green parties in many countries, and indeed contributing towards the global expansion of democracy. Post-materialist values have become more popular in the post-war era, Inglehart suggests, because the younger generation has grown up during a period of widespread affluence, without major economic insecurities, under the welfare state. Inglehart allows that long-term trends can be affected by short-term fluctuations, particularly those produced by changing economic conditions.[47] Nevertheless, the theory predicts that we can expect a steady rise in post-materialist values in post-industrial societies through the process of generational replacement.

If we look at the trends in party support by age group in Britain (see figure 6.7) it is apparent that since the mid-sixties younger voters have tended to be among the least Conservative, while older voters have fairly consistently proved the most Conservative. However far from dividing over time, if anything the generational differences in party support, which were marked in the early seventies, have slightly closed in recent elections.

One explanation for generational differences in party choice is the 'life-cycle' effect, namely that people tend to be more radical when young, but they become more cautious and conservative as they grow older and acquire more responsibilities like a career, family and mortgage, and hence a greater stake in society. In contrast, 'cohort' explanations suggest that it is less a person's age which is important than the period when they first entered political life. Different cohorts may be influenced by decisive political events – such as the Great Depression in thirties, the establishment of the welfare state after the end of the Second World War, or the sixties' sexual revolution – which may leave their imprint on a generation. To examine cohort explanations we can analyse groups of voters classified according to the period when they first cast their vote. As shown in figure 6.8, the results show that those who first voted in the inter-war years, before the Labour party achieved a sustained period in government, have remained the strongest Conservative supporters, with the majority supporting the Thatcher and Major governments. In contrast the youngest generation, who first entered the ballot box after 1970, prove the least supportive of the Conservative party. The cohort explanation may have significant implications for long-term trends in party support, which tend to be favourable for Labour, since generational replacement can be expected gradually to transform the electorate over many decades.

Race and ethnicity

In Britain patterns of immigration have gradually left their imprint resulting in a more multicultural society, with diversity of ethnicity, language and religion.[48] Despite the existence of black residents as far back as the eighteenth century, post-war Britain remained an overwhelmingly white society. In 1961 fewer than 300,000 citizens from the New Commonwealth settled in Britain. In the 1951 and 1961 census, ethnic minorities constituted less than one per cent of the population of Great Britain. By the 1991 census, ethnic minorities – with diverse origins from countries in the Caribbean and south-east Asia – constituted in total 3 million people or 5.5 per cent of the population.[49] Due to geographical concentration, ethnic minority groups have transformed cities like Bradford, Leicester, Birmingham, and London boroughs like Brent, Hackney and Newham. It would be mistaken to assume that the black population reflects one homogeneous group: there are significant divisions in terms of language, origins, culture and religion between blacks and Asians, and indeed within

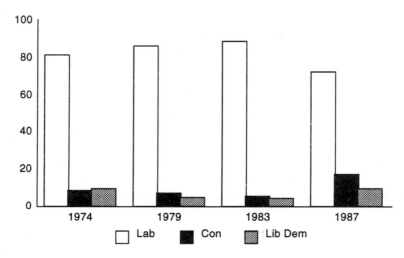

Figure 6.9   Ethnic minority voters, 1974–87
Source: Saggar 1992.

the Asian population. These divisions mean that we cannot assume that ethnic minorities participate in politics as a bloc, or share a common sense of political identity. The largest single grouping is South Asian, including Indian, Pakistani and Bangladeshi, numbering 1.5 million. The distribution of the ethnic minority population also shows wide regional variations, with less than one per cent in the North, Scotland and Wales compared with 15 per cent in Greater London. Ethnic minorities are most heavily concentrated in constituencies such as Brent South (51 per cent), Birmingham Ladywood (46 per cent), Birmingham Sparkbrook and Small Heath (44 per cent), East Ham (43 per cent), and Ealing Southall (42 per cent). The expansion of the black electorate is shown by the fact that in 1971 there were 18 constituencies where the black population (defined as those born, or with one parent born, in the New Commonwealth or Pakistan) made up 15 per cent or more of the population. By 1991 (defined in the census by ethnic origin) there were 56 such seats.

The BES is limited when examining the pattern of voting choice for ethnic groups, because of the problems of sample size. Evidence is available, however, in separate surveys from 1974 to 1987 based on quota sampling in areas of ethnic minority concentration (see figure 6.9). These show a broadly consistent pattern: eight out of ten ethnic minority voters have usually supported the Labour party, while the remainder have divided evenly between the Conservatives and Liberal Democrats. The only minor change over time in these results has been a modest shift among Asian electors away from the Labour party.[50] Nevertheless quota surveys based on areas of high ethnic minority concentration may systematically exaggerate Labour support. The 1979 pooled Gallup pre-election surveys based on nation-wide samples found two-thirds of ethnic minority voters (66 per cent) intended to support Labour, while just over a quarter (28 per cent) were Conservative, and only 6 per cent were Liberals.[51] A similar pattern was evident in the 1992 BES, where 62 per cent of non-white voters supported Labour, compared with 35 per cent Conservatives and 4 per cent Liberals. The results suggest that the black electorate continues to remain a bulwark of Labour support, but we need more detailed surveys based on probability samples before we can determine the exact strength of the relationship.

Conclusions

To analyse the relative importance of structural factors we can compare the relationship between constituency characteristics from English and Welsh census data in 1966, 1981 and 1991 and party support in the 1966, 1979 and 1992 general elections.[52] The 1992 analysis uses the 'notional' election results based on the new constituency boundaries adopted in 1995. The results in table 6.3 demonstrate that at the aggregate level constituency demographics continue to provide a remarkably consistent predictor of which major party wins and loses. Conservative support continues to be highest in affluent suburbs with a high concentration of professional and managerial workers – like Kensington and Chelsea, Bristol West and Wokingham – and this relationship has not weakened over time. In contrast there are impregnable Labour fortresses among the constituencies with a high proportion of semi-skilled and unskilled workers – such as Bootle, Glasgow Shettleson and Stoke-on-Trent – and Conservative support in these seats has not strengthened but actually declined since the mid-sixties. There is some evidence of class de-alignment at this level among the skilled non-manual group, but overall, as Miller suggested in an earlier analysis,[53] the pattern does not suggest a

Table 6.3 Constituency characteristics and party support, England and Wales

	Con Vote			Lib Dem Vote			Lab Vote		
	1966	*1979*	*1992*	*1966*	*1979*	*1992*	*1966*	*1979*	*1992*
SEG I/II	.70	.80	.65	.56	.46	.42	−.82	−.81	−.68
SEG III N	.49	.63	.17	.23	.21	.00	−.45	−.57	−.11
SEG III M	−.51	−.57	−.44	−.38	−.29	−.33	.57	.58	.50
SEG IV	−.50	−.70	−.64	−.28	−.39	−.32	.49	.72	.63
SEG V	−.53	−.71	−.73	−.40	−.40	−.28	.60	.71	.65
Owner-occupier	.42	.60	.59	.34	.33	.26	−.51	−.60	−.57
Council house	−.44	−.69	−.68	−.38	−.41	−.36	.52	.71	.69
Retired	.27	.22	.13	.36	.29	.35	−.45	−.33	−.31
Children	−.22	−.41	−.38	−.39	−.44	−.35	.41	.53	.47
Hsehold no car	−.53	−.69	−.75	−.46	−.45	−.41	.65	.73	.76
Hsehold density	−.43	−.55	−.37	−.33	−.43	−.29	.52	.61	.41
Unemployed	−.45	−.69	−.74	−.20	−.42	−.39	.38	.71	.72
All non-white	−.01	−.21	−.21	−.08	−.28	−.27	.08	.28	.30
Black			−.20			−.20			.26
Asian			−.16			−.25			.25
Other non-white			−.05			−.18			.14

Notes: Correlations between constituency characteristics in census and share of the vote. All are statistically significant at the 0.1 level.
In 1966 and 1981 the ethnic minority population was measured by the percentage of population in households with head born in New Commonwealth or Pakistan.
In 1991 the census included the ethnic identity of residents.
Household density is more than one person per room.

Sources: 1966 Census: British Parliamentary Constituencies, 1955–74 (Crewe)
1981 Census: British Parliamentary Constituencies, 1979–83 (Crewe and Fox)
1992 Vote: Media Guide to the New Parliamentary Constituencies (Rallings and Thrasher)
1991 Census Data for the New Parliamentary Constituencies in England and Wales, House of Commons Research Paper 95/94-II.

secular trend at local level. Instead this suggests there may well be a 'neighbourhood effect', where people vote like the people around them.

We can compare the analysis of class with other indicators of social inequality in the census. Here the evidence confirms that housing tenure is strongly associated with party support, and indeed this relationship has strengthened over time, supporting the restructuring thesis. The age profile of the population also proves a powerful and consistent predictor

Table 6.4   Analysis of structural factors on Conservative vote

	1964	1966	1970	1974F	1974O	1979	1983	1987	1992
Class	.21**	.25**	.17**	.12**	.11**	.10**	.13**	.12**	.10**
Tenure	.19**		.13**	.20**	.19**	.20**	.17**	.18**	.21**
Union	.10**		.11**	.14**	.16**	.16**	.11**	.11**	.11**
Religion	.14**	.10**	.13**		.12**	.11**	.07**	.11**	.12**
Age	.10**	.11**	.14**	.05	.03	.01	.07**	.08**	.07**
Region	.03	.04	.03	.01	.02	.01	.09**	.06**	.14**
Gender	.03	.03	.01	.05*	.03	.01	.04*	.04**	.01
Adj R²	.14	.08	.10	.09	.10	.1)	.09	.10	.14

Notes: ** = sig p.01 * = sig p.05
The figures represent standardized beta coefficients with Conservative vote as the dependent variable. The data was coded as follows:

Class	OPCS R's Social Class I,II, IIINM (1)/ Else (0)
Tenure	Owner Occupier (1)/ Other (0)
Religion	R's Religion C of E or C of S (1)/ Else (0)
Age	In years
Union	R's Trade Union Member (1)/ Else (0)
Gender	Male (1)/ Female(0)
Region	Scotland, North, North-West, Yorkshire and Humberside (1)/ Else (0)

Source: *British Election Studies, 1904–92.*

of votes: Conservative support is particularly strong in seats with many elderly retirees, particularly south coast towns such as West Worthing, Bexhill and Battle, and Bournemouth West. Conversely Labour tends to be stronger where many households have large families, and in poorer, inner-city seats, where few can afford private transportation, with a high housing density, and many on the dole. More remarkably, far from weakening over time, if anything these correlations at local level have become stronger. Lastly, seats with a high proportion of ethnic minorities have also become more solidly Labour over time. The 1991 census reveals that such support is particularly strong among the black and Asian populations, while the association is less clear-cut among other groups of non-whites.

Yet before we can draw any conclusions here, because of the dangers of the ecological fallacy, any associations at the constituency level need to be confirmed using survey data of individuals. So far we have looked at the trends in each of the major structural variables which have been thought to determine voting behaviour in Britain. In order to examine changes in the multivariate relationship between these factors we can use OLS regression analysis, with the Conservative/non-Conservative vote as the dependent variable. The results in table 6.4 demonstrate that indicators of socio-economic inequalities, including occupational class, housing tenure and union membership, have consistently proved significant predictors of Conservative support. The period-specific decline in class voting from 1966 to February 1974, followed by a slight recovery in 1983, discussed earlier, is further confirmed by this analysis.

Of the other predictors, religion remains consistently significant across the last thirty years. Despite secularization, the cleavage in nineteenth-century party politics, between the Church of England and the disestablishment churches, continues to show its imprint in twentieth-century voting behaviour. As noted earlier, age proved more important in the sixties than in the seventies, before recovering slightly in the eighties. The regional 'north–south' divide, which some observers date from the mid-fifties, only emerges as statistically significant in this measure since 1983. Overall gender proves insignificant except for a few elections, in part because of the curvilinear relationship between age and gender noted earlier. Lastly we can conclude that the proportion of variance explained by structural factors at individual level (the R^2 in table 6.4) remains relatively constant during the last three decades, lending weight to the restructuring perspective. Class voting declined during the early seventies, but there is no evidence from this analysis of any decline in the overall influence of structural factors on individual voting choice.

Notes

1   Alain Touraine, 1971. *The Post-Industrial Society*. New York: Random House; Daniel Bell, 1973. *The Coming of Post-Industrial Society*. New York: Basic Books.

2   Seymour Lipset and Stein Rokkan, 1967. *Party Systems and Voter Alignments*. New York: Free Press, pp. 1–64

3   For a discussion of some of these issues see 'Party Politics in Eastern Europe', in a special issue of *Party Politics* 1(4), October 1995; see also Herbert Kitschelt, 1992. 'The Formation of Party Systems in East Central Europe', *Politics and Society* 20: 7-50; Geoffrey Evans and Stephen Whitefield, 1993. 'Identifying the Bases of Party Competition in Eastern Europe', *British Journal of Political Science* 23(4): 521–48.

4   For a discussion see Jerome M. Chubb, William H. Flanigan and Nancy H. Zingale, 1990. *Partisan Realignment: Voters, Parties and Government in American History*. Boulder, CO: Westview Press.

5   Seymour Martin Lipset, 1981. *Political Man: The Social Bases of Politics*. Baltimore, MD: Johns Hopkins University Press

6   Richard Rose, 1974. *Electoral Behaviour*. New York: Free Press; Arend Lijphart, 1981. 'Political Parties', in David Butler, Austin Ranney and H. R. Penniman (eds), *Democracy at the Polls*. Washington, DC: AEI Press.

7   Kenneth D. Wald, 1983. *Crosses on the Ballot: Patterns of British Voter Alignments since 1885*. Princeton, NJ: Princeton University Press.

8   For details see Ben Pimlott and Chris Cook (eds), 1991. *Trade Unions in British Politics*, 2nd edn. London: Longman.

9   Keith Middlemass, 1994. 'The Party, Industry, and the City', in Anthony Seldon and Stuart Ball, *Conservative Century*. Oxford: Oxford University Press; Michael Pinto-Duschinsky, 1981. *British Political Finance, 1830–1980*. Washington, DC: AEI Press.

10 Market Research Society, 1963. *Social Class Definitions and Market Research*. London: Market Research Society; Robert Price and George Sayers Bain, 1988. 'The Labour Force', table 4.1b, in A. H. Halsey, *British Social Trends Since 1900*. London: Macmillan.

11 Robert Alford, 1964. *Party and Society*. London: Murray.

12 For details of similar declines in Scandinavia see Ole Borre, 1984. 'Critical Electoral Change in Scandinavia', in R. Dalton, S. Flanagan and P. Beck (eds), *Electoral Change in Advanced Industrial Democracies*. Princeton, NJ: Princeton University Press.

13 Russell Dalton, 1996. 'Political Cleavages, Issues and Electoral Change', in Lawrence LeDuc, Richard Niemi and Pippa Norris (eds), *Comparing Democracies: Elections and Voting in Global Perspective*. Thousand Oaks, CA: Sage; Mark Franklin, Tom McKie and Henry Valen et al., 1992. *Electoral Change*. Cambridge: Cambridge University Press; Ronald Inglehart, 1990. *Culture Shift*. Princeton, NJ: Princeton University Press; Paul Nieuwbeerta, 1995. *The Democratic Class Struggle in Twenty Countries, 1945–1990*. Amsterdam: Thesis Publishers.

14 Russell Dalton, 1996. 'Political Cleavages, Issues and Electoral Change', in Lawrence LeDuc, Richard Niemi and Pippa Norris (eds), *Comparing Democracies: Elections and Voting in Global Perspective*. Thousand Oaks, CA: Sage.

15 See, for example, Mark Franklin, Tom McKie and Henry Valen et al., 1992. *Electoral Change: Responses to Evolving Social and Attitudinal Structures in Western Countries*. Cambridge: Cambridge University Press.

16 For theoretical account of these developments see Alain Touraine, 1969. *La*

Société Post-industrielle. Paris. Denoel; Daniel Bell, 1973. *The Coming of Post-Industrial Society*. New York: Basic Books; Anthony Giddens, 1990. *The Consequences of Modernity*. Cambridge: Polity Press; Krishan Kumar, 1995. *From Post-Industrial to Post-Modern Society*. Oxford: Blackwell. For a summary of these changes in the UK see A. H. Halsey (ed.), 1988. *British Social Trends since 1900*. London: Macmillan; A. H. Halsey, 1995. *Change in British Society*. Oxford: Oxford University Press.

17   *Social Trends 1995*, table 4.9, p. 68. London: HMSO.

18   Robert Price and George Sayers Bain, 1980. 'The Labour Force', in A. H. Halsey (ed.), *British Social Trends since 1900*. London: Macmillan.

19   See Philip Abrams and Richard Brown (eds), 1984. *UK Society: Work, Urbanism and Inequality*. London: Weidenfeld and Nicholson; Derek Bird, Mark Beatson and Shaun Butcher, 'Membership of Trade Unions', *Employment Gazette*, May 1993: 189–96.

20   *Social Trends 1995*, figure 4.21. London: HMSO.

21   For a summary of the debate see Gordon Marshall, David Rose, Howard Newby and Carolyn Vogler, 1989. *Social Class in Modern Britain*. London: Unwin Hyman; Stephen Edgell and Vic Duke, 1991. *A Measure of Thatcherism*. London: HarperCollins Academic, pp. 21–69; Erik Wright et al., 1989. *The Debate on Classes*. London:Verso.

22   John Goldthorpe and Keith Hope, 1974. *The Social Grading of Occupations*. Oxford: Clarendon Press; John Goldthorpe, 1980. *Social Mobility and the Class Structure in Modern Britain*. Oxford: Clarendon Press.

23   Anthony Heath, Roger Jowell, John Curtice, 1991. *Understanding Political Change*. Oxford: Pergamon Press; Anthony Heath, Roger Jowell and John Curtice, 1985. *How Britain Votes*. Oxford: Pergamon Press; Anthony Heath, Roger Jowell and John Curtice, 1994. *Labour's Last Chance?* Aldershot: Dartmouth; John Curtice, 1996. 'Class dealignment Revisited'. Paper presented at the PSA Annual Conference, Glasgow.

24   This debate is summarized in David Denver and Gordon Hands (eds), 1992. *Issues and Controversies in British Voting Behaviour*. Herts.: Harvester Wheatsheaf. See also David L. Weakliem, 1995. 'Two Models of Class Voting', *British Journal of Political Science* 25(2): 254–70.

25   See James Alt, 1984. 'Dealignment and the Dynamics of Partisanship in Britain', in Russell Dalton, Scott Flanagan and Paul Beck (eds), *Electoral Change in Advanced Industrial Democracies*. Princeton, NJ: Princeton University Press.

26   Patrick Dunleavy and Christopher Husbands, 1985. *British Democracy at the Crossroads*. London: George Allen & Unwin.

27   Ibid.

28   David Butler and Donald Stokes, 1974. *Political Change in Britain*, 2nd edn. London: Macmillan.

29   A. H. Halsey, 1988. 'Higher Education', in A. H. Halsey (ed.), *British Social Trends since 1900*. London: Macmillan.

30   *1991 Census Report for Great Britain, Part 2.* 1993. London: OPCS HMSO. Table 84, p. 309.

31   See John Curtice and Michael Steed, 1982. Electoral Choice and the Production of Government: The Changing Operation of the Electoral System in the United Kingdom since 1955', *British Journal of Political Studies* 12: 249–98; R. Johnston, 1985. *The Geography of English Politics*. London: Croom Helm; R. J. Johnston, C. J. Pattie and J. G. Allsopp, 1988. *A Nation Dividing?* London: Longman; David Smith, 1989. *North and South*. Harmondsworth: Penguin; 'The Break-Up of England?', 1993. Special issue of *Political Geography* 12(2): 136–90.

32   For a discussion of the consequences see Andrew Marr, 1992. *The Battle for Scotland*. Harmondsworth: Penguin; Lindsay Paterson, 1994. *The Autonomy of Modern Scotland*. Edinburgh: Edinburgh University Press; David McCrone, 1992. *Understanding Scotland: The Sociology of a Stateless Nation*. London: Routledge.

33   John Curtice and Michael Steed, 1992. 'Appendix 2: The Results Analysed', in David Butler and Dennis Kavanagh, *The British General Election of 1992*. London: Macmillan.

34   Ivor Crewe, 1983. 'The Electorate: Partisan Dealignment Ten Years On', *West European Politics* 6: 183–215.

35   Vernon Bogdanor and William Field, 1993. 'Lessons of History: Core and Periphery in British Electoral Behaviour, 1910–1992', *Electoral Studies* 12(3): 203–24.

36   R. J. Johnston, Charles Pattie and John Allsopp, 1988. *A Nation Dividing?* London: Longman; Charles Pattie, Ed Fieldhouse, Ron Johnston and Andrew Russell, 1991. 'A Widening Regional Cleavage in British Voting Behaviour, 1964–87: Preliminary Explorations', in Ivor Crewe, Pippa Norris, David Denver and David Broughton (eds), *British Elections and Parties Yearbook, 1991*. Herts.: Harvester Wheatsheaf; Anthony Heath, Roger Jowell and John Curtice, 1985. *How Britain Votes*. Oxford: Pergamon Press.

37   Ian McAllister and Donley Studlar, 1992. 'Region and Voting in Britain, 1979–87: Territorial Polarization or Artifact?', *American Journal of Political Science* 36(1): 168–99.

38   William Miller, 1981. *The End of British Politics? Scots and English Political Behaviour in the Seventies*. Oxford: Clarendon Press; Anthony Heath, Roger Jowell and John Curtice, 1985. *How Britain Votes*. Oxford: Pergamon.

146   *The Social Identity of Voters*

39 John Curtice, 1992. 'The North-South Divide', in Roger Jowell, Lindsay Brook, Gillian Prior and Bridget Taylor, *British Social Attitudes: the Ninth Report*. Hants.: Dartmouth; John Curtice, 1988. 'One Nation', in Roger Jowell, Sharon Witherspoon and Lindsay Brook (eds), *British Social Attitudes: the Fifth Report*. Aldershot: Gower.
40 Anthony Heath and Bridget Taylor, 1996. 'British National Sentiment'. Paper presented at the PSA annual conference, Glasgow; Jack Brand, James Mitchell and Paula Surridge, 1994. 'Social Constituency and Ideological Profile: Scottish Nationalism in the 1990s', *Political Studies* 42(4): 616–29.
41 Joni Lovenduski and Vicky Randall, 1993. *Contemporary Feminist Politics*. Oxford: Oxford University Press.
42 Henry Durant, 1969. 'Voting Behaviour in Britain 1945-66', in Richard Rose (ed.), *Studies in British Politics* (2nd edn). London: Macmillan.
43 See Maurice Duverger, 1955. *The Political Role of Women*. Paris: UNESCO; David Butler and Donald Stokes, 1974. *Political Change in Britain*. London: Macmillan; Jean Blondel, 1974. *Voters, Parties and Leaders*. Harmondsworth: Penguin; Richard Rose, 1974. 'Britain: Simple abstractions and complex realities', in *Electoral Behaviour*. New York: Free Press; Peter Pulzer, 1967. *Political Representation and Elections in Britain*. London: Allen and Unwin, p. 522.
44 Vicky Randall, 1987. *Women and Politics*, 2nd edn. London: Macmillan, p. 73.
45 See Pippa Norris, 1996. 'Mobilizing the Woman's Vote: The Gender-Generation Gap', *Parliamentary Affairs* 49(2): 333–42. This pattern was first noticed by S. Baxter and M. Lansing, 1980. *Women and Politics: The Invisible Majority*. Ann Arbor, MI: University of Michigan Press, p. 157.
46 Ronald Inglehart, 1977. *The Silent Revolution*. Princeton, NJ: Prnceton University Press; Ronald Inglehart. 1990. *Culture Shift*. Princeton, NJ: Princeton University Press; Paul R. Abramson and Ronald Inglehart, 1995. *Value Change in Global Perspective*. Ann Arbor, MI: University of Michigan Press.
47 Paul R. Abramson and Ronald Inglehart, 1995. *Value Change in Global Perspective*. Ann Arbor: University of Michigan Press, p. 14; Ronald Inglehart. 1990. *Culture Shift in Advanced Industrial Society*. Princeton, NJ: Princeton University Press.
48 Terri Sewell, 1993. *Black Tribunes: Black Political Participation in Britain*. London: Lawrence and Wishart; Shamit Saggar, 1992. *Race and Politics in Britain*. Herts.: Harvester Wheatsheaf; Muhammad Anwar, 1986. *Race and Politics*. London: Tavistock; John Solomos, 1989. *Race and Racism in Contemporary Britain*. London: Macmillan; Zig Layton-Henry, 1984. *The Politics of Race in Britain*. London: George Allen & Unwin.
49 *1991 Census Report for Great Britain, Part I*. 1993. London: OPCS HMSO;

Andy Teague, 1993. 'Ethnic group: first results from the 1991 Census', *Population Trends* 72, Summer, pp. 12–17.

50 Shamit Saggar, 1992. *Race and Politics in Britain*. Herts.: Harvester Wheatsheaf. It should be noted, however, that these surveys varied by polling company, date of fieldwork and sampling methods, so the results are not strictly comparable. Where ethnic minorities are sub-divided the results show that Asian voters are less pro-Labour than Afro-Caribbean voters. See also Kaushika Amin and Robin Richardson, 1992. *Politics for All: Equality, Culture and the General Election 1992*. London: Runnymede Trust.

51 Zig Layton-Henry, 'Black electoral participation in Britain 1964–92: the myth of declining Labour party support'. Paper presented at the ECPR, University of Leiden, April 1993.

52 It should be noted that at the time of writing the 1991 Census data for the new Scottish constituencies had not been released.

53 William Miller, 1981. *The End of British Politics? Scots and English Political Behaviour in the Seventies*. Oxford: Clarendon Press.

Part III

Changes in the Party System

7 Party Competition and Ideology

The evidence we have considered so far suggests that during the late sixties and early seventies strong party loyalties and class voting weakened, accompanied by a growth in campaign waverers and late deciders. This opened the ground for the periodic and erratic waves in minor party support which we have observed in recent decades. Commentators have commonly stressed that these developments, particularly the structural erosion in Labour's social base, explains Conservative predominance in government since 1979. Nevertheless, based on the evidence in the previous two chapters, we can conclude that the overall pattern of trends during the last thirty years suggests less a long-term glacial shrinkage in Labour's support, based on changes in society and the economy, than a political shift in the nature of party competition.

Structural accounts for the decline of the Labour party have come under increasing challenge from theories which emphasize how electoral fortunes can change, sometimes radically and sharply, in response to strategic developments in party competition at the level of haute politique. The focus is 'top-down', stressing how party leadership can transform the nature of the options confronting voters. The rise and fall of the Social Democratic party in the 1980s, for example, can be attributed primarily to the deep schism within Labour's centre-left, the decisions of key leaders, sudden by-election victories, and coalitional politics within the SDP–Liberal Alliance, as much as to the process of partisan dealignment among the electorate.[1]

The primacy of party-led or strategic accounts of electoral change has been argued by a growing number of scholars, in Britain and elsewhere.[2] In a study of western Europe, Herbert Kitschelt has emphasized the importance of how social democratic parties seek to attract and maintain grassroots support, including how they shape their campaign, policy positions and images in attempting to attract voters.[3] In recent decades some parties of the left have retained popular support, while in other countries Christian Democrat and Conservative parties have experienced a resurgence. Overall there has been no steady and consistent decline in the left,[4] which throws doubt on the thesis that the shrinkage of the working class in post-industrial societies necessarily leads to the decline of social democracy.[5] Kitschelt suggests that if the British Labour party moves towards the 'catch-all' model, widening their appeal to a national constituency rather than their working-class base, this may encourage voters to switch more easily from closely-related parties. 'Catch-all' parties reduce their ideological baggage, and de-emphasize their class appeal in favour of recruiting voters amongst the whole electorate.[6]

In similar argument Peter Mair suggests that many of the most significant electoral shifts in European countries have been the product of party-led 'top-down' factors – such as innovations in governing coalitions, in the pattern of government formation and in conflict over issues – which have served to destabilize the electorate. More open patterns of party competition change the context of voter choice, with the potential thereby to increase electoral mobility.[7] In similar vein studies in Britain have stressed the importance of the nature of the constituency contest facing voters. Heath, Jowell and Curtice suggest that the pattern of electoral change in Britain from 1964–87 suggests alterations in the context of party and ideological competition, rather than changes in the social psychology of individual voters:

> Our period has seen the extension of the franchise, increased numbers of Liberal candidates, the formation (and more recently demise) of the SDP, changed tactical considerations, and changed ideological positions held by the Labour and Conservative parties. In all these political respects there are changed circumstances facing voters. [8]

The growth of the Liberals and minor parties, which have gradually built up a more effective grassroots organization and fielded more candidates, has provided voters with new choices in election campaigns. Rose and McAllister draw similar conclusions: 'Important changes in electoral competition in the past two decades have been party-led not voter-led."[9]

The most widely recognized formal theory of party competition is provided by Anthony Downs in *An Economic Theory of Democracy* (1957). Downs outlines a spatial model which assumes that parties are competing for votes with policy alternatives which array themselves along a left–right ideological spectrum. The model assumes that parties strategically shape their manifestos to position themselves as close as possible to the concentration of voters. Parties are assumed to be mobile so that they can place themselves at any point on the continuum, although Downs assumes that parties cannot 'leapfrog' each other. Electors are assumed to support parties which are closest to their policy preferences, based on a rational calculation about the alternatives available. And the party with the most votes enters government with a mandate to implement their proposals. The Downsian tradition has generated a range of studies by Ian Budge, David Robertson, and others, which attempt, in increasingly sophisticated ways, to test (and modify) different assumptions about parties and voters within this perspective.[10]

The Downsian model can be loosely applied to the strategic changes in party positions in British politics in the post-war years. Observers of party fortunes in recent decades have commonly argued that Labour party popularity sank to record lows after they abandoned their core supporters by shifting away from the centre-left, while in contrast under Thatcher the Conservatives tapped new sources of support by moving right.

During the seventies the Labour party shifted sharply towards the radical left in the policies it espoused. Studies by Pat Seyd, David Coates and Eric Shaw, among others, have documented how the post-war consensus on domestic and foreign affairs began to collapse after the end of the second Wilson administration, as the left moved into the ascendant within the party.[11] In 1973 Labour shifted towards a more socialist stance towards the economy, advocating radical measures to redistribute income and wealth to working people, including increased public ownership, direct government intervention in planning the economy, price and import controls, rent restraint, pensions increases, abolition of prescription charges, reform of the tax structures, industrial democracy, and free collective bargaining in the workplace. In foreign affairs the party also abandoned the post-war consensus, advocating sweeping cuts in defence and unilateral disarmament. By the early eighties Labour's leftward shift was considerable, culminating in the election of Michael Foot as leader in

1980, the subsequent split producing the break-away Social Democratic Party, and the 1983 election manifesto proposing public ownership, a wealth tax, industrial democracy, a non-nuclear defence policy, withdrawal from Europe, and the abolition of private education.

Based on these trends, commentators have argued that by shifting towards the left in the drive for ideological purity, as the activists took over the tiller, the party moved away from the position of the average Labour supporter. In this view, Labour abandoned its voters, as much as voters deserted the party. It was only under the successive leaderships of Neil Kinnock, John Smith and Tony Blair that Labour has gradually and painfully abandoned the socialist shibboleths of nationalization, unilateralism and trade union power, symbolized by the dropping of Clause IV, changed its image, modernized its organization, unified its leadership, and moved back to the centre ground of British politics.[12]

At the same time many observers noted that while the Labour party seemed intent on committing electoral suicide in a pure but lonely socialist wilderness, under Mrs Thatcher the Conservative party moved sharply towards the right. During the eighties commentators commonly pointed to the apparent popularity of Conservative policies on key issues such as privatization, trade union reform, and the sale of council houses, and suggested that on these issues Mrs Thatcher's instincts were in tune with, and served to reinforce, the individualistic zeitgeist of the eighties.

The conventional wisdom concerning the triumph of popular capitalism was that a sea-change in social values was particularly evident among the new property and share-owning skilled working class, along with the upwardly-mobile service workers in the private sector. As Peter Jenkins expressed the view which became common in the eighties: 'Mrs Thatcher has presided over a considerable, although far from complete, change in attitudes. Its assumptions are individualistic rather than collectivist, preferring private to state ownership, putting the rights of members before the interests of the trade union, and sound money above the priming of the economy.'[13] The more apocalyptic visions saw Mrs Thatcher's victory in 1979 as signifying the birth of a new epoch, and the death of the post-war consensus as a set of dominant ideas, public policies and political alliances.[14]

In the early eighties, under Mrs Thatcher, the Conservative party shifted decisively right. The core themes, reiterated in speech after speech, embodied a widespread nostalgic reaction to British decline during the mid-1970s. In this sense the central message of Thatcherism was less abstract theories of monetarism or individual freedom than the need to break with the failures – economic, social, foreign policy and moral – associated with social democracy in the late sixties and seventies. For Thatcher the causes of the decline could be clearly identified. In the economic sphere government was seen as over-mighty, bloated with bureaucracy, smothering independent initiative and freedom of choice through excessive taxation and undue interference. Therefore the balance of the state needed to be tilted away from welfarist, Keynesian, corporatist, demand-side intervention towards the private market-place. The primary objective on taking office was limiting government to produce a more competitive, entrepreneurial and growth-oriented economy. In terms of the policy agenda the free market was to be restored by giving high priority to the control of inflation, reductions in personal levels of income tax, the reform of industrial relations, privatization and deregulation, while simultaneously reducing the size of government and the costs of domestic programmes.

Underlying the economic message was a broader moral agenda, central to the populist appeal of the regime, although arguably less central to their policy priorities, about the need to restore traditional 'family' values at home and national security abroad.[15] This repeated the nostalgic message about the need to reverse the liberal social mores associated with the late sixties and seventies. These themes resonated throughout Thatcherism. The promise was to change the trends towards rising levels of crime, sexual permissiveness and abortion, by restoring traditional sources of moral authority. This was coupled with a vigorous assertion of British interests abroad, the need to rebuild strong defences, to revive patriotism, and to restore national confidence. Under John Major it can be argued that the Thatcherite agenda has become more muted in certain regards, such as the abandonment of the ill-fated poll tax, and the pace of policy implementation has slowed, in part because of deep internal splits between Euro-fanatics and Euro-sceptics, yet most of the core ideological components have continued to drive the party.[16] Indeed it can be argued that the real triumph of Thatcherism has been to act like an ideological neutron bomb, sucking the oxygen out of the air, and leaving a vacuum of alternative ideas in its wake. The way that the rhetoric of both major parties now reflects many of the Thatcherite ideas which would have been anathema to Labour a decade ago – the abandonment of collectivism and

Keynesian state management of the economy – is a sign of its ideological triumph.

In the light of these significant shifts in party competition on the left–right battleground, the question for this chapter is how to analyse systematically the electoral impact of these developments. The focus of the party competition approach is essentially 'top-down', about how parties can change the electoral choice available to voters, even without any significant prior electoral flux. It is difficult to analyse the short-term effects of changes in party strategy, ideology and specific 'shocks' to the system – such as the resignation of Mrs Thatcher, the breakaway of the SDP, or Labour's abandonment of Clause IV. The series of British Election studies covers over three decades in politics yet there are only limited questions which are consistent measures of issues and ideology across the whole series. Moreover as post-election surveys they lack sufficiently detailed intervals to determine the electoral flux, rather than inter-electoral flow, caused by particular developments. More direct evidence about the short-term impact on party popularity of shifts in strategy and issue positions can be derived from indicators such as monthly Gallup polls available since 1945, the yearly EuroBarometer surveys since 1970, the annual British Social Attitudes surveys since 1983,[17] and post-war by-election results.[18] A growing body of work has used econometric techniques to model the relationship between government popularity and economic performance.[19]

To examine party-led accounts of electoral change this chapter will use three main sources of data. First, to understand long-term changes in the ideological positions of British parties we will turn to data from the Manifesto Research Group which has systematically analysed the contents of post-war party programmes in Europe.[20] Second, to look at the ideology of the electorate we will compare trends in public support for a range of social and economic issues in the British Election Study. Lastly, to analyse the relative position of different parties in relation to the median voter we can compare the British Election Study with data from the British Representation Study (BRS). The BRS examined the attitudes and values of Members of Parliament and parliamentary candidates in the 1992 general election, using identical items at mass and elite levels.[21]

Left–Right Trends in Party Programmes

We can start by examining where parties place themselves on the ideological spectrum based on the content analysis of party manifestos since the war.[22] Manifestos represent authoritative statements of party policy which cover a wide range of themes. Moreover these programmes are representative statements for the whole party which, even if not read by many voters, are central components of the election campaign. The content analysis measured the proportion of space in each party manifesto (the number of 'arguments') devoted to a standard range of 56 different categories of issue areas, including statements about economic, social and foreign policy (see Appendix A, in this chapter). The amount of space devoted to each issue is taken as an indirect indication of the importance of the issue for the party's policy agenda: if Labour emphasizes the need for spending on health and pensions, while the Conservatives focus on the necessity of encouraging private enterprise and low taxation, this identifies their overall priorities. The contents were classified to include how far the manifesto emphasized the following themes, which can be judged to define the basic divisions in party politics in Britain:

Right	*Left*
Pro–market economy	Pro–mixed economy
Limited welfare state	Expanded welfare state
Strong and efficient government	Decentralization
Moral traditionalism	Cultural pluralism
Nationalism	Internationalism
Military strength	Peace and détente

These categories were then summed to produce an overall left–right measure calculated by deducting the right-wing from the left-wing scores.[23] Figure 7.1 shows the position of the main British parties on the main left–right ideological spectrum. If we look at the trends over time for the major parties it is apparent that the post-war consensus which developed in the early fifties reduced the distance between Labour and the Conservatives, with both shifting towards support of Keynesian economic management, the National Health System, and Beveridge's reformed welfare state. The early years of the 1951 Churchill government saw a

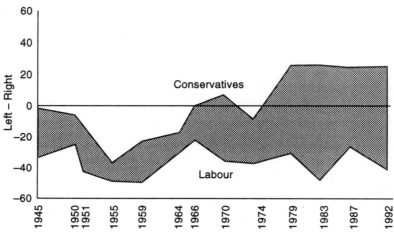

Figure 7.1   Party competition – Left–Right
Source: British Election Studies, 1964–92.

continuation of the broad policy framework adopted by Attlee, without massive denationalization of the public sector.[24] From the mid-fifties onwards both major parties shifted back towards the centre ground, but the distance between them remained fairly constant. Yet by the 1970 general election onwards we see the start of greater party polarization. With the end of the Butskellite consensus, dissatisfied by the achievements of the Wilson administration, Labour shifted leftwards. In opposition the Conservatives became more sympathetic to free-market solutions, and thereby moved decisively right. The first two years of the Heath government saw cuts in public spending, abolition of price and income controls, and more disengagement of the government from the economy, although this was swiftly reversed by the U-turns in 1972. The 1974 elections saw the Conservatives fight on more centrist ground again, before the massive shift right for the Conservatives in 1979 under the leadership of Mrs Thatcher. During the eighties the Conservatives remained on the right, while Labour zig-zagged, first sharply to the left following adoption of the Alternative Economic Strategy and unilateralism in 1983, then back towards the centre-left in 1987, then slightly left again (driven mainly by welfare pledges on health and education) in 1992. Party polarization throughout the eighties has been far more marked than during the consensual fifties. Most importantly, the

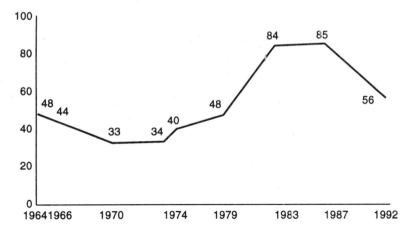

British Election Studies, 1964–92: Considering everything the Conservative and Labour party stand for, would you say there is . . . a great deal of difference between them, some, not much.

Figure 7.2　Perceived party difference

broad pattern of trends in party competition was reflected in public opinion. The proportion of the public who perceived 'a great deal of difference between the parties' rose in the mid-seventies, then jumped dramatically from 1979 to 1983 (see figure 7.2).

In order to examine what aspects of policy change this shift represents we can examine its components. The strongest party difference has revolved around management of the British economy, with conflict between the Keynes demand management approach adopted by both parties after the war and the more free-market philosophy associated with 'Selsdon Man' and Thatcherism. As shown in figure 7.3, during the early fifties both parties accepted the Butskellite consensus, but this started to break down in 1959 when the Conservatives moved to less interventionist policies. While Labour remained fairly centrist under Harold Wilson, the shift towards more public ownership, redistribution of wealth and socialist management of the economy pushed Labour to the left in the 1974 and 1983 manifestos. By 1987 and 1992, however, Labour had moved to the right on the economy, accepting the need for market-driven economic growth and a reduced role for nationalized industry. Nevertheless, in the

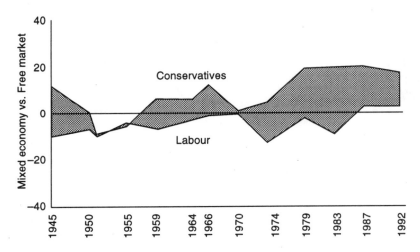

Figure 7.3   Party competition – management of the economy
Source: Party manifesto content analysis (Eco1–Eco2).

last decade, competition over the economy remains marked, with far greater polarization than in the fifties. On some other issues, like the priority given to internationalism (for example, support for the European Union), the major parties occasionally zig-zag past each other, leapfrogging across the left–right divide. But on the economy the position of the major parties is clearly established in a distinctive ideological space on the left and right. Moreover battles over the economy remain at the heart of party competition, based on the amount of attention devoted to this issue in manifestos.

The welfare state remains the other critical dividing line between the major parties (see figure 7.4). In the eighties Thatcherism seemed to drag both parties to the right on the economy. In contrast, although Conservative rhetoric on reducing the role of the welfare state was particularly strong in 1979, during the eighties they moved steadily left, as has the Labour party. This suggests that the Thatcherite revolution, if there was one, focused on the need for a more entrepreneurial and deregulated economy, but the revolution did not advance further by reducing the role of the state in the provision of basic welfare services. In their manifesto pledges both parties have remained committed to maintaining levels of spending on health and education.

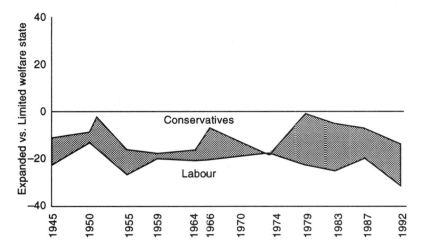

Figure 7.4 Party competition – welfare state, 1945–92
Source: Party manifesto content analysis (Soc3–Soc4).

Figure 7.5 shows that in the fifties the position of the major parties on the issues of moral traditionalism and cultural pluralism were largely indistinguishable, and these issues were rarely mentioned on the party platforms. Since the early seventies, with the rise of sexual, race and group identity politics, and issues like divorce, abortion and affirmative action, party polarization has also increased. Since 1970 the Conservatives have put more emphasis on the importance of traditional moral values, on issues like the family, religion and crime, while Labour presents a more favourable appeal towards minority groups and cultural pluralism. A similar pattern can be observed in figure 7.6 concerning the need for a strong central state, following the rise of nationalism in the late sixties. The Conservatives give a higher priority to a strong and efficient centralized state; in 1970 Labour showed more support for regional devolution.

Lastly, on the issues of foreign and defence policy, while there remains a party difference, particularly in 1983 with Labour's pledge for unilateral nuclear disarmament, party polarization according to manifesto pledges is usually relatively modest. We can conclude that the traditional left–right Labour and Conservative battle over the economy and the welfare state clearly outweighs major party competition over international affairs.

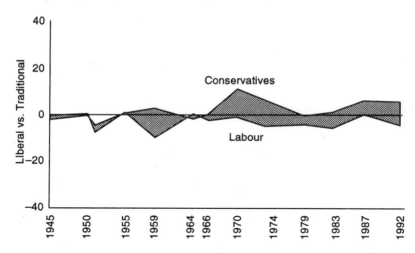

Figure 7.5   Party competition – moral traditionalism, 1945–92
Source: Party manifesto content analysis (Soc1–Soc5).

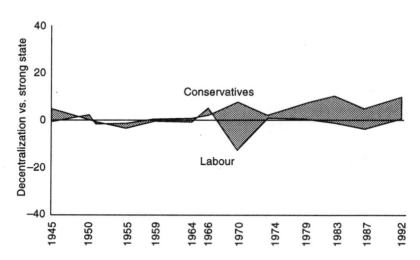

Figure 7.6   Party competition – strong central state, 1945–92
Source: Party manifesto content analysis (Pol6–Pol4).

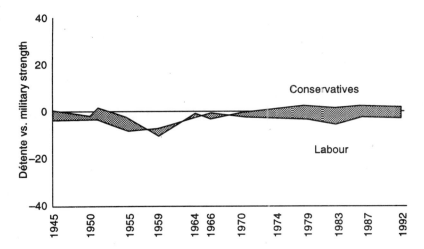

Figure 7.7 Party competition – defence policy, 1945–92
Source: Party manifesto content analysis (For1–For2).

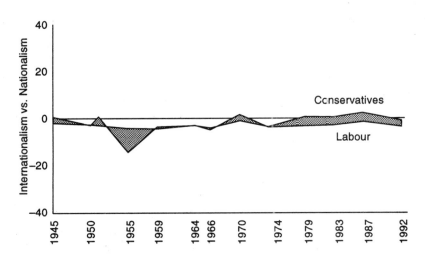

Figure 7.8 Party competition – foreign policy, 1945–92
Source: Party manifesto content analysis (For3–For4).

Trends in British Public Opinion

So far we have considered how parties have changed, but in the Downsian model we need to compare these shifts with the position of the median British voter. We need to consider the *direction* of change in public opinion from 1964 to 1992, where there is a consistent series of items in the British General Election Studies which focus on the issues central to party competition. Moreover, we need to examine the *balance* of opinion to see whether Conservative values of free enterprise and moral traditionalism, or Labour's values of a mixed economy and cultural pluralism, were more in tune with the majority of the electorate.

Many commentators believe that in the post-war decade the consensus about the managed economy and welfare state was one broadly shared among the elite and the public. In contrast in the mid-seventies many suggest that the energy crisis, stagnation, and lower economic growth led to a retreat from socialist 'tax and spend' panaceas. At the same time, it can be argued, widespread disillusionment with the effects of the welfare state led to a backlash against social democratic solutions, and the 'winter of discontent' led to calls to curb trade union power. Journalists commonly suggested that in the eighties the Conservatives benefited from these developments by campaigning on the need for lower government spending, privatization and deregulation, and reform of the trade unions. Yet more systematic studies of public opinion trends in the mid-eighties dispute these claims.[25] Does the available evidence, based on trends in public opinion in the British Election Study from 1964 to 1992, support these assumptions?

Privatization versus nationalization

The issue of nationalization versus privatization can be seen as one of the classic divisions in British party politics, although privatization policies have been implemented by Conservative and Socialist governments across western countries.[26] The effects of the British government's programme have been radical: between 1979 and 1989 the sale of shares in Jaguar, British Telecom, British Gas, British Airways and Rolls-Royce, along with the flotations of government holdings and company sales, led to the transfer of about 40 per cent of the nationalized sector.[27] The aim was to develop popular capitalism by expanding individual share-ownership. In this the government seems to have been remarkably successful: among the adult British population the proportion of al shareholders more than doubled from 4 million in 1983 to 10 million in 1993[28], although ownership is spread thinly.

Table 7.1 Attitudes towards nationalization vs. privatization (%)

Year	Privatize	No Change	Nationalize	PDI (a)
1964	20.7	50.7	28.5	–7.8
1966	22.4	48.6	28.9	–6.5
1974F	24.8	46.8	28.4	–3.6
1974O	21.9	45.9	32.2	–10.3
1979	40.0	43.2	16.9	23.1
1983	43.0	39.4	17.5	25.5
1987	31.9	51.0	17.1	14.8
1992	24.0	52.3	23.7	–0.3

Note: Q 1987: 'Are you generally in favour of . . . more rationalization of companies by government, more privatization of companies by governmen., or should things be left as they are now? (If more) A lot more . . . or a little more . . . ?'

The percentage Difference Index (PDI) equals those in favour of more privatization minus those in favour of more nationalization.

Source: British Election Studies, 1964–92.

Did privatization became popular due to widespread disillusionment with the old nationalized industries? The evidence from the series of British General Election Studies shows that from 1964 to October 1974 public opinion was fairly stable on this issue, with a rough balance between those favouring more nationalization and those supporting privatization (or denationalization). Trends show a dramatic shift in attitudes during the mid-seventies: under the 1974–9 Wilson–Callaghan administration the balance in public opinion tipped sharply towards the sale of public assets. The proportion of the electorate favouring nationalization almost halved, from 32 to 17 per cent (see table 7.1). This confirms that in the early eighties Conservative policies on privatization were in tune with the mood of the electorate. Nevertheless, by 1987 public opinion had started to swing away from further privatization, towards maintaining the status quo, a trend which accelerated by the next election. By 1992 one-quarter was in favour of more privatization, more than half supported no change, while the remaining quarter supported more nationalization. The overall balance of public opinion in 1992 had come full circle and it was remarkably similar to attitudes in the mid-sixties: change plus ça change.

Trade union reform

The conventional wisdom is that trade unions became increasingly unpopular during the mid-seventies, due to problems of increased militancy, industrial stoppages and high pay settlements, culminating in the 1978 'Winter of Discontent'. As a result many commentators feel that public opinion swung towards trade union reform to make them more accountable and to limit their powers. To achieve this Conservative governments introduced a series of measures: the 1980, 1982, 1988 and 1990 Employment Acts, the 1980 Employment Protection Act, the 1984 Trade Union Act, and the 1993 Trade Union Reform and Employment Rights Act. Together these initiatives transformed industrial relations, restricted unlawful picketing, removed union immunities from civil actions, limited union closed shops, and required a pre-strike ballot of the workforce in support of any industrial action, and created a more flexible labour market.[29]

Table 7.2   Attitudes towards trade union power

Year	Too powerful	Not too powerful	PDI (a)
1964	54.2	31.9	22.3
1966	63.8	25.2	38.6
1974(Feb.)	65.6	23.8	41.8
1974(Oct.)	77.5	18.4	59.1
1979	77.5	17.2	60.3
1983	70.1	24.9	45.2
1987	45.4	11.8	33.6
1992	30.3	59.2	28.9

Note: Q 1987–92 'Do you think that trade unions in this country have too much power or too little power?'
(a) Percentage Difference Index (PDI) equals 'too much' minus 'too little'.

Source: British Election Studies, 1964–92.

The evidence about public opinion in the British Election Studies (BES) suggests that in the early sixties trade unions were unpopular: the majority felt unions were too powerful. This proportion increased substantially during the next decade: from just over half in 1964, to two-thirds in 1966, and three-quarters in 1974 (Oct.) and 1979. Nevertheless, support for this position peaked in the 1979 survey, and declined slowly during the first Conservative administration. Based on a slightly differently worded item by 1987 less than half of the electorate thought that the unions were too powerful, and the proportion dropped to less than a third by 1992. There are problems in analysing trends here due to differences in measurement,[30] but this change in public opinion is confirmed in questions about attitudes towards trade union reform. In 1979, after the Winter of Discontent, two-thirds of the electorate thought there should be stricter laws to regulate the activities of trade unions (see table 7.3). Support for this proposition fell in subsequent surveys until by 1992 opinion was more evenly divided: a third favoured further reform while slightly more than a third were against more legislation. Again it seems that on trade unions Mrs Thatcher benefited by the tide of public opinion in the late 1970s which swept her into office. But, perhaps reflecting the significant decline in the power of organized labour during the last decade, the electorate moved away from the Conservatives on this issue.

Table 7.3 Attitudes towards trade union reform

Year	Stricter Laws	Does Not Matter	Not Stricter Laws	PDI
1979	68.9	8.8	16.1	52.8
1983	56.4	5.7	30.6	25.8
1987	50.3	11.4	33.0	17.3
1992	35.4	20.0	37.6	−2.2

Note: Q 'Do you think the government should or should not do the following, or doesn't it matter either way? ... Introduce stricter laws to regulate the activities of trade unions?'

Source: *British Election Studies, 1979–92.*

There are serious problems in measuring consistent trends in public opinion on the welfare state, due to discontinuity in the BES series, nevertheless, the available evidence suggests a similar pattern to that already observed concerning privatization and trade union reform. Again from 1974 to 1979 there was a right-wing shift: under Callaghan public support for spending on welfare benefits declined sharply. By the time Mrs

Thatcher came to power half thought that benefits had gone too far, compared with only 17 per cent who thought they needed to be extended further. In contrast, by 1992 the balance of opinion had reversed, with almost half favouring greater spending compared with 17 per cent against (see table 7.4). The public continued to display overwhelming support for greater spending on the central pillars of the welfare state: the NHS, education and poverty relief.

Table 7.4   Attitudes towards welfare benefits

	Gone too Far	About right	Not far enough	PDI
1974 (Oct.)	34.0	43.1	23.0	11.0
1979	50.1	32.9	17.0	33.1
1983	19.5	51.1	29.4	−9.9
1987	24.8	40.3	34.9	−10.1
1992	16.6	37.5	45.9	−29.3

Note: The Percentage Difference Index (PDI) represents the proportion 'Too Far' minus the proportion 'Not far enough'.
Source: *British Election Studies, 1974–92*.

Moral traditionalism

Lastly, on the social agenda there was a range of issues underlying the populist appeal of Conservatism, designed to restore respect for traditional authority and 'family values'. The conventional wisdom holds that during the late seventies the public swung towards the right on these issues, in reaction against increased levels of sexual permissiveness, lawlessness, racial conflict, illegitimacy and divorce. Yet the available BES evidence on attitudes towards abortion, and equal opportunities for women and ethnic minorities, suggests that the period from 1974 to 1992 was generally one of increasing liberalism, particularly on the issue of sexual equality (see table 7.5). While the Conservatives moved towards greater moral traditionalism from the early seventies onwards, it appears that public opinion was shifting in the opposite direction.

Table 7.5 Attitudes towards moral traditionalism

Year	Too far	About right	Not far enough	PDI
THE AVAILABILITY OF ABORTION				
1974 (Oct.)	42.9	42.6	14.6	–28.3
1979	44.4	44.0	11.6	–32.8
1983	31.7	55.4	12.9	–18.8
1987	32.9	56.8	10.3	–22.6
1992	22.6	62.5	14.9	–7.7
ATTEMPT TO ENSURE SEXUAL EQUALITY				
1974 (Oct.)	19.2	46.0	34.8	15.6
1979	22.7	47.8	29.5	6.8
1983	9.5	58.2	32.3	22.8
1987	8.6	48.5	42.9	34.3
1992	4.6	38.7	56.7	52.1
ATTEMPTS TO ENSURE RACIAL EQUALITY				
1974 (Oct.)	27.0	44.3	28.7	1.7
1979	29.9	41.0	29.1	0.8
1983	19.8	52.9	27.3	7.5
1987	29.3	41.9	28.8	–0.5
1992	25.7	40.8	33.6	7.9

Note: The Percentage Difference Index (PDI) represents the proportion 'Too far' minus the proportion 'Not far enough'.

Source: *British Election Studies, 1974–92.*

The results confirm the findings of earlier studies of public opinion which concluded there was no evidence that during Mrs Thatcher's first term the government had converted the electorate on the central values of strong government, discipline and free enterprise. As Ivor Crewe noted:

> Quite simply, there has been no Thatcherite transformation of attitudes or behaviour among the British public. If anything, the British have edged further away from Thatcherite positions as the decade has progressed. The Thatcher governments have undoubtedly transformed the British political economy, overturned the political agenda, and permanently altered the social structure. But this has been done without a cultural counter-revolution in the thinking of ordinary people.[31]

This observation remains true almost a decade later. While the Conservatives have remained wedded to most of the original tenets of Thatcherism, and they have been repeatedly re-elected to power, they have not carried popular opinion with them.

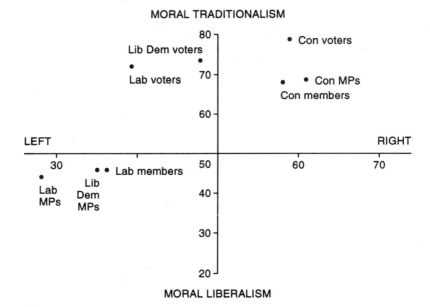

Figure 7.9   Party competition and value scales, 1992

Party competition and social values

The measures we have considered so far help to describe trends over time on particular issues, but this analysis is limited as there are few appropriate items in BES surveys before October 1974 which can be used to test attitudinal change on a consistent basis. More systematic value scales based on factor analysis help us examine the closeness of parties to different groups in the electorate. The scales distinguished economic left–right values and the moral traditionalism–liberalism divide.[32] The left–right scale proved a particularly strong predictor of voting choice.[33] The 'left-right' scale included attitudes towards private medicine, the National Health Service, defence spending, poverty, welfare benefits, nuclear power, trade unions and the redistribution of wealth. The 'moral traditionalism' scale included items on the death penalty, school discipline and respect for traditional values. In total these factors explained 44.1 per cent of variance. These 100 point scales proved reliable when tested for internal consistency,[34] and they can be used to plot the position of voters, party members and MPs to provide a spatial map of party competition.

The results, in figure 7.9, show that Conservative party groups are clustered fairly closely together in the traditional–right quadrant, with members more centrist than other groups. In the Labour party, voters are scattered in the left–traditionalism quadrant, with Labour MPs located at the most extreme point in the left–liberal quarter. Labour members were at the mid-way point between these groups, although slightly closer to leaders than voters.[35] On this map Liberal Democrat voters are found, as might be expected, equidistant between Labour and Conservative voters. They can be seen as 'centre–traditionalists', in the middle on the economic and social cleavage but, possibly surprisingly, believing in old-fashioned moral values. In contrast Liberal Democrat MPs are closer to Labour MPs and Labour members. We can conclude that at the time of the 1992 general election Conservative MPs were positioned close to Conservative voters on basic value cleavages. The Conservative party had a more distinctive issue space, which made it harder for their supporters to desert to the opposition. In contrast, in the last campaign Liberal and Labour MPs proved more distant from their voters, and sharing a more common left–liberal set of values.

Conclusions

This chapter has considered a Downsian model of party competition, comparing shifts in the official party platforms against trends in public opinion. As we would expect the patterns are not wholly consistent; many attitudes remain highly stable over time. Yet, on balance we can conclude that on certain key themes which were central to Thatcherism – attitudes towards privatization, trade union reform and government spending – there is evidence for a rightward turn in public opinion during the mid to late seventies. To this extent Conservative predominance during the eighties was based on their appeal to the zeitgeist. There was indeed a resurgence of Conservative values in the seventies, as many observers suggest, but a closer analysis of the timing indicates that the Thatcher government was the beneficiary, rather than cause, of this change. In this sense, far from continuing the momentum of the Conservative revolution, the Major government may well reflect its apotheosis. If we focus on trends from 1979 to 1992 it is apparent that on many issues – notably public support for spending on the welfare state, for trade union reform and for privatization – the Conservative party has become increasingly out of tune with the direction of British public opinion. While there is evidence from the party manifestos that the Conservatives have gradually shifted left on the welfare state, paralleling trends in public opinion, there has been no similar movement on the economic philosophy. Downs assumes that parties can shift in line with public opinion, to mobilize support. In practice the complex internal politics of modern parties means that ideological baggage, once accumulated, is difficult to dump. A major political party can be seen as similar to an oil tanker heading for a Pacific reef, they can steer slowly to the left or right, but they cannot brake, still less reverse. It has usually proved extremely difficult for parties – particularly parties in government – to shift ideological directions, even under new leadership. As demonstrated by Labour's painful renaissance, it may take decades on the opposition backbenches to force parties to change. Nevertheless, as Mrs Thatcher showed in the late-seventies, if the party leadership is in tune with a significant sea-change in public opinion, it can be done.

Appendix A – Content Analysis: Major Categories

MANAGEMENT OF THE ECONOMY

Pro-Market Economy: such as favourable mentions of capitalism, individual enterprise, private property rights, privatization, and encouraging economic competition. (Eco1) (Right)

Pro-Mixed Economy: Including favourable references to public ownership, government management of the economy, controls over prices, wages, and tariffs, demand-oriented economic policy, collaboration of employers and trade unions in economic planning. (Eco2) (Left)

WELFARE STATE

Limited welfare state: such as the need to limit expenditure on social services, desirability of competition and private services in welfare provision, the need for private education, and the abuse of trade union power. (Soc3) (Right)

Expanded welfare state: such as positive references to the need to expand or maintain social services, educational services, leisure facilities, references to the concept of equality and the end to discrimination, and favourable references to labour groups, working class and unemployed. (Soc4) (Left)

STRONG CENTRAL STATE

Strong and Efficient Government: including favourable mentions of strong government, the need for efficiency in administration, cutting down the civil service, and the party's competence to govern. (Pol6) (Right)

Decentralization: support for federalism, regional autonomy or devolution, deference to local expertise, cultural diversity and cultural autonomy for areas. (Pol4) (Left)

MORAL TRADITIONALISM

Moral Traditionalism: such as appeals to traditional moral values, favourable mentions of maintenance and stability of family, religion, censorship of immorality, enforcement of law, tougher action against crime, resources for the police, need for national unity. (Soc1) (Right)

Cultural Pluralism: Favourable references to classes and groups, underprivileged minorities such as the handicapped, immigrants, homosexuals, ethnic minorities, women, old people, and young people. (Soc5) (Left).

FOREIGN POLICY

Nationalism: Favourable mentions of national independence and sovereignty as opposed to internationalism, the need for national security, opposition to the European Union, appeals to patriotism and nationalism. (For3) (Right)

Internationalism: The need for international cooperation, international courts, support for UN, favourable mentions of the European Union and the desirability of expanding its competence. (For4) (Left)

DEFENCE

Military strength: The need to maintain or increase military expenditure, modernization of armed forces, the need to keep military treaty obligations. (For1) (Right)

Peace and Détente: Declarations of belief in peace and negotiations to resolve conflict, favourable mentions of cutting military expenditure, disarmament and the need for self-government for colonies, negative references to controlling other countries. (For2) (Left)

Notes

1   See Ivor Crewe and Anthony King, 1995. *SDP: The Birth, Life and Death of the Social Democratic Party*. Oxford: Oxford University Press.
2   See also Anthony Heath, Roger Jowell and John Curtice, 1991. *Understanding Political Change*. Oxford: Pergamon Press, pp. 211–21; Hermann Schmitt and Søren Holmberg, 1995. 'Political Parties in Decline?', in Hans-Dieter Klingemann and Dieter Fuchs, 1995, *Citizens and the State*. Oxford: Oxford University Press; Richard Rose and Ian McAllister, 1990. *Voters Begin to Choose*. London: Sage.
3   Herbert Kitschelt, 1994. *The Transformation of European Social Democracy*. Cambridge: Cambridge University Press.
4   Gallagher, Laver and Mair compare the levels of electoral support for left and right parties across fifteen countries in Western Europe. The pattern suggests long-term continuity. The parties of the left (including in the total the vote share for the Communists, New Left, Social Democrats and Greens) consistently won 40.2–40.6 per cent of the vote in every decade from the fifties until the eighties. In contrast parties of the centre and right consistently won 55.7 to 56.7 per cent of the vote. Michael Gallagher, Michael Laver and Peter Mair, 1995. *Representative Government in Modern Europe*. New York: McGraw Hill, table 9-6, p. 229.
5   See also Pippa Norris, 1996. 'Conservatism in Disarray?', *The Brown Journal of World Affairs* III(1): 163-9.
6   Otto Kirchheimer, 1990. 'The Catch-All Party', in Peter Mair (ed.), *The West European Party System*. Oxford: Oxford University Press.

7   Peter Mair, 1996. 'Party Systems and Structures of Competition', in Lawrence
     LeDuc, Richard G. Niemi and Pippa Norris (eds), *Comparing Democracies:
     Elections and Voting in Global Perspective*. Thousand Oaks, CA: Sage.

8   Anthony Heath, Roger Jowell and John Curtice, 1991. *Understanding Political
     Change*. Oxford: Pergamon, p. 211.

9   Richard Rose and Ian McAllister, 1990. *The Loyalties of Voters*. London: Sage,
     p. 27.

10 See, for example, David Robertson, 1976. *A Theory of Party Competition*.
     London: John Wiley and Sons; Ian Budge and Dennis J. Farlie, 1983.
     *Explaining and Predicting Elections: Issue Effects and Party Strategies in Twenty-
     Three Democracies*. London: Allen & Unwin; Ian Budge, David Robertson and
     Derek Hearl (eds), 1987. *Ideology Strategy and Party Change: Spatial Analysis
     of Post-War Election Programmes in Nineteen Democracies*. Cambridge:
     Cambridge University Press; Hans-Dieter Klingemann, Richard Hofferbert
     and Ian Budge, 1994. *Parties, Policies and Democracy*. Boulder, CO: Westview
     Press.

11 Patrick Seyd, 1987. *The Rise and Fall of the Labour Left*. London: Macmillan;
     David Coates, 1980. *Labour in Power?* London: Longman; Eric Shaw, 1988.
     Discipline and Discord in the Labour Party. Manchester: University of
     Manchester Press; Dennis Kavanagh and Peter Morris, 1989. *Consensus
     Politics from Attlee to Thatcher*. Oxford: Blackwell.

12 See Eric Shaw, 1994. *The Labour Party since 1979*. London: Routledge; Martin
     J. Smith and Joanna Spear, 1992. *The Changing Labour Party*. London:
     Routledge.

13 Peter Jenkins, 1987. *Mrs Thatcher's Revolution: The Ending of the Socialist Era*.
     London: Jonathan Cape, p. 375.

14 David Graham and Peter Clarke, 1986. *The New Enlightenment: The Rebirth
     of Liberalism*. London: Macmillan, p. xii.

15 For the debate concerning the centrality of these values to Thatcherism see
     Stuart Hall, 1988. *The Hard Road to Renewal*. London: Verso; Bob Jessop,
     Kevin Bonnett, Simon Bromley and Tom Ling, 1988. *Thatcherism*.
     Cambridge: Polity Press.

16 See Dennis Kavanagh, 1994. *The Major Effect*. London: Macmillan.

17 For details see Lindsay Brook et al., 1992. *British Social Attitudes: Cumulative
     Sourcebook*. London: SCPR/Gower.

18 See Pippa Norris, 1990. *British By-Elections: The Volatile Electorate*. Oxford:
     Clarendon Press.

19 David Sanders, 1995. 'Forecasting Political Preferences and Election
     Outcomes in the UK: Experiences, Problems and Prospects for the Next
     General Election', *Electoral Studies* 14(3): 251–72; Harold Clarke, Marianne
     C. Stewart and Gary Zuk, 1986. 'Politics, Economics and Party Popularity in

Britain, 1979-93', *Electoral Studies* 5: 123-41; Helmut Norpoth, 1987. 'The Falklands War and Government Popularity in Britain: Rally Without Consequence or Surge Without Decline', *Electoral Studies* 6: 3-16; David Sanders, Hugh Ward, David Marsh and Tony Fletcher, 1987. 'Government Popularity and the Falklands War: A Reassessment', *British Journal of Political Science* 17: 281–314.

20 See Hans-Dieter Klingemann, Richard Hofferbert and Ian Budge, 1994. *Parties, Policies and Democracy*. Boulder, CO: Westview Press.

21 See Pippa Norris and Joni Lovenduski, 1995. *Political Recruitment: Gender, Race and Class in the British Electorate*. Cambridge: Cambridge University Press; Paul Whiteley, Patrick Seyd and Jeremy Richardson, 1994. *True Blues: The Politics of Conservative Party Membership*. Oxford: Clarendon Press; Patrick Seyd and Paul Whiteley, 1992. *Labour's Grass Roots: The Politics of Party Membership*. Oxford: Clarendon Press.

22 These data are derived from the Comparative Manifestos Project (CMP95), author A. Volkens, Science Center Berlin, Research Unit Institutions and Social Change (Director, Hans-Dieter Klingemann) in cooperation with the Manifesto Research Group (chaired by Ian Budge). The author is most grateful to Hans-Dieter Klingemann for providing access to this dataset.

23 Right-wing = (Pol 6 + Eco 1 + Soc 3 + For 3). Left-wing = (Pol 4 + Eco 2 + Soc 4 + For 4).

24 See, for example, Dennis Kavanagh and Peter Morris, 1989. *Consensus Politics From Attlee to Thatcher*. Oxford: Blackwell.

25 See John Rentoul, 1989. *Me and Mine: The Triumph of the New Individualism?* London: Unwin Hyman; Ivor Crewe and Donald Searing, 1988. 'Mrs Thatcher's Crusade: Conservatism in Britain, 1972-1986', in B. Cooper, A. Kornberg and W. Mishler (eds), *The Resurgence of Conservatism in Anglo-American Democracies*. Durham, NC: Duke University Press.

26 See John Vickers and Vincent Wright, 1988. 'The Politics of Industrial Privatisation in Western Europe: An Overview', in *West European Politics* 11:(4)1/30.

27 J. Vickers and G. Yarrow, 1988. *Privatisation: An Economic Aspect*. Cambridge, MA: MIT Press.

28 *Social Trends 1995*. 1995. London: Central Statistical Office, HMSO, p. 98.

29 Robert Taylor, 1994. 'Employment and Industrial Relations Policy', in Dennis Kavanagh and Anthony Seldon, *The Major Effect*. London: Macmillan; Peter Riddell, 1989. *The Thatcher Decade*. Oxford: Blackwell, pp. 43–68; B. C. Roberts, 1989. 'Trade Unions', in Dennis Kavanagh and Anthony Seldon, *The Thatcher Effect*. Oxford: Clarendon Press.

30 It should be noted that the question wording was modified from 1983 to 1987.

Q 1983: 'Do you think that trade unions in this country have too much power or   not?'
Q 1987: 'Do you think that trade unions in this country have too much power or too little power?' (coded on a five-point Likert scale).

31 Ivor Crewe, 1989. 'Values: The Crusade that Failed', p.241 in Dennis Kavanagh and Anthony Seldon (eds), *The Thatcher Effect: A Decade of Change.* Oxford: Oxford University Press. See also Ivor Crewe, 1988. 'Has the Electorate become Thatcherite?', in Robert Skidelsky, *Thatcherism.* London: Chatto & Windus; Ivor Crewe and Donald Searing, 1988. 'Ideological Change in the British Conservative Party', *American Political Science Review* 82(2): 361–84.

32 For details see Anthony Heath et al., 1991. 'The Measurement of Core Beliefs and Values', British Journal of Political Science 24(1): 115–23; Pippa Norris, 1995. 'May's Law of Curvilinear Disparity: Leaders, Officers, Members and Voters in British Parties', in *Party Politics* 1(1).

33 An OLS regression analysis, controlling for the independent effects of social class, housing tenure, and age, produced a strong association between the left–right scale and the Conservative vote (standardized beta coefficient of .53, total R2 = .33).

34 Cronbach's alpha was 0.754 for the 'left–right' scale and 0.637 for the 'liberal–authoritarian' scale.

35 For further discussion see Pippa Norris, 'Labour party factionalism and extremism', in Anthony Heath et al. (eds), *Labour's Last Chance? The 1992 Election and Beyond.* Aldershot: Dartmouth, 1994.

8 Party Representatives

We have considered the ability of parties to shift their ideological positions, and the limitations of these strategies. Parties may also compete through changing the types of parliamentary candidates they select as their standard-bearers, in the hope of thereby attracting new groups of supporters. In the early eighties the Conservative party, concerned about its image as an 'old boys' network for the leisured and landed upper-classes, radically changed the way they selected Conservative candidates. The party adopted a more 'meritocratic' process, including weekend selection boards designed to reflect personnel practices, to attract more middle-class professionals.[1] In recent years Labour has introduced significant reforms to try to bring more women into its parliamentary ranks, although one of the more radical steps – the use of all-women shortlists in half its target seats – has been subsequently abandoned on legal appeal.[2] Much of the motivation for trying to change Labour's cloth-cap image through changing their candidates was electoral, driven by the desire to attract 'the women's vote'. The aim of this chapter is to analyse how far the composition of parliamentary parties has evolved over time, in term of the socio-economic, gender and racial backgrounds of MPs and parliamentary candidates, and to explore whether these changes have influenced electoral fortunes at constituency level.

Trends in Socio-economic Status

Since class has been the basic electoral cleavage in British politics, not surprisingly parties have traditionally been most concerned about the class image of their candidates. The most striking change in the parliamentary elite in the post-war era has been the decline of railwaymen, dockers and miners on the Labour benches, replaced by professionals such as lawyers, teachers, consultants and journalists.[3] Labour was first founded in 1900 to 'secure the representation of working class opinion in parliament'.[4] Ross estimates that for the 1918-35 period, about three-quarters of all Labour MPs (72 per cent) could be classified as rank and file workers – miners, metal workers, textile workers, train drivers and printers – normally sponsored by the major unions (see figure 8.1).[5] This closely matched the population; from 1911-1931 about 70-75 per cent of the labour force worked in manual occupations.[6] The influx of new members in the post-war Attlee landslide changed the face of the Labour party. In the 1945-50 parliament almost half the Labour members were middle class (49 per cent). Labour's working-class MPs declined throughout the fifties and sixties, with some fluctuations. By the time of the 1992 election only a fifth (22 per cent) of Labour MPs, and a tenth (9 per cent) of adopted Labour candidates, came from a working-class background.[7] The twentieth century has seen a shrinkage in the proportion of manual workers in the labour force: from 75 in 1911 to 48 per cent in 1991.[8] But the decline among

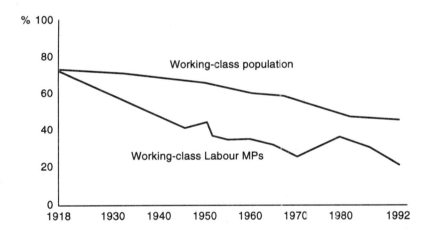

Figure 8.1 Proportion of working-class Labour MPs, 1918–92
Sources: Butler 1988; Butler and Kavanagh 1992.

Labour MPs has gone faster and further. If parliament reflected the electorate, there would be five times as many working-class MPs.

In the mid-nineteenth century the Conservatives were the party of the great landowners and the barons of commerce and industry.[9] In the long-term, as Guttsman demonstrates, the main change has been the decline in the traditional aristocracy, replaced by the private-sector professional middle-classes.[10] Not surprisingly there have always been few working-class members in the Conservative party, at most 3-4 per cent in the 1918–51 period. Since the early fifties this has dropped to only three or four Conservative MPs, or about one per cent. This pattern existed despite efforts by Conservative Central Office to change the position.[11] The Conservatives formed the Unionist Labour Movement (ULM) in 1919, when the absence of working-class Conservative MPs was considered a serious electoral liability. Several ULM members became Conservative candidates in the 1930s, but this had little effect on the class composition of the parliamentary party. Another initiative was attempted, in reaction to their post-war defeat, with the establishment of the Conservative Trade Unionists' Organisation in 1947. During the same period the Maxwell Fyfe financial reforms were intended to produce more socially diverse candidates. Neither initiative had a major effect, due to resistance by constituency parties.

In the post-war years both Labour and the Conservatives experienced an expansion of middle-class MPs, and it might appear that the parties have thereby become more homogeneous. Nevertheless, the traditional class categories are broad, and serve to disguise some significant occupational differences which continue to distinguish party elites. If we look more closely at occupational patterns from 1945 to 1992 the biggest change on the Conservative side has been the decline in the army generals and landed squires, and a steady increase in professional politicians with early careers as political researchers and organizers.[12] By far the largest group of Conservative MPs, including about half their members, are company directors, company executives and barristers. On the Labour benches the biggest growth has come from teachers, lecturers and researchers, followed by those in local government, and in routine white-collar jobs. This pattern follows the post-war expansion of post-secondary education and the welfare state. These occupational patterns have reduced the broad class differences, but reinforced a public–private division between the major parties.

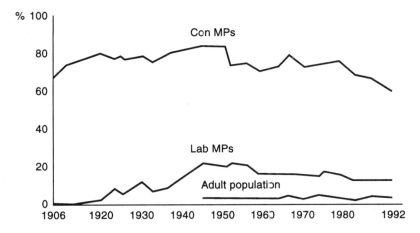

Figure 8.2 Proportion of public-school educated MPs, 1906–92
Sources: Butler 1988; Butler and Kavanagh 1992.

Parallel concerns have traditionally been expressed about the over-representation of members drawn from the public schools and Oxbridge, particularly the number of Old Etonians and Harrovians. From 1920 to 1950 about 80 per cent of all Conservative MPs attended a public school, with a slight fall in the sixties and seventies, followed by a steady decline. In the 1992 general election about two-thirds (62 per cent) of all Conservative members had been public-school educated, and just over half (55 per cent) of the new Conservative MPs. There have always been far fewer public school boys in the Labour party, although with the post-war intake the proportion rose to about a fifth, before falling again gradually. By 1992, 40 Labour MPs (14 per cent) had been to public school, compared with about 5 per cent of the British population. Compared with the population, public school products are over-represented eight-fold.

Most legislatures in established democracies have experienced a process of professionalization, including many more university graduates.[13] At the turn of the century just over half the Conservative parliamentary party were graduates (57 per cent) compared with almost three-quarters today (73 per cent). Oxford and Cambridge retain their lead on the Conservative benches although over the years increased proportions of MPs have been drawn from other universities.[14] The change has been even more dramatic

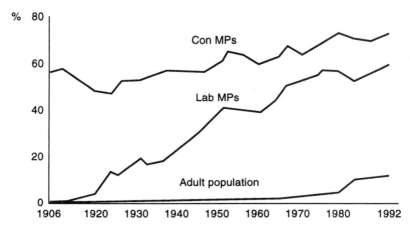

Figure 8.3 Proportion of MPs who are graduates, 1906–92
Sources: Butler 1988; Butler and Kavanagh 1992.

on the Labour benches; the parliamentary party contained no graduates in the early years, about a third in 1945, and almost two-thirds today. University graduates are over-represented in Parliament compared with the nation by a ratio of 10:1.

Trends in Women in Parliament

Women were first allowed to stand for parliament following the *Representation of the People's Act 1918* (giving the vote to women over 30) and the *Equal Franchise Act of 1928* (which lowered the voting age of women to 21, the same as men). Yet from 1918 to 1983, with remarkably little variation, less that 5 per cent of all MPs were women (see figure 8.4). The first significant signs of change appeared in the 1987 election, when the proportion of women MPs rose to 6.3 per cent, before jumping to 9.2 per cent in 1992. The Conservatives increased their number but in the 1992 election the most substantial shift occurred in the Labour party, where the number of women almost doubled from 21 to 37 MPs, representing 13.6 per cent of the parliamentary party. In 1992 sixty women were elected to the Commons. This represents significant progress but never-

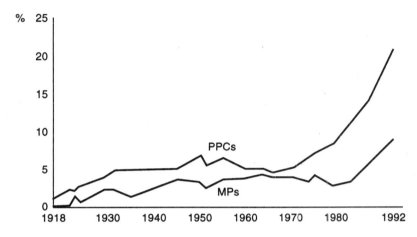

Figure 8.4 Proportion of women MPs and candidates, 1918–92
Source: F. W. S. Craig, 1989.

theless there are fewer women in the British House of Commons than in comparable legislatures in most developed democracies.[15]

The proportion of women candidates remained fairly static from 1918 until the mid-1970s; since then there has been a sharp rise, tripling from October 1974 (7.1 per cent) to 1992 (21.1 per cent). In the major parties the increase has been strongest among Labour women, although the proportion of Conservative women candidates has also doubled during this period. Due to greater longevity, and a slight tendency towards higher turnout, women are 52–53 per cent of voters.[16] If parliament reflected the nation, after the 1992 general election there would have been 339 women in the House, not 60.

Trends in Ethnic Minority Representation

The history of ethnic minority representation has been one of painfully slow and modest change. In the pre-war period there were three Asian Members of Parliament: the last, Shapurji Saklatvala, lost his seat in Battersea North in 1929. The post-war period saw only a few black candidates standing for the major parties: the best known was Dr (later Lord)

David Pitt, fighting the Labour seat of Wandsworth Clapham, who suffered a higher than average swing of 10.2 per cent against him in 1970.

Ethnic minority candidates started to stand following the October 1974 election (see table 8.1), with the number rising to eighteen in 1983, and twenty-eight in 1987. As a result for the first time since 1924 MPs were elected from black or Asian backgrounds, all Labour: Bernie Grant for Tottenham, Diane Abbott for Hackney North and Stoke Newington, Paul Boateng for Brent South and Keith Vaz for Leicester East. In all these constituencies black candidates could have been expected to do well since ethnic minorities constituted over one-quarter of the electorate. In 1992 Labour made little progress in increasing the number of minority candidates and the result was the return of five black Labour MPs, with the addition of Piara Khambra.

Conservative attempts to increase support among blacks started with the establishment in 1976 of the Anglo-Asian and Anglo-West Indian Conservative Societies, and later the One Nation Forum founded under the leadership of the party deputy chairman, Sir John Cope. The party's electoral drive was launched with the claim that Conservative values of opportunity, family life and law and order made it a natural party for ethnic minority voters, particularly Asian small businessmen. The Conservatives have a long way to go to mobilize support, since the black electorate is overwhelmingly likely to support Labour (see chapter 6). Partly in response to progress within the Labour party, the Conservatives selected seven black candidates to fight the 1992 general election. In the election Nirj Deva was elected as the first Asian Conservative MP since 1900.

There has therefore been limited progress in the parliamentary representation of ethnic minorities in the post-war period. Nevertheless this trend lags far behind the increase in the black electorate. Only ten ethnic minority members have ever entered the British Parliament.[17] If parliament reflected the public, the Commons would include six times the number of black or Asian MPs. As Britain has become more racially diverse in recent decades, the issue of minority representation in parliament has proved increasingly controversial.

The Electoral Impact of Candidates

The question which remains is whether changes in the type of candidates

Table 8.1   Ethnic minority MPs and candidates

	Conservative		Labour		Total all parties	
	PPC	MP	PPC	MP	PPC	MP
1950	0	0	0	0	1	0
1951	0	0	0	0	0	0
1955	0	0	0	0	0	0
1959	0	0	1	0	1	0
1964	0	0	0	0	1	0
1966	0	0	0	0	0	0
1970	0	0	1	0	8	0
1974 (Feb.)	0	0	1	0	6	0
1974 (Oct.)	0	0	1	0	3	0
1979	2	0	1	0	12	0
1983	4	0	6	0	18	0
1987	6	0	14	4	28	4
1992	8	1	9	5	17	6
Total	20	1	34	9	95	10

Source: Pippa Norris and Joni Lovenduski, 1995. *Political Recruitment: Gender, Race and Class in the British Parliament.* Cambridge: Cambridge University Press.

selected have had any significant impact on the electoral fortunes of the parties at constituency level. We can examine the ˙personal vote' for particular groups of candidates in the 1992 election.

In any analysis we need to control for the status of the contestants. Candidates can be classified into three main types. *Incumbents* are MPs elected in the previous general election who are restanding in the same seat, and for the same party, in the subsequent general election. *Inheritors* are candidates selected for one of their party's existing seats, from which the previous MP has retired (an 'open seat'). *Challengers* are candidates fighting a seat held by another party. If there is an incumbency effect, we would expect a party's incumbents would perform better than its inheritor · or challengers, other things being equal. To analyse the incumbency effect, the mean change in the share of the constituency vote can be compared for each group.

In 1992 Labour incumbents won 3.6 per cent more of the vote than Labour inheritors, an incumbency advantage of 1,750 votes in an average seat. In some Labour seats the 'retirement slump' was far stronger. For example, in 'mixed urban–rural' Scottish seats the mean fall in the Labour vote was 2.9 per cent but in Falkirk East, where Harry Ewing retired after

18 years, it dropped by 8.1 points and in Cunninghame South, where David Lambie retired after 22 years, it fell by 7.9 points.

Conversely, Labour first-time incumbents, who had suffered from 'retirement slumps' in 1987, often did exceptionally well in 1992. In the East Midlands the mean rise in the Labour vote was 7.4 per cent but in Mansfield the Labour left-winger Alan Meale increased his vote by 16.9 percentage points (and his majority from 56 to 11,724) with the largest pro-Labour swing in the country (10.6 per cent). In Leicester East, Keith Vaz, an Asian, increased his vote by 10.4 points on a 9.6 per cent swing. In Bristol South, Dawn Primarolo's vote rose by 9.3 per cent, and her majority from 1,404 to 8,919, on a swing of 7.5 per cent; in the four other Bristol seats (including Kingswood) the mean swing was 5.5 per cent.

In the Conservative party, too, incumbents did better than inheritors, although the difference was more modest – about 0.6 per cent or about 350 votes. It is difficult to identify any Labour gains from the Conservatives which can plausibly be attributed to the retirement of the Conservative incumbent. However, some first-term Conservative incumbents did particularly well: John Bowis consolidated his 1987 gain of Battersea, with a 3.7 per cent swing from Labour, while Graham Riddick increased his majority in the formerly Liberal Colne Valley from 1,677 to 7,225 on a 3.2 per cent swing; in the surrounding West Yorkshire seats the mean swing was 0.6 per cent to the Conservatives.

Therefore controlling for the type of contestant, the type of seat (marginal or safe), and regional swings, we can go on to examine whether ethnic minority or women candidates experienced any electoral benefits or penalties from the electorate.[18]

Ethnic minority candidates

Twenty-two Asian and Afro-Caribbean candidates stood for the main parties, six fewer than in 1987. The Conservatives selected seven ethnic minority candidates, including two inheritors of marginal Conservative seats: Nirj Joseph Deva for Brentford and Isleworth and John Taylor for Cheltenham. The Labour party selected nine ethnic minority candidates, a decline from their 14 at the previous election. These included four 1987 incumbents, Bernie Grant (Tottenham), Diane Abbott (Hackney North),

Paul Boateng (Brent South) and Keith Vaz (Leicester East). In addition Ashok Kumar defended the Langbaurgh seat he won in the 1991 by-election and Piara Khambra was selected to inherit the safe Labour (and predominantly Asian) seat of Ealing Southall. The three other black Labour challengers faced daunting Conservative majorities. The Liberal Democrats selected seven ethnic minority challengers, although none of the seats were good prospects for the party.

The analysis of voting swings suggests that black Labour candidates incurred a lower penalty than their Conservative counterparts, although both groups had mixed fortunes. Three of the four black Labour MPs elected in 1987 were returned with swings well above the regional average: Keith Vaz (9.5 per cent), Bernie Grant (9.2 per cent) and Diane Abbott (5.6 per cent). The high swings in the two London seats probably reflected not only local acceptance of a black MP but the retreat from the London Labour hard-left. But in marginal Langbaurgh Ashok Kumar's swing was below average (0.5 per cent against the local mean of 1.6 per cent) despite the boost he should have received from his by-election victory, and he failed to hold the seat. Piara Khambra was elected for Ealing Southall, where the decision of the retiring MP, Sydney Bidwell, to stand as a 'True Labour' candidate splintered the Labour vote and produced a small swing to the Conservatives.

The result that received most publicity was John Taylor's defeat in marginal Cheltenham, which fell to the Liberal Democrats on a swing of 5.2 per cent. Taylor refused to admit in public that racism was to blame. Liberal Democrat strength in the south-west, the closeness of the Liberal challenge in Cheltenham ever since February 1974 and local Conservative party divisions over its selection, may all have played a part; but in the surrounding Cirencester & Tewkesbury seat, where the incumbent also retired, the Conservative vote remained solid. Racism probably did cost the Conservatives the seat. Other black Conservatives did better. Nirj Joseph Deva's election for Brentford and Isleworth made him the first Asian (or black) Conservative this century: the swing against him (5.3 per cent) was average for the area.

Black Conservative challengers did slightly – but only slightly – worse than average: for example in Islington North the anti-Conservative swing was –4.6 per cent compared with –3 per cent for inner London; in Bradford North and Bradford South it was, respectively, –6.3 per cent and –5.3 per cent compared with –2.1 per cent in Bradford West, although the Bradford

North swing will have owed something to Labour's by-election victory there in 1990.

Women candidates

The 1992 election proved a substantial advance for women: 336 stood as candidates for the main parties, including 41 (1987) incumbents, 10 inheritors, and 32 Labour and Conservative challengers in promising marginals (seats with majorities of under 10 per cent). As a result 60 women MPs were elected, compared with 41 in 1987 and 23 in 1983, the largest number ever returned to Parliament. Most of the new women MPs were Labour (up from 21 to 37) while the number of Conservative women MPs barely grew (up from 17 to 20). Although the trend represents progress, fewer than one in ten members of the current Parliament is a woman. On a linear continuation of the trend the number of women MPs would be only 100 by the year 2000 (at 15 per cent, still lower than the average for member states of the European Community) and would not achieve parity with men until the middle of the twenty-first century. The paucity of women MPs was not the result of discrimination by voters. A comparison of the mean share of the constituency vote, controlling for region and type of seat, shows that Labour and Conservative women did slightly better than men as incumbents, only marginally worse than men as inheritors, and about as well as challengers. If the number of women inheritors increased – which is the key to increasing the number of women MPs – they would face no barriers in the electorate.

Conclusions

The type of representatives which a party selects as its standard bearers might be expected to have direct, and indirect, effects on its electoral fortunes. The direct effects are evident in the change in the vote for particular candidates in particular seats. The evidence from this chapter suggests that the selection of ethnic minority inheritors and challengers may produce a slight electoral penalty for both major parties, although the loss of votes is usually fairly minimal. As second-term incumbents, ethnic minority MPs have experienced higher than average swings in their favour.

In contrast the adoption of more women candidates seems unlikely to have a significant impact on the results in particular seats: women do not necessarily gain votes, but then neither do they lose them.

Indirectly, we might expect changes in parliamentary representation gradually to shape party images. Through the recruitment process parties can gradually change the face of the parliamentary representatives which they present to the world. A study by Labour's Shadow Communication Agency found that in 1987 Labour was widely seen as the most masculine of all the parties. Since then the party has adopted a series of strategies as a matter of priority to try to change this image, including the selection of more women candidates in the last general election, the modernization of the party organization, and the implementation of 40 per cent quotas for women at every level of the party including internal posts and conference delegates, and greater focus on women's policy concerns in party leaflets and publicity. It is too early to say whether these reforms will have any significant electoral benefits, but changes to the recruitment process represent another significant strategy which parties can use to try to bolster their popular support.

Notes

1   See Pippa Norris and Joni Lovenduski, 1995. *Political Recruitment: Gender, Race and Class in the British Parliament.* Cambridge: Cambridge University Press.

2   See Clare Short, 1996. 'Women and the Labour Party', *Parliamentary Affairs* 49(1): 17–25.

3   There are a number of problems associated with the classification of members' prior occupational backgrounds, including lack of detailed information, and problems of consistent categorization in different time series. For the time series data this study uses the standard sources, as referenced.

4   Robert McKenzie, 1963. *British Political Parties.* London: Mercury Books, pp. 456–57.

5   F. W. S. Ross, 1955. *Elections and Electors.* London: Eyre and Spottiswoode, table 19 and table 20, pp. 60–1.

6   Robert Price and George Sayers Bain, 1988. 'The Labour Force', in A. H. Halsey, *British Social Trends since 1900.* London: Macmillan, table 4.1(b), p. 164.

7   See David Butler, 1988. 'Electors and Elected', in A. H. Halsey, *British Social Trends since 1900.* London: Macmillan, tables 8.6, 8.7, pp. 316–17. This is based on the Nuffield series of British General Election Studies. It should be

noted that Burch and Moran, using a different classificatory scheme, estimate that the proportion of working-class MPs is significantly lower. See Martin Burch and Michael Moran, 1985, 'The Changing Political Elite', *Parliamentary Affairs* 38(1): 1–15. The Butler series is used in this study since it provides a longer time-span.

8 Robert Price and George Sayers Bain, 1988. 'The Labour Force', in A. H. Halsey, *British Social Trends since 1900*. London: Macmillan, p. 163; *1991 Census Report for Great Britain (Part 2)* 1993, table 86. London: OPCS.

9 J. A. Thomas, 1939. *The House of Commons, 1832–1901*. Wales: University of Wales Press.

10 W. L. Guttsman, 1963. *The British Political Elite*. New York: Basic Books.

11 John Greenwood, 1988. 'Promoting Working-Class Candidature in the Conservative Party: the limits of central office power', *Parliamentary Affairs* 41: 456-68.

12 See Peter Riddell, 1993. *Honest Opportunism: The Rise of the Career Politician.* London: Hamish Hamilton.

13 See Pippa Norris (ed.), 1997. *Routes to Power: Legislative Recruitment in Advanced Democracies.* Cambridge: Cambridge University Press.

14 From 1945 to 1992 the proportion of all Conservative MPs attending Oxbridge declined from 53 to 45 per cent, and the proportion who attended other universities rose from 11 to 28 per cent.

15 Joni Lovenduski and Pippa Norris, 1993. *Gender and Party Politics.* London: Sage.

16 See Pippa Norris, 1991. 'Gender Differences in Political Participation in Britain: traditional, radical and revisionist models', *Government and Opposition* 26(1): 56–74.

17 This includes a Liberal in the 1890s, a Conservative in the 1900s, a Communist with Labour support in the 1920s, four Labour members since 1987, one Labour member in 1991, plus one Labour MP and one Conservative MP in 1992.

18 See also Pippa Norris, Elizabeth Vallance and Joni Lovenduski, 1992. 'Do Candidates Make a Difference?', 45(2): 496–517; Ivor Crewe, Pippa Norris and Robert Waller, 1992. 'The 1992 General Election', in Pippa Norris (ed.), *British Elections and Parties Yearbook, 1992.* Herts.: Harvester Wheatsheaf.

Part IV

Changes in Political Communications

9 Changes in Communications

Explanations based on political communications suggest that the major transformation in election campaigns has come less from long-term structural trends or changes in party strategies, than from the system of political communications in the modern campaign. In particular, in common with most established democracies, Britain has experienced the erosion of channels of direct communications between politicians and voters, and the simultaneous rise of mediated election campaigns, with significant consequences for representative democracy.

This chapter considers whether the modernization of political communications has significantly weakened traditional linkages between parties and voters, and altered the dynamics of party competition. The role of the media in campaigns, especially television, has expanded in many countries during the last fifty years. Swanson and Mancini suggest that the process of modernization has entailed several related developments in election campaigns: a significant shift from direct to mediated communications; from dispersed local party organizations to central co-ordination of the campaign by the national leadership; from amateur volunteers contributing time and labour to paid professional consultants; and from cleavage-based and issue-based conflict towards the character-based 'personalization' of party politics.

Yet the impact of these developments on democracies varies substantially depending upon the institutional context of election campaigns, such as the structure of political communications.[2] As a result, despite the process of modernization, election campaigns in different countries continue to show striking contrasts. The rise of television-dominated, personality-driven and negative campaigns has probably gone further in the United States, Italy and Russia, for example, than in Britain, Germany and Sweden, due to the legal rules governing broadcasting, the strength of traditional mass-branch party organizations, the political culture and the structure of competition for elected office.[3]

In emphasizing the importance of the media and the campaign context in the study of voting behaviour we are returning to an older tradition. The focus on the campaign was evident in the earliest modern studies of British general elections, by R. B. McCullum and Alison Readman in 1945, and H. G. Nicholas in 1950,[4] as well as in the first studies of constituency campaigning in Glasgow, Greenwich, Newcastle-under-Lyme, Bristol South-East, and Leeds.[5] These books concentrated on 'the election machinery', the structure and activities of local and national party organizations, party platforms on the major issues, the background and character of the candidates, and the press coverage, concluding with the results. These contemporary accounts captured and preserved on record the blow-by-blow immediacy of the campaign, drawing upon detailed qualitative, journalistic and historical sources, including personal interviews, participant observation, analysis of newspaper coverage and constituency leaflets, and aggregate analysis of voting results and the social background of candidates. Like the earliest campaign surveys by Paul Lazarsfeld and colleagues in the United States,[6] the behaviour of the electorate was contextualized by locating it within a specific campaign. McCullum and Readman founded the long-standing series of 'Nuffield' studies, carried out in every general election since 1951 by David Butler and colleagues. The Nuffield series expanded to cover developments like television coverage and the use of opinion polls, and more systematic psephological and content analysis, but these remain recognizably within the tradition of the earlier volumes.[7]

Recent work on political communications includes the 'Essex' series concentrating on the structure and contents of election communications, including the role of campaign managers, pollsters, and journalists;[8] detailed studies of the legal and constitutional basis of British elections,[9] the financial regulation of British campaigns,[10] the nature of national and local party organizations,[11] and most recently, the development of professional political marketing by parties.[12] The focus is upon the key actors in the election – leading politicians, professional consultants and commentators – the battle to dominate the campaign agenda, and the process of electoral communications. We can build on this foundation to understand British elections as a dynamic interaction between three agencies: the electorate, parties, and the media. Each part of the trilogy can be seen to play a distinct role in constructing the meaning, and determining the outcome, of campaigns.[13] Parties seek to attract, reinforce, and mobilize supporters. Parties aim to do this by shaping the information received by the public, defining the policy agenda, framing who gets blamed or rewarded for policy problems, and ultimately influencing people's voting choices. Citizens employ established attitudes, beliefs and opinions to sift information and weigh preferences within a campaign. And the media provide the essential linkage function allowing parties and voters to communicate with each other.

Today politicians can occasionally bypass the media, meeting individuals face-to-face at campaign rallies or on doorsteps. MPs can take soundings from their local party. Constituency party activists continue to invest considerable time and effort on door-step politics in local campaigns with all the paraphernalia of posters, canvassing and local meetings.[14] But these activities, which only ever reached a few, have declined dramatically in Britain.[15] There are fewer constituency volunteers today since, as noted in chapter 5, levels of party membership have declined substantially in Britain since the fifties.[16] Interpersonal communications, such as political discussions within the family or workplace, may prove important, but much of this information ultimately derives from the media.[17] Therefore for most of the time in the modern campaign politicians and voters have to communicate with each other indirectly. Rather than treating studies of voters, parties and the media in isolation, as has been common in the past, we need to reintegrate these concerns. From a 'new institutionalism' perspective[18] we need to understand how voting and party behaviour is shaped by its context.

According to agenda-setting theory, each actor – parties, the media and the electorate – brings their concerns to the election, and the campaign resolves which priorities predominate. In effective democratic campaigns, party and voter agendas move closer together, with the media serving as marriage broker. This linkage function has to be seen as a process of mutual interaction. Media messages are predominately 'top-down' during an election, telling voters about parties, for example, by reporting press

	Pre-modern	Modern	Post-modern
Campaign organization	Local and decentralized	Nationally co-ordinated	Nationally co-ordinated but decentralized operations
Preparations	Short-term and ad-hoc	Long campaign	Permanent campaign
Central co-ordination	Party leaders	Central headquarters, more specialist consultants and party	More outside consultants, pollsters and specialist campaign departments
Feedback	Local canvassing	Opinion polls	Opinion polls, focus groups, Internet web sites
Media	National and local press, local handbills, posters and pamphlets, radio leadership speeches	Television broadcasting through major territorial channels	Television narrowcasting through fragmented channels, targeted mail, targeted ads
Campaign events	Local public meetings, limited whistle-stop leadership tours	Media management, daily press conferences, themed photo opps, TV PPBs, bill-board wars	Extension of media management to 'routine' politics, leadership speeches, policy launches, etc
Costs	Low budget and local	Higher costs for producing TV PPBs	Higher costs for consultants, research, and TV ads

Figure 9.1   Changes in campaigning

conferences, policy debates, or campaign rallies. But the direction is also 'bottom-up', informing party leaders about public concerns through coverage of opinion polls, phone-in programmes, and vox pop interviews. Seen in this light, the quality of the campaign is important, not just for determining the winning party, but also as an integral part of representative democracy.

Media coverage therefore matters in the most obvious sense if it influences voting choice, and thus the outcome for the winning party in government. This has been the primary preoccupation with previous studies in Britain. But arguably even more important, the coverage of the campaign may matter for the quality of British democracy if the media influences citizens' knowledge about the policy options available, their sense of civic engagement, and their participation in the electoral process. Campaigns may matter for parties by improving their understanding of public concerns, forcing politicians to pay attention to citizens, and providing feedback to politics at Westminster. Coverage by the media which is excessively negative, superficial, or biased, may erode the ability of parties and the public to connect. Elections may thereby function as a form of civic education for leaders and led. Democratic campaigns are the principal opportunity for politicians and voters to talk to, and learn about, each other.

The Pre-Modern Doorstep Campaign of 1945

In order to understand changes over time in the role of the media, and the modernization of political communications, we can compare post-war contests with the campaign of today. The development of electioneering in Britain can be categorized into three-stages,[19] as illustrated in figure 9.1. The 1945 general election exemplified the pre-modern campaign with its decentralized, ad-hoc and unco-ordinated organization, volunteer labour-force and constituency focus.[20] The end of the war-time coalition government on 21 May 1945, and the dissolution of Parliament two days later, brought the first general election for a decade.

The Electronic Media

Media coverage of the campaign was limited compared with today. Television played no role during, or after, the campaign. The BBC started its post-war television service in 1946, reaching some 15,000 households. The first programmes about party politics appeared on television in 1951, but television news did not cover the campaign until 1959. Nevertheless, as Clement Attlee acknowledged, the first revolution in the electronic media had already created a mass audience and the beginnings of a national campaign. The introduction of radio broadcasting in 1924 permanently altered the way elections were fought.[21] Leadership speeches, which previously reached an audience of only a few thousand, were now heard night after night by millions. In the 1945 campaign BBC radio scheduled one (20-30 minute) broadcast after the main evening news each weekday evening. Ten broadcasts were allocated to the Conservatives and Labour, four to the Liberals, one each to the Communists and the Common Wealth party. Labour broadcasts were more co-ordinated and thematic than the Conservatives. The opening broadcasts by the party leaders were seen to set the tone for the subsequent campaign. According to BBC audience research, the listenership was substantial: just under half the adult population heard each broadcast, with numbers rising towards polling day.[22] Moreover, just as later television set the agenda for newspapers, so the radio broadcasts were reported at length in the printed press.

Newspapers

Newspaper readers had the choice of the tabloid *Daily Mirror* and *Daily Sketch*, or one of the seven broadsheet national morning newspapers, or a local paper.[23] The print media were highly partisan, especially the popular press. Conservative-leaning national newspapers (the *Daily Express*, the *Daily Mail*, the *Daily Sketch* and the *Daily Telegraph*) had the highest circulation, selling about 6.8 million copies. But the Conservative edge in the national press was not great. The Labour-supporting *Daily Herald* and *Daily Mirror* enjoyed a combined circulation of 4.4 million, while the Liberals received the support of the *News Chronicle* and the *Manchester Guardian*, with a total circulation of 1.6 million. *The Times* remained fairly independent, traditionally Conservative although anti-Churchill in this election.[24]

The only newspaper with a systematic opinion poll was the *News Chronicle*, which published the British Institute of Public Opinion, later known as Social Surveys (Gallup Poll) Ltd.[25] These polls showed a twenty-point Labour lead over the Conservatives in February and April 1945. The Gallup survey taken closest to polling day, with fieldwork between 24th and 27th June in 195 constituencies, showed a smaller gap between the parties, with 47 per cent voting Labour, 41 per cent voting Conservative, and 10 per cent Liberal. Nevertheless most journalistic commentators expected a close result (the *News Chronicle, Daily Mail*), or a Conservative victory (the *Daily Express, The Times, Financial Times, Glasgow Herald*), as did contemporary observers, based largely on Churchill's personal popularity and international stature.[26]

The localized, volunteer campaign

The party's grassroots organization of voluntary helpers within each constituency remained the bedrock of the campaign. This reflected patterns of constituency party organization which developed in the mid-Victorian era. The British electorate was small in number prior to the First World War: there were about 900 votes per constituency in 1835, 3,500 in 1868, and 5,200 in 1900. With electorates of this size, candidates and their agents could manage local campaigns on a personal basis, contacting many supporters directly. The main work of Conservative Associations lay in maintaining the registration of supporters, and battling in the courts with the registration claims of opponents.[27] The Corrupt Practices Act of 1883 put an end to the bribery and treating which had characterized election management.[28] The 1918 Reform Act transformed the electorate, with the extension of the franchise to women voters over thirty, as well as the removal of complex property qualifications. The further expansion of the franchise to all women in 1928 saw a dramatic increase in numbers. By 1945 there were almost 40,000 voters per seat. Mobilizing support on this scale required an effective party organization within each constituency.

The Conservative party organization had been allowed to fall into disrepair during the Second World War, it had been 'moth-balled' because partisan activity was seen as unpatriotic, and there was minimal co-ordination between its different branches. At grassroots level each of the 640 constituency associations functioned as an independent unit, with its own funds, officers, candidates and publicity staff. Above this loose structure was the Central Council and the Executive Committee of the National Union, which tried to co-ordinate the local party associations, mainly through persuasion. Central Office also produced a variety of pamphlets, handbills, posters and material for speeches. Yet as Lord Wooton summarized the prevailing wisdom of the time, all politics was local: 'Let there be no mistake about it; elections are won in the constituencies and not in the central or area offices. Elections are won on doorsteps of the land, not at great public meetings'.[29] Local parties were gradually transformed from small, informal groups of men engaged at registration societies to mass membership organizations with regular meetings and a more bureaucratic structure of officers. Membership, which as we saw in chapter 5, reached its peak in the period 1945–63, was mobilized during the campaign to leaflet the constituency, canvass voters, plan the local campaign, and activate supporters on election day. Candidates were often adopted just before the election, and they came home from the war to throw themselves enthusiastically into a hectic round of five or six public meetings a night, in village halls, with tours in speaker vans and leaf-letting during the day.

In 1945 the national campaign and the role of central party headquarters remained low-key for both major parties. Prior to the development of the tools of market research, the party leadership developed their party platform and campaign messages in the light of conference debates, political 'hunches', and informal feedback from the constituencies, but without any input derived from the paraphernalia of survey research, focus groups, and political consultants. The Market Research Society was first organized in 1947, but it was not until 1962/3 that these techniques were seriously considered by the major British political parties.[30]

Based on the leadership of Winston Churchill, at the zenith of his long career, the Conservatives remained confident of victory. Under Churchill's leadership Germany had surrendered and Japan was about to fall. The few polls published by Gallup during the months leading up to the campaign pointed to a Labour victory, but they were largely ignored. The party leaders toured the country, addressing public meetings. Attlee covered around seven or eight meetings a day around the country, driven by his wife, and accompanied by a single publicity officer who dealt with the press. The Labour leader made about seventy speeches in total, mostly extemporary with minimal notes.[31] Winston Churchill went on a four-day whistle-stop tour around the country, in a special train, addressing six to eleven cities every day.[32] Meetings within the constituency were the heart of the local campaign. Activity was reported to have declined with the use of radio broadcasts, nevertheless one study reported that in Glasgow alone over 600 school halls had been booked for public meetings during the 1950 campaign.

There was a three-week hiatus between the end of polling day and the announcement of the results, occasioned by the need to collect and count the votes of three million troops abroad. When declared, the results of the 1945 general election proved remarkable in nearly all regards – the largest two-party swing in votes since 1918, the substantial Labour landslide, the size of the Conservative defeat.[33] On 5 July 1945, Labour received 48.3 per cent of the vote, the best result they have ever received, before or since. The number of Labour MPs more than doubled overnight, from 154 to 393. Labour had held two minority administrations in 1924 and 1929 but this was the first Labour government with a comfortable overall majority (of 147 seats), with prospects of a full term in office to implement plans for radical economic and social change. Conservative seats were decimated, from 585 in 1935 to 213 in 1945. The first post-war election can be regarded as a 'critical election',[34] producing a long-term shift in the balance of partisan forces, developing and consolidating a new policy agenda, and establishing the basis for 'normal' two-party politics for successive decades. Conventionally, 1945 is seen as the watershed in British politics, producing the birth of the Westminster two-party system.

The Modernization of Campaigns

The modernization of election campaigns has occurred with similar trends across advanced democracies, although there remain significant cross-national variations produced by such factors as legal regulations controlling political broadcasting and advertising, the structure of the media system (such as the role of public television) and differences in the nature of election contests (such as presidential or parliamentary). In Britain, compared with the post-war period, local activities by volunteers in constituencies, while continuing, have been swamped by the modern campaign where the national battleground is television. As shown in figure 9.1, the main developments in the modern campaign include the evolution of a centrally co-ordinated party campaign, with professional management of media communications; the use of specialist campaign consultants and market researchers; the widespread employment of opinion polls to guide presentation; the adoption of professional advertising and marketing techniques for party political broadcasts and party messages; and the higher costs of professional campaigns. Many of these techniques originated in campaigns in the United States, but since they have been widely deployed, with a trans-Atlantic flow of advisors and techniques, it seems preferable to use the term 'modernization' rather than 'Americanization'.[35]

Constituency campaigning

The modernization of campaigning does not mean that local activity has ceased, far from it, but it does mean that the focus of the campaign battle-field has shifted to the party leadership in national television studios. Most of the major elements of the traditional constituency election, evident in 1945, remain recognizable today. Candidates continue to campaign on doorsteps, with the classic ritual of leafletting and canvassing by party volunteers. Yet public meetings, which were the core of the grassroots contest in 1945, often described as attracting packed crowds of enthusiastic supporters and hecklers, have declined to marginal significance today: only 3.8 per cent of voters report turning out for political meetings in recent campaigns (see table 9.1). The traditional activity of canvassing to identify and mobilize support remains widespread: almost half the public reported that a party worker had called at their doorstep during recent campaigns, with a fairly even balance for canvassers from the Labour and Conservative parties. Party members continue to be active at the grassroots, according to this measure, despite the modernization of the national campaign. Moreover many people reported reading party literature which had been stuffed through their letter box: in the 1992 election almost half said they read a campaign leaflet, while another third said they at least glanced at one.

Studies suggest that constituency campaigning remains important to the results in some marginal seats. Seyd and Whiteley have argued that highly active Labour parties, and to a lesser extent strong party memberships, are very likely to be in constituencies which experience above-average swings in the Labour vote.[36] The authors also found a significant relationship between the level of Conservative campaign spending in a constituency (as a proxy measure of grassroots party activism) and their share of the local vote, confirming the earlier research of Johnstor.[37]

These studies help challenge the conventional wisdom that only the national election matters, but we need to explore local campaigning more directly to understand these preliminary findings. These results may represent a spurious correlation, caused by other local factors (such as the adoption of a popular parliamentary candidate. the performance of the local council, or political controversies in the constituency) which simultaneously boost local party activism/resources *and* their share of voting support. Studies by Denver and Hands, which used surveys of people actually involved in constituency campaigning, found that although Labour and the Liberal Democrats slightly improved their vote through local campaigning, Conservative campaigning has a relatively strong negative effect, which requires further exploration.[38]

Table 9.1 Campaign communications

	Attended campaign meeting	*Party canvasser called*	*Read campaign leaflet*	*Followed campaign newspaper*	*Followed campaign TV/radio*
1964	7.9	34.1	64.1	64.2	81.4
1966				57.7	72.5
1970				50.0	73.6
1983	3.9	47.9		70.2	80.3
1987	2.7	46.7		67.7	81.0
1992	3.8		82.3		

Source: British Election Studies, 1964–92.

Newspapers

Yet overall, no matter its possible significance in marginals, local party activity is swamped by the sheer volume of information conveyed by the mass media. In the BES survey about two-thirds of the public report following campaigns in newspapers. The role of newspapers may be particularly important politically because of the shift in the partisan bias in the

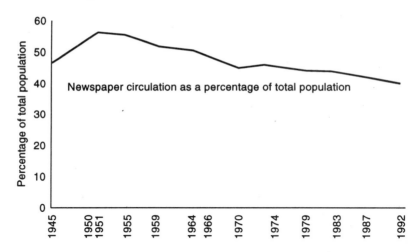

Figure 9.2   Total newspaper circulation, 1945–92

British press. Newspaper readership remains fairly healthy since two-thirds of the public (62 per cent) reads a national newspaper every day. Total circulation figures remain fairly stable over the last two decades – about 14–15 million national newspapers are sold every day – although sales as a proportion of the population have declined somewhat. In 1970 about one-third of the British population bought a national daily newspaper compared with about one-quarter today (see figure 9.2). Readership of tabloids, in particular, has declined over the last decade leading to fierce competition in this sector of the market.

The range of available papers has slightly expanded: there are eleven national daily newspapers in Britain today compared with nine just after the war.[39] The market has changed substantially during this period. Some papers such as the *News Chronicle* and *Daily Sketch* have disappeared. Others have declined sharply in popularity such as the *Daily Express* and *Daily Telegraph*. Others have expanded such as the 'soar-away' *Sun*. Some new ventures such as *The Independent* and *The European* have found their niche in the market. Others like the *News on Sunday* flopped within a few months of launch. In total the five daily 'broadsheets' share about 6 million readers (see figure 9.3).

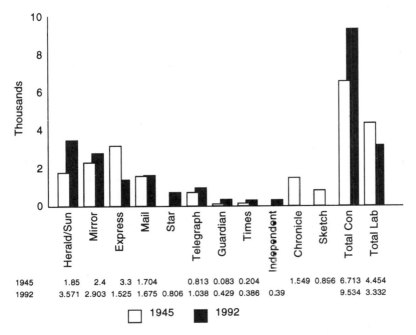

	Herald/Sun	Mirror	Express	Mail	Star	Telegraph	Guardian	Times	Independent	Chronicle	Sketch	Total Con	Total Lab
1945	1.85	2.4	3.3	1.704		0.813	0.083	0.204		1.549	0.896	6.713	4.454
1992	3.571	2.903	1.525	1.675	0.806	1.038	0.429	0.386	0.39			9.534	3.332

□ 1945   ■ 1992

Figure 9.3   Circulation by newspaper

Owned by Rupert Murdoch, *The Times* has a readership of about one million. *The Times* wavered in party allegiance during the 1970s. In the eighties under Murdoch *The Times* has been Conservative, as are two-thirds of its readers, although in the 1992 election it became an outspoken critic of the government's campaign. *The Independent*, launched in 1986, has built up a readership of one million. In the last week of the 1992 campaign, *The Independent*, edited by Whittam-Smith and owned as a private limited company, ran editorials outlining the case for all three major parties. Its readership is equally non-partisan, split evenly between three parties.

The *Guardian* has wavered between being pro-Labour and pro-Liberal Democrat. With a readership of 1.2 million, *The Guardian* caters to the middle class, public sector professionals in social services, education, and local government, and about three-quarters of *Guardian* readers voted non-Conservative in the last election. The *Daily Telegraph* has the highest proportion (72 per cent) of Conservative readers of any paper. It appeals to a slightly older traditional readership and has the most pro-government editorials of the broadsheet press. Although the *Telegraph* has lost many readers in recent decades nevertheless the paper continues to attract the largest share of the quality market, with a circulation of 2.5 million. The *Financial Times* has the smallest circulation among the broadsheets and, somewhat surprisingly, came out against the government in the 1992 election.

The six daily tabloids reach in total about 32 million readers, or just over half the total population. The contrast to the broadsheets is less in size than style of journalism. The tabloids have three main characteristics: a simplification of issues into black and white terms; a lack of proportion or qualification in news stories; and issues are personalized. *The Sun* used to be the *Daily Herald*, which was a solid working-class Labour paper, but in 1969 it was taken over by Rupert Murdoch. In 1974 it switched from Labour to Conservative, and has subsequently become one of the strongest Government supporters. *The Sun* has been the most aggressive and successful British newspaper in expanding its readership. Driven down-market, among all tabloids, the contents are frequently the most racist, sexist and homophobic. *The Sun* currently sells about 3.5 million copies

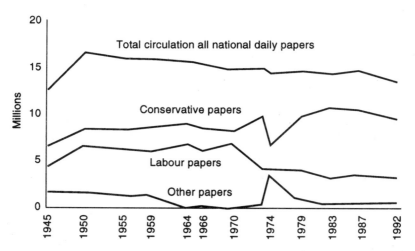

Figure 9.4   The partisan balance of the press
Note: Party affiliation defined by editorial endorsements.

and has ten million readers a day, or about one in five of the British population. It particularly appeals to young men, one quarter of whom read *The Sun*.

The *Daily Mirror* is the other largest selling tabloid, also with about ten million readers. Nevertheless sales have been on the slide; its peak circulation was about 14 million in the Wilson years. Traditionally solidly Labour, recently the paper has been considering abandoning its Labour affiliation, or at least following *The Sun* more downmarket in expanding its coverage of entertainment, sex, and sport. *The Mirror* has experienced financial problems following Robert Maxwell's death and the collapse of his empire.

The other tabloids – the *Daily Mail*, *Daily Express*, *Daily Star* and *Today* – were all Conservative papers in the 1992 election. They vary in tone and readership – the *Mail* and *Express* are the most 'newsy' with a slightly more lower middle class, female Conservative readership. The *Star* and *Today* share the male, skilled working-class readership. The Sunday versions of most papers reflects their stablemates but it is worth noting that *The News of the World* has the largest readership of any British newspaper (13 million).

Concern about the media has increased in recent years as supporters of the opposition parties criticize the press for the predominant Conservative bias. Newspapers in Britain have always been strongly partisan. But over the years the balance between the Conservative and Labour press has moved decisively in favour of the former (see figure 9.4). In the fifties about half the public read a Conservative paper. Today about three-quarters do so. Out of six tabloids only one (the *Daily Mirror*) is Labour. Immediately after the last election *The Sun* proclaimed in a banner headline: 'IT WAS THE SUN WOT WON IT.' Many feel that the pro-Tory bias in the press is unhealthy for democracy, and that it stacks the cards too much against the opposition who have little chance of getting their message across. In particular some believe that in the last week of the 1992 campaign the Tory tabloids created a late but decisive swing to the Conservatives.[40] In Neil Kinnock's words, in his resignation speech after the last election:

> I seek no excuses, and I express no bitterness, when I say that the Conservative supporting press has enabled the Tory party to win yet again, when the Conservative party could not have secured victory by itself on the basis of its record, its programme or its character.

It is true that the partisan balance in the press tipped towards the Conservatives in the seventies, due to the transformation of the *Daily Herald* into *The Sun*, the demise of the *News Chronicle*, and the more partisan tone of *The Times* under Murdoch. In 1992, 70 per cent of the press supported the Conservatives and only two out of eleven national papers backed Labour. Further it seems true that Tory tabloids like *The Sun* have become far less restrained in their partisan criticisms, muddying the line between editorial and news coverage. In the last election *The Sun* adopted a combination of humour, personal invective and punchy copy to pour scorn on Kinnock's leadership. *The Sun* had a sustained campaign contrasting 'untrustworthy' Kinnock to 'honest' John Major. On the last day *The Sun* used a banner headline 'NIGHTMARE ON KINNOCK STREET' which topped eight consecutive pages describing the graphic consequences of a Labour victory, including a warning that loft conversions would need the support of lesbian and gay groups on left-wing councils. Among other stories, it claimed to show Kinnock-free zones if Labour won the last election. And *The Sun* psychic revealed 'exclusively' that Mao and Trotsky would vote Labour from the grave, Queen Victoria and Elvis would vote Conservative, Hitler would vote Loony, and Ghengis Khan doesn't know. On the last day *The Sun* had a front page with Kinnock's head inside a light-bulb, and a banner headline: 'If Kinnock wins today will the last person to leave Britain please turn out the lights.'

But does the press bias matter? Before jumping too hastily to this conclusion, there are reasons to doubt the effects of newspaper partisanship on the *short-term* election results. First, since the fifties there has been the growth of television coverage of the election campaign, and by law this has to remain non-partisan and 'balanced'. There are arguments about whether television achieves a fair balance, but the net impact has been to downplay the influence of newspapers as the main source of campaign information.

Second, if there was a late swing in 1992 this was not confined to readers of the Tory tabloids but was nationwide. The most thorough study of the effects of newspaper readership in the 1992 campaign, by John Curtice and Holli Semetko, was based on the BES panel survey. The study found no evidence that consistently reading the Tory tabloids, or switching to the Tory tabloids, had any effect on vote switching towards the Conservatives during the short campaign, or during the period 1987-92. At most, the Tory press had a marginal impact on perceptions of party images. Curtice and Semetko conclude: 'The Conservative bias of Britain's popular press does not seem to represent a major barrier to a future Labour victory.'[41]

Lastly, in the post-war period the press has always been slightly biased towards the Conservatives. And this did not prevent Labour winning in the early and mid-sixties, or the early seventies. The shift in press bias is more the result of change in one popular tabloid's coverage (*The Sun*) than a widespread change in the whole market. While a more politically diverse market would be healthy in a pluralistic democracy, and while some may deplore the racism, sexism and homophobia rife throughout the tabloid press, nevertheless the bias in the British press probably does not present an insurmountable hurdle for the Labour party.

Television

The campaign coverage which reaches the widest audience is in the electronic media: more than three-quarters of the public reports following the campaign on television or radio. More detailed studies of the audience for different types of media have repeatedly found that television is generally regarded by the public as its most important source of news, and that television is highly rated in providing the most complete, accurate, fair and clearest account of the news.[42] The shift towards reliance primarily on mediated communications seems to have occurred fairly rapidly following the introduction of television news coverage of the campaign in 1959.

The way party campaign communications have been transformed through the growth of professional marketing and public relations techniques, the proliferation of opinion polls, the development of professional management of the party's media messages, and the dominance of the central television campaign, has been covered extensively in a series of recent studies of Britain by Dennis Kavanagh and Margaret Scammell, among others,[43] as well as other countries,[44] and will not be described further here. During the seventies and eighties political marketing has clearly transformed the presentation of party images and campaign messages. Yet the modernization of elections has been only one part of the change. As a result of technological, political and journalistic developments in recent years Britain has been moving cautiously towards the third category of campaigns, the post-modern election

Post-modern campaigns are characterized by more focused communications which allow different messages to be tailored to different groups of target voters, such as the elderly or women. The focus of professionalized campaigns is strategic marketing: finding a clear space in the party contest which promotes a 'product' identity and which maximizes support. In this regard, parties can act as market leaders, challengers, followers or specialists, depending on their level of support and their strategic choices.[45] Downsian theories of party competition in the ideological space, discussed in chapter 7, provide the foundation for much of the more recent interest in political marketing.

Post-modern campaigns also involve a shift from the 'long' towards the 'permanent' campaign, where government and opposition activities throughout the parliament are seen as part of the battle for popularity. And where communication consultants, pollsters and market research analysts are involved in politics on a regular basis, rather than just during the 'official' campaign. While there have been some moves in this direction, particularly in the Labour party, the development has not gone as far as in the United States.[46] In the depths of the Conservatives' unpopularity in 1995, the party was still not polling to seek to identify solutions to this problem, mainly because it had run out of money. There is no pollster in Number 10.

In other regards, despite the gradual growth of satellite and some cable, along with the development of a fifth terrestrial channel, British television has not yet moved down the road from broadcasting to narrow-casting, with the fragmentation of stations, which is evident in the United States, Italy or the Netherlands, producing a fragmentation of audiences.[47] The strength of public sector television has also prevented some of the excessive tabloidization of news and 'infotainment' which has become endemic in America, although commercial pressures have clearly affected ITN, local news and the early evening news. Nor, given the legal regulations controlling the use of political television, has Britain followed the American model of 30-second ads, with the subsequent over-simplification of political messages.

At present British campaigns, despite the significant changes during the eighties, probably remain on balance in the 'modern' rather than 'post-modern' category. Technological developments like the proliferation of digital and satellite stations, and the World Wide Web, could change British communications fairly rapidly in future, but it seems probable that differences in political and media systems wil continue to restrict the wholesale importation of American campaigning. We need to go on to consider what effects the modernization of campaign communications have had on the electorate, particularly the central role of television.

Notes

1 David Swanson and Paolo Mancini, 1996. *Politics, Media and Modern Democracy*. New York: Praeger.

2 See Holli Semetko. 1996, 'The Media', in Lawrence LeDuc, Richard Niemi and Pippa Norris (eds), *Comparing Democracies: Elections and Voting in Global Perspective*. Thousand Oaks, CA: Sage.

3 David Swanson and Paolo Mancini, 1996. *Politics, Media and Modern Democracy*. New York: Praeger.

4 R. B. McCullum and Alison Readman, 1947. *The British General Election of 1945*. London: Geoffrey Cumberlege/Oxford University Press; H. G. Nicholas, 1951. *The British General Election of 1950*. London: Macmillan and Co.

5 See S . B.Chrimes (ed.), 1950. *The General Election in Glasgow, February 1950*. Glasgow: Jackson, Son and Company, Glasgow University Publications; R. S. Milne and H. C. Mackenzie. 1954. *Straight Fight*. London: Hansard Society; R. S. Milne and H. C. Mackenzie, 1958. *Marginal Seat*. London: Hansard Society; A. H. Birch, 1959. *Small Town Politics*. Oxford: Oxford University Press; Frank Bealey, Jean Blondel and W. P. McCann, 1965. *Constituency Politics: A Study of Newcastle-Under-Lyme*. London: Faber and Faber; Richard Rose, 1967. *Influencing Voters*. London: Faber & Faber; Ray Vicker, 1962. *How An Election Was Won*. Chicago: Henry Regnery Company.

6 Paul Lazarsfeld et al., 1944. *The People's Choice*. New York: Columbia University Press; B. Berelson, Paul Lazarsfeld and W. N. McPhee, 1954. *Voting*. Chicago: University of Chicago Press.

7 See, for example, David Butler and Dennis Kavanagh, 1992. *The British General Election of 1992*. London: Macmillan.

8 See, for example, Ivor Crewe and Brian Gosschalk, 1995. *Political Communications: The General Election Campaign of 1992*. Cambridge: Cambridge University Press; Colin Seymour-Ure, 1996. *The British Press and Broadcasting since 1945*. Oxford: Blackwell.

9 Robert Blackburn, 1995. *The Electoral System in Britain*. New York: St. Martin's Press; Rodney Brazier, 1994. *Constitutional Practice*, 2nd edn. Oxford: Clarendon Press.

10 See Michael Pinto-Duschinsky, 1981. *British Political Finance, 1830-1980*. Washington, DC: AEI Press.

11   See, for example, Eric Shaw, 1994. *The Labour Party since 1979*. London: Routledge; Anthony Seldon and Stuart Ball (eds), 1995. *Conservative Century*. Oxford: Oxford University Press; John Stevenson, 1993. *Third Parties since 1945*. Oxford: Blackwell/ICBH.

12   See, for example, Margaret Scammel, 1995. *Designer Politics: How Elections are Won*. London: Macmillan; Bob Franklin, 1994. *Packaging Politics*. London: Edward Arnold; Dennis Kavanagh, 1995. *Election Campaigning*. Oxford: Blackwell.

13   This perspective is developed in Marion Just et al., 1996. *Crosstalk: Citizens, Candidates and the Media in a Presidential Campaign*. Chicago: University of Chicago Press.

14   David Denver and Gordon Hands, 1993. 'Measuring the intensity and Effectiveness of Constituency Campaigning in the 1992 General Election', in David Denver et al. (eds), *British Elections and Parties Yearbook, 1993*. Herts.: Harvester Wheatsheaf.

15   David Butler, 1989. *British General Elections since 1945* Oxford: Blackwell, p. 112.

16   Richard Katz and Peter Mair, 1995. *How Parties Organize*. London: Sage; Anders Widfeldt, 1995. 'Party Membership and Party Representativeness', in Hans-Dieter Klingemann and Dieter Fuchs (eds), *Citizens and the State*. Oxford: Oxford University Press.

17   Lenart, Silvo, 1994. *Shaping Political Attitudes*. Thousand Oaks, CA: Sage.

18   James G. March and Johan P. Olsen, 1989. *Rediscovering Institutions*. New York: The Free Press; Sven Steinmo, Kathleen Thelen and Frank Longstreth (eds), 1994. *Structuring Politics*. New York: Cambridge University Press.

19   See David Farrell, 1996. 'Campaign Strategies and Tactics', in Lawrence LeDuc, Richard Niemi and Pippa Norris (eds), *Comparing Democracies: Elections and Voting in Global Perspective*. Thousand Oaks, CA: Sage.

20   For richly detailed accounts see Austin Mitchell, 1995. *Election '45*. London: Fabian Society; Ray Vicker, 1962. *How an Election Was Won*. Chicago: Henry Regnery Company; R. B. McCallum and Alison Readman, 1947. *The British General Election of 1945*. London: Geoffrey Cumberlege/Oxford University Press.

21   Clement Attlee, 1954. *As it Happened* London: William Heinemann Ltd, p. 141.

22   R. B. McCullum and Alison Readman, 1947. *The British General Election of 1945* London: Geoffrey Cumberlege/Oxford University Press, p. 154.

23   See Colin Seymour-Ure, 1996. *The British Press and Broadcasting since 1945*, 2nd edn. Oxford: Blackwell.

24   H. G. Nicholas, 1951. *The British General Election of 1950*. London: Macmillan, p. 144.

25   The *Daily Express* produced a survey based on the Centre of Public Opinion,

but it did not publish an estimate of voting intentions. R.B. McCallum and Alison Readman, 1947. *The British General Election of 1945.* London: Geoffrey Cumberlege/Oxford University Press, p. 243.

26 Ibid.

27 Stuart Ball, 1994. 'Local Conservatism and Party Organization', in Anthony Seldon and Stuart Ball, *Conservative Century.* Oxford: Oxford University Press.

28 See H. J. Hanham, 1978. *Elections and Party Management.* Sussex: Harvester Press.

29 Lord Wooton, in a speech at Conservative Party Conference, Blackpool, October 1946.

30 Richard Rose, 1967. *Influencing Voters.* London: Faber and Faber.

31 Attlee, 1954. *As it Happened.* London: Heinemarn, p. 144.

32 Martin Gilbert, 1988. *Winston Churchill: Never Despair 1945–1965.* London: Houghton Mifflin, p.50.

33 For details see R. B. McCallum and Alison Readman, 1947. *The British General Election of 1945.* London: Geoffrey Cumberlege/Oxford University Press.

34 For a discussion of the concept of critical elections, and their characteristics, see Walter Dean Burnham, 1970. *Critical Elections and the Mainsprings of American Politics.* New York: Norton.

35 Ralph Negrine and Stylianos Papathanassopoulos, 1996. 'The "Americanization" of Political Communication'. *The Harvard International Journal of Press/Politics* 1(2): 45–62.

36 Patrick Seyd and Paul Whiteley, 1992. *Labour's Grassroots.* Oxford: Clarendon Press.

37 Paul Whiteley, Patrick Seyd and Jeremy Richardson, 1994. *True Blues: The Politics of Conservative Party Membership.* Oxford: Clarendon Press; Patrick Seyd and Paul Whiteley, 1995. 'The Influence of Local Campaigning on the Conservative Vote in the 1992 General Election', in David Broughton et al. (eds), *British Elections and Parties Yearbook, 1994.* London: Frank Cass; Ron Johnston, 1987. *Money and Votes: Constituency Campaign Spending and Election Results.* London: Croom Helm.

38 David Denver and Gordon Hands, 1993. 'Measuring the intensity and effectiveness of constituency campaigning in the 1992 general election', in David Denver et al. (eds), *British Elections and Parties Yearbook, 1993.* Herts.: Harvester Wheatsheaf.

39 James Curren and Jean Seaton, 1993. *Power Without Responsibility,* 4th edn. London: Routledge; Colin Seymour-Ure, 1996. *The British Press and Broadcasting since 1945.* Oxford: Basil Blackwell.

40 For a discussion see Martin Harrop and Margaret Scammel, 1992. 'A Tabloid

War', in David Butler and Dennis Kavanagh, *The British General Election of 1992*. London: Macmillan; David McKie, 1995. 'Fact is Free but Comment is Sacred', in Ivor Crewe and Brian Gosschalk, *Political Communications: The General Election Campaign of 1992*. Cambridge, Cambridge University Press; Richard Webber, 1993. 'The 1992 General Election: constituency results and local patterns of national newspaper readership', in David Denver et al. (eds), *British Elections and Parties Yearbook, 1993*. Herts.: Harvester Wheatsheaf.

41   John Curtice and Holli Semetko, 1994. 'The Impact of the Media', in Anthony Heath et al. (eds), *Labour's Last Chance?* Dartmouth: Aldershot.

42   Barrie Gunter, Jane Sancho-Aldridge and Paul Winstone, 1994. *Television: The Public's View 1993*. London: John Libbey; Barrie Gunter and M. Svennevig, 1988. *Attitudes to Broadcasting Over the Years*. London: John Libbey.

43   Dennis Kavanagh, 1995. *Election Campaigning: The New Marketing of Politics*. Oxford: Blackwell; Margaret Scammell, 1995. *Designer Politics: How Elections are Won*. London: Macmillan; Nicholas O'Shaughnessy, 1990. *The Phenomenon of Political Marketing*. New York: St. Martin's Press. For the history of selection broadcasting see Asa Briggs, 1995. *The History of Broadcasting in the UK: Competition 1955–74*, vol. 5. Oxford: Oxford University Press.

44   Shaun Bowler and David M. Farrel, 1992. *Electoral Strategies and Political Marketing*. Basingstoke: Macmillan; David Butler and Austin Ranney (eds), 1992. *Electioneering*. Oxford: Clarendon Press; Paolo Mancini and David Swanson, 1996. *Politics, Media and Modern Democracy*. New York: Praeger.

45   Neil Collins and Patrick Butler, 1996. 'Positioning Political Parties: A Market Analysis', *The Harvard International Journal of Press/Politics* 1(2): 63-77.

46   Dennis Kavanagh, 1996. 'New Campaign Communications: Consequences for British Political Parties', *The Harvard International Journal of Press/Politics* 1(3).

47   Jay Blumler (ed.), 1992. *Television and the Public Interest: Vulnerable Values in West European Broadcasting*. London: Sage; Preben Sepstrup, 1990. *Transnationalization of Television in Western Europe*. London: Academic Research Monographs; Alessandro Silj, 1992. *The New Television in Europe*. London: John Libbey; John Tydeman and Ellen Jakes Kelm, 1986. *New Media in Europe*. New York: McGraw Hill; Richard Parker, 1995. *Mixed Signals*. New York: Twentieth Century Fund.

10   Media Effects

Given these changes in political communications, what effects have they had on the electorate? Previous research on this topic in Britain, reflecting the concerns of thirty years ago, has usually adopted an unduly narrow conception of media 'effects', conceived as the influence of the media on the vote. The dominant model remains the simple one of 'stimulus–response', without taking account of intervening conditions such as the source, contents, and user.[1] In the United States most recent mainstream studies of voting behaviour and public opinion have absorbed political communications as an integral part of their analysis.[2] There are some classic studies of Britain in the 1960s,[3] which deserve to be re-examined during the changed context of modern television-saturated campaigns. Yet with some notable exceptions,[4] it is striking how far most recent mainstream research on British voting behaviour has excluded the influence of political communications. Like Sherlock Holmes's dog which did not bark, work on media effects in Britain has been remarkable mainly by its absence.

In this chapter media influence is conceptualized as a sequential process from message through successive steps of information, agenda-setting, framing, and persuasion, to an attitudinal or behavioural response. There is great diversity in the research questions, theoretical styles and methods of evidence within the 'media effects' literature. At the broadest level commentators commonly distinguish between three broad schools of thought. Pre-war theories of *propaganda*, impressed by the rapid growth and potential reach of mass communications, stressed that the public could easily be swayed by media techniques.[5] In reaction to this, post-war American studies, analysing the first systematic survey evidence, stressed theories of *minimal consequences*, which downplayed media influence.[6]

Research since the seventies, which has found significant but *limited effects*, can be placed between these extremes. Recent studies in the United States suggest the media influences public opinion through four main avenues: enabling people to keep up with what is happening in the world (learning), defining the major political issues of the day (agenda-setting), influencing who gets blamed or rewarded for events in the news (framing responsibility), and finally shaping people's political choices (persuasion).[7] These four categories represent a sequence of effects in a dynamic process: from growing awareness of a problem (like global warming, conflict in Bosnia, or rising interest rates), to rising concern about these issues, to assigning responsibility for them (whether the British government could have done more to prevent these problems). Finally, this process may persuade voters, if people feel the government has failed to tackle a critical issue. Of these factors, most attention in the British literature has been devoted to the media's (particularly newspapers') partisan powers of persuasion, without taking into account the intermediate steps which may, or may not, lead to changes or reinforcement in voting behaviour.

The neglect of media effects in Britain has probably been driven by a variety of factors. In Britain the field of electoral behaviour has been dominated by survey methods, despite their limitations when dealing with short-term change.[8] There are well-established difficulties in isolating media messages from surrounding events during the campaign, and complex problem of disentangling the reciprocal relationship between media use and political attitudes, using survey data.[9] Alternative research designs require controlled experiments, focus groups or personal interviews which can isolate the short-term effects of specific messages. This neglect has left a vacuum at the heart of our understanding of the linkages between parties and voters. Commentators widely acknowledge the dominance of television in modern British campaigns, but at the same time we admit that we know little about its role. Writers commonly extrapolate from the American research on media effects to Britain, although this may be highly misleading given major differences in the media and political systems.

Recent studies allow some tentative conclusions about media influences on the vote in Britain. Based on the 1983 and 1987 BES, Newton found a significant link between newspaper readership and voting choice, after controlling for political attitudes.[10] Using aggregate data, Webber noted a relationship between readership of the popular tabloids (the *Mirror* and *Sun*), and constituency party swing.[11] Based on the 1987–92 BES panel,

Curtice and Semetko concluded that over the longer term newspapers had a modest influence upon their readers' voting choice, as well as their economic evaluations, although there were few short-term effects.[12] Saunders, Marsh and Ward, as well as Gavin, suggest media coverage shapes perceptions of the economy, thereby producing an indirect effect on the vote.[13] Studies have most commonly focused on the partisan impact of newspapers, where we might expect to find the strongest relationship, although it is difficult to disentangle the direction of causal effects: people may vote for a party influenced by the political content of newspapers, but they may also buy a newspaper sympathetic to their party choice, or both.

Miller produced the most thorough recent study of television effects.[14] Based on a panel survey and content analysis in the 1987 British general election Miller concluded that television coverage had little influence on agenda-setting, or perceptions of party credibility. Yet the press, but not television, had a significant impact on voting choice, and party and leadership images. Studies therefore generally conclude that newspapers have a modest but significant influence upon voting choice in Britain, although the effect of television is less well established.

The influence of the British media on learning, agenda-setting, persuasion and political participation can be re-examined since the 1992 BES cross-sectional included many items of media use. The television scale in this analysis sums ten separate items, such as how often people watched or listened to the news, and saw party political broadcasts (see table 10.1). These items proved reasonably reliable as a scale.[15] The survey also measured readership of daily morning newspapers (type of paper, frequency of use, attention to political coverage, and perceptions of partisan bias), allowing simple measures of newspaper consumption by combining frequency of use plus attention. The five-wave *panel survey*[16] also monitored people's media use and attention during the campaign.

Learning Effects on Political Information

What do voters learn from campaign communication? The answer depends very much upon what is defined as 'knowledge', whether the research tests for the acquisition of specific factual 'information' (for example, the name of the leader of the opposition) or a more general understanding of British politics (such as the position of parties on the major

Table 10.1 Effects of the media on political information

	ALL	R4 Today	BBC2 Newsnight	BBC1 9 News	BBC1 6 News	ITN News at 10	ITN 5.40	Ch4 7 News	Quality newspaper	Tabloid newspaper
Class	.20	.20	.22	.21	.22	.21	.22	.22	.23	.21
Education	.26	.25	.27	.28	.27	.28	.28	.27	.31	.24
Gender	.27	.27	.27	.27	.27	.27	.27	.27	.23	.26
Age	.20	.19	.21	.22	.22	.22	.24	.21	.05	.23
Interest	.13	.14	.14	.14	.15	.15	.14	.14	.08	.15
Media Use	.10	.14	.08	.09	.03	.02	.02	.07	.01	.02
Adjusted R^2	.32	.34	.33	.33	.32	.32	.32	.33	.29	.27

Note: The figures represent standardized beta coefficients in a two-stage ordinary least squared regression model with scores on the Politics Quiz as the dependent variable. All coefficients are significant at the 0.1 level unless otherwise indicated.

Variables are defined as follows:

  Class: respondent's Goldthorpe Heath classification.
  Education: respondent's highest educational qualification.
  Interest: whether respondent cared which party won the election (0/1).
  Media use: how often respondent watched/listened to the specified programme per week.

Source: 1992 BES Cross-sectional Survey.

issues).[17] Studies suggest that the impact of attention to television news and the press is strongest on levels of cognitive knowledge. If so, we would expect that the most regular and attentive viewers of television news would be among the most informed citizens, concerning specific political events, the identity of party leaders, and general awareness of the political system.

One test of political knowledge is the ten-point 'political quiz' in the 1992 BES. This included a series of general statements which people had to judge true or false, ranging from fairly simple items ('The leader of the Labour party is Neil Kinnock') through more general constitutional statements ('British prime ministers are appointed by the Queen'). We might expect the social background and prior interest of respondents to influence both their political knowledge and their use of the media. The model therefore included measures of social class, education, age and gender. Interest was measured by how much respondents cared which party won the general election. After controlling for these factors, what impact did television usage have on general levels of political knowledge?

The results of the regression analysis in table 10.1 show that the strongest influences on political knowledge are education, gender, class, age and interest, as other studies have commonly found. Nevertheless the model also shows that after controlling for these factors, those most attentive to television news also scored highly on the political knowledge scale. The overall model proved reasonably satisfactory (Adjusted R^2 = .32).

Three main issues of interpretation arise from the results. First, this pattern showed considerable variation once we looked in more detail at the source of television news programme. Levels of information proved most strongly associated with the 'high-brow' programs such as listening to *Today* on Radio 4, and watching *Newsnight* on BBC2, the BBC1 *9 O'Clock News*, and Channel 4's *7 O'Clock News*. But the evidence is mixed: it remains unclear why there was not a similar pattern among those who tuned into the ITN *News at Ten* which is pitched at around the same level, or the slightly softer early evening BBC1 and ITN news.

The second question concerns how we interpret the direction of causality where there was a significant association between knowledge and viewership. Regular viewers of the news might be expected to learn more about the political system. Yet, equally plausibly, those who were more knowledgeable about British politics might be expected to watch the news on a regular basis. Without a more precise gauge of what was learnt from specific transmissions, or time-series data measuring changes in political knowledge *or* media use during the campaign, it is difficult to interpret this evidence.

Lastly, it might be expected that there would be a stronger relationship between the print media and levels of political information, because reading newspapers is normally seen as a more demanding activity than watching television. The quality press includes a far wider range of stories, and covers these in more depth, than broadcast news. Nevertheless previous research into the relative information value of print and television news has produced mixed results. After controlling for social background and interest, this study found no significant association between newspaper readership (quality or tabloid) and scores on the political knowledge scale, which seems counter-intuitive. Overall therefore the limited evidence in the BES provides unclear conclusions about the impact of media use on the acquisition of information. These findings remain difficult to interpret for methodological reasons. Rather than survey measures of knowledge and media use, with the 'effects' of media coverage measured well after the event, in the next election we will have more detailed studies of what is learnt and understood from specific media messages concerning particular events, using focus groups and experiments to supplement panel survey data.

Agenda-setting effects

The idea that the media plays a critical role in agenda-setting has a long history. In Cohen's words: 'The press is significantly more than a purveyor of information and opinion. It may not be successful in telling its readers what to think, but it is stunningly successful in telling them what to think about.'[18] The most convincing evidence of agenda-setting comes from experiments by Iyengar and others who have found that a slight shift in the priorities of news coverage can produce a significant change in viewers' beliefs about the importance of these issues.[19] Yet survey evidence in Britain tends to provide little support for this view. In the 1987 general election Miller found that television's agenda was very different to the public agenda, with a far greater focus on security issues. Nevertheless the television coverage of defence had only a very modest impact on public worry about this issue. Moreover, public concern about health and education preceded television's switch towards these issues. Miller concluded that the public and television agendas remained poles apart throughout the 1987 campaign.[20]

To re-examine agenda-setting effects in the last campaign we can measure changes in issue priority in the 1987-92 panel survey. Content analysis of television news found that the most prominent issue on all channels was the economy, with considerable attention devoted to taxation.[21] A similar pattern was clear in front-page lead stories about the election.[22] In addition the explosion of publicity around 'the war of Jennifer's ear' gave a large boost to coverage of health and social services. In 1987 defence played a major role in the campaign.[23] In 1992, in marked contrast, following the fall of the Berlin Wall, changes in central and eastern Europe, and new relations with Russia, the issue of defence almost dropped out of sight on television coverage. Therefore what was the overall impact of the media's agenda on public priorities?

Table 10.2   Agenda-setting effects

Change 1987–92	Taxation		Health & Soc Serv		Defence	
	Low TV	*High TV*	*Low TV*	*High TV*	*Low TV*	*High TV*
Less salient	1.1	.6	5.4	5.6	19.0	21.3
No change	92.1	91.9	71.7	72.4	79.7	77.5
More salient	6.8	7.5	22.9	22.0	1.3	1.2
	100.0	100.0	100.0	100.0	100.0	100.0

Note: Q: At time of general election, importance of . . . as an issue facing Britain? Change in 'most important' issue.

Source: 1987–92 BES Panel Survey, N =1604.

Without detailed time-series data to see whether changes in news coverage followed, or preceded, public concern it is difficult to resolve this question. Nevertheless we can analyse whether public concern about these issues changed from 1987 to 1992, and whether the shift was strongest among the most attentive television viewers. People were asked about the most important issues facing Britain each election survey. Public concern about defence clearly declined substantially between elections, while at the same time increased priority was given to health and social services, and taxation. Changes in the media and public agendas were therefore associated. But, as shown in table 10.2, there is no evidence that the media set the public agenda. The changes in priority given to the issues of defence, health, and taxation were found equally among those most attentive to television news during the campaign, and those least attentive. The agendas of the media, the parties, and the public, shifted between elections, but it is not clear from this evidence who led (if anybody), and who followed.

Persuasion and Voting Choice

Most previous work on media effects in Britain has focused on the vote, particularly the impact of Tory tabloid newspapers on the Conservative lead in successive elections. There has been far less analysis of the influence of television on the vote. To see whether more regular viewers of television news were persuaded to switch parties we can analyse a voter transition matrix of vote change in the 1987–92 elections, based on the panel survey.

Table 10.3   Voter persuasion effects, 1987–92

	1992 Election					
	Con	Lab	Lib Dem	Other	Not vote	
LOW TV						
Con 1987 vote	78.3	4.7	8.8	2.6	5.6	100.0
Lab 1987 vote	4.1	75.8	7.2	4.2	8.7	100.0
Lib Dem 1987 vote	13.6	16.8	60.9	3.0	5.7	100.0
HIGH TV						
Con 1987 vote	82.1	5.0	6.9	1.7	4.3	100.0
Lab 1987 vote	3.5	82.4	6.7	2.8	4.6	100.0
Lib Dem 1987 vote	16.4	31.5	45.9	2.7	3.5	100.0

Source: 1987–92 BES Panel Survey, N =1604.

The results suggest an intriguing pattern (see table 10.3). The most regular viewers of television news were slightly more likely to remain Labour and Conservative supporters than those who watched less television. In contrast, among Liberal Democrat voters in 1987, those who watched more television news were more likely to desert their party than those who watched less. The principal, although not exclusive, beneficiary was the Labour party. We can speculate about possible explanations for this pattern, but these initial results suggest television reinforced support most strongly for the major parties.

Participation, political efficacy and satisfaction

Lastly, what is the effect of the media on public participation, efficacy and satisfaction with the political process? One of the primary functions of the media's coverage of the campaign is to increase information about the choices on offer, stimulating interest in public involvement in the process. Yet in the United States, many commentators have suggested that the increasingly negative slant of television coverage has produced a growing cynicism and disillusionment with American government and public life.[24] What is the evidence in Britain?

Table 10.4   Political satisfaction effects, 1987–92

| | TV usage | | Newspaper usage | |
Change 1987–92	*Low*	*High*	*Low*	*High*
Less satisfaction	17.4	17.0	19.0	15.1
No change	61.4	62.5	59.7	64.8
More satisfaction	21.2	20.5	21.3	20.1
	100.0	100.0	100.0	100.0

Note: Q: 'All in all, how well or badly do you think the system of democracy in Britain works these days?'

Source: 1987–92 BES Panel Survey, N = 1604.

We can measure changes in overall satisfaction with the British political system by the question asked in the 1987-92 BES Panel survey: 'All in all, how well or badly do you think the system of democracy in Britain works these days?' As shown in table 10.4, many people changed their mind about this issue between 1987 and 1992. But the change was not unidirectional: about equal proportions were more or less satisfied with British democracy. Moreover, this pattern was not significantly associated with regular use of television or newspapers.

What is the relationship between television use and electoral participation? As shown in table 10.5, the regression model includes variables for class, age, gender and education, which may all be expected to influence both turnout and media use. After controlling for these factors, television viewership proved to be significantly related to (reported) voter turnout, and indeed to be a better predictor than any of the social background variables. Television use was also significantly related to political efficacy – the

Table 10.5   Participation, efficacy and TV use

| | Vote Turnout | Political Efficacy |
	Beta Sig.	Beta Sig.
Class	.02	.18**
Age	.08*	.21**
Gender	.04	.13**
Education	.04	.26**
Television use	.14**	.19**
Adjusted R²	.03	.24

Note: The figures represent standardized beta coefficients in an ordinary least squared regression model. See table 1 for coding. Turnout is defined as reported turnout (0/1). Political efficacy is a scale from items Q220a to Q220e.
** p $\geqslant$ .01   * p $\geqslant$ .05

Source: 1992 BES Cross-sectional Survey, N = 3534.

sense that citizens could influence government and the political process. Nevertheless, as with earlier evidence, questions about how we interpret this relationship remain. Watching politicians debate the major issues during the campaign may stimulate viewers to feel better informed, more aware of the choices on offer, and therefore better equipped to exercise choice at the ballot box. Nevertheless, those most interested in voting, who want to influence the process, may be more likely to watch campaign news. From this evidence, the old issues of reciprocal causality remain unresolved.

Conclusions

To summarize: we can conclude that there is a significant link between watching television news and levels of political knowledge, participation and efficacy in Britain. Nevertheless the evidence concerning learning is not always consistent (for example, across programmes), and we found no support for the agenda setting effects which are often stressed in American studies. The analysis also suggests that television may have had a modest impact on the vote, since the most attentive viewers were slightly more likely to switch away from the Liberal Democrats between elections. Yet overall we should treat these results with caution because there remain serious problems in disentangling causality through survey measures which cannot relate detailed media messages to specific media effects. Political communications have clearly changed in recent decades, but the effects of this development on British electoral behaviour continues to remain unresolved and in need of further research.

Notes

1   Denis McQuail, 1992. *Mass Communication Theory*. London: Sage, pp. 260–1.
2   See, for example, John Zaller, 1993. *The Nature and Origins of Mass Opinion*. Cambridge: Cambridge University Press; Sam Fopkin, 1994. *The Reasoning Voter*. Chicago: University of Chicago Press.
3   Joseph Trenaman and Denis McQuail, 1961.*Television and the Political Image*. London: Methuen; Jay Blumler and Denis McQuail, 1968. *Television in Politics*. London: Faber & Faber.
4   Pat Dunleavy and Chris Husbands, 1985. *British Democracy at the Crossroads*. London: Allen and Unwin; Anthony Heath et al., 1994. *Labour's Last Chance: The 1992 Election and Beyond*. Hants.: Dartmouth; William Miller, 1991. *Media and Voters: The Audience, Content and Influence of Press and Television at the 1987 General Election*. Oxford: Clarendon Press; William Miller et al., 1990. *How Voters Change: The 1987 British Election Campaign in Perspective*. Oxford: Clarendon Press.
5   Walter Lippmann, 1922. *Public Opinion*. New York: Free Press.
6   Joseph Klapper, 1960. *The Effects of Mass Communications*. New York: Free Press; Paul Lazarsfeld, B. Berelson and H. Gaudet, 1948. *The People's Choice*. New York: Columbia University Press.
7   Stephen Ansolabehre, Roy Behr and Shanto Iyengar, 1993. *The Media Game*. NewYork: Macmillan; Stephen Ansolabehre and Shanto Iyengar, 1995. *Going Negative*. New York: Free Press. Shanto Iyergar and Donald Kinder, 1987.*News that Matters*. Chicago, University of Chicago Press; Shanto Iyengar, 1991. *Is Anyone Responsible? How Television Frames Political Issues*. Chicago: University of Chicago Press; Marion Just et al., 1996. *Crosstalk: Constructing the Campaign*. Chicago: University of Chicago Press.
8   Carl Hovland, 1959. 'Reconciling Conflicting Results from Survey and Experimental Studies of Attitude Change', *American Psychologist* 14: 8–17.
9   Ken Newton, 1993. 'Political Communications', in Ian Budge and David McKay (eds). *The Developing British Political System: the 1990s*, 3rd edn. London: Longman.
10 Ken Newton, 1991 'Do people believe everything they read in the papers?', in Ivor Crewe et al., *British Elections and Parties Yearbook, 1991*. Herts.: Harvester Wheatsheaf.

11 Richard Webber, 1993. 'The 1992 general election: constituency results and local patterns of national newspaper readership', in David Denver et al. (eds), *British Elections and Parties Yearbook*. Herts.: Harvester Wheatsheaf.

12 John Curtice and Holli Semetko, 1994. 'The Impact of the Media', in Anthony Heath et al. (eds), *Labour's Last Chance?* Aldershot: Dartmouth.

13 Neil Gavin, 1992. 'Television News and the Economy: The Pre-Campaign Coverage', *Parliamentary Affairs* 45(4): 596–611; Neil Gavin, 1995. 'Television, the Economy and the Public Mood: the Conservative government in a bad year'. Paper given at EPOP, London, September; Neil Gavin and David Sanders, 1995. 'The Impact of Television Economic News on Public Perceptions of the Economy and Government, 1993–94'. Paper presented at the PSA Conference on Elections, Parties and Public Opinion, Guildhall University; David Sanders, David Marsh and Hugh Ward, 1993. 'The Electoral Impact of Press Coverage of the UK Economy, 1979–87', *British Journal of Political Science* 23; 175–210.

14 William Miller, 1991. *Media and Voters*. Oxford: Clarendon Press.

15 The Cronbach's Alpha for this scale was .66.

16 The ten-item media scale was constructed from the following items:
Q2 07a–g How often do you watch/listen to the following television/radio programme:

BBC1 9 O'clock News
BBC1 6 O'clock News
ITN News at Ten
ITN 5.40 p.m. News
BBC2 Newsnight
Channel 4 7 O'clock News
Radio 4 Today programme

Q2 08. Leading up to a general election, a lot of time on television news is spent on politics and the election campaign. How much attention do you generally pay to these items?
Q2 10a. How often have you seen additional television programmes about the election campaign?
Party Election Broadcasts
Interviews with John Major, Neil Kinnock or Paddy Ashdown

The 1987–92 panel survey includes a more restricted range of items on media usage than the cross-sectional survey.

17 Michael Delli Carpini and Scott Keeter, 1996. *What Americans Know About Politics and Why it Matters*. New Haven, CT: Yale University Press.

18 Bernard Cohen, 1993. *The Press and Foreign Policy*. Berkeley, CA: University of California Press (reprinted from 1963), p. 13.

19 Shanto Iyengar and Donald Kinder, 1987. *News that Matters*. Chicago: University of Chicago Press.

20 William Miller, 1991. *Media and Voters*. Oxford Clarendon Press.

21 Martin Harrison, 1992. 'Politics on the Air', in David Butler and Dennis Kavanagh, *The British General Election of 1992* London: Macmillan; Holli Semetko, Margaret Scammell and Tom Nossiter, 1994. 'The Media's coverage of the campaign', in Anthony Heath et al., *Labour's Last Chance?* Hants.: Dartmouth.

22 Martin Harrop and Margaret Scammel, 1992. 'A Tabloid War', in David Butler and Dennis Kavanagh, *The British General Election of 1992*. London: Macmillan.

23 Martin Harrison, 1988. 'Broadcasting', in David Butler and Dennis Kavanagh. *The British General Election of 1987*. London, Macmillan.

24 Tom Paterson, 1993. *Out of Order*. New York: Vintage; Robert Putnam, 1995. 'Tuning In, Tuning Out: The Strange Disappearance of Social Capital in America', *PS: Political Science and Politics* 27(4): 564–83; Pippa Norris, 1996. 'Does Television Erode Social Capital? A Reply to Putnum', *Political Science and Politics* 28(4).

Conclusions:
Electoral Reform and
Electoral Change

As the first part argued, electoral behaviour should be located within the broader context of the 'Westminster model' of responsible party government. In the ideal model this system promotes consensual and effective government, shackling power with accountability. Parties need to compete with alternative platforms laying out their main proposals, with the main battleground over the classic economic and social issues dividing conservatives and socialists. Voters need to chose parties based on evaluations of their record and policies. And free and fair elections need to translate votes into seats, with a modest swing in two-party support producing alternation of the party in government. In the early post-war years many believed this system worked since balanced two-party competition in central and local government reflected widespread support for the two major parties among the electorate, with elections providing the essential democratic foundation for this political system.

In recent years, many are less sanguine about the practice of responsible party government in Britain. The mechanism seems cracked. As we have observed, during the seventies the electorate becomes more loosely attached to the major parties, accompanied by a growth in waverers and late deciders, with party support ebbing and flowing into unfamiliar channels. This decade also experienced a modest restructuring in the social basis of party support, with class divisions fading slightly over time, while other social cleavages like the north–south regional divide became more pronounced. Trends during the last half-century suggests that partisan loyalties and class voting have declined less as the result of steady, secular trends than due to strategic shifts in party competition, particularly in the ideological position of the major parties in comparison with public opinion. Moreover there have been dramatic changes in the context within which voters decide, with the modernization of campaign communications. The shift from decentralized, amateur, and candidate-centred pre-modern campaigns of the post-war years to the centralized, professional, co-ordinated and televised modern campaign has been immense, with the promise of further change still to come in political communications.

Nevertheless despite significant changes in voters, parties and the media, the actual outcome of recent elections looks remarkably familiar. Labour and the Conservatives continue to dominate parliamentary politics, although local government is more commonly a three-horse race. Despite changes in the electorate, the institutional structure of the British electoral system constrains and maintains British politics in familiar channels. Yet although inherently conservative, institutions have the capacity to change, sometimes with a clear breakdown, following shocks to their external environment. In the powerful model of 'punctuated' equilibrium, developed by Stephen Krasner,[1] institutions are characterized by long periods of stability which are periodically interrupted by crises that bring about abrupt change, after which institutional stasis again takes hold.

This notion helps us to understand the nature of electoral change in Britain. The two-party duopoly of central government has persisted largely undisturbed for the last half-century, despite more erratic support for the two major parties in recent decades. Without secure electoral foundations, structural changes to the Westminster model – such as potential splits within the Conservative party over Europe, or significant reforms to the constitution and electoral system – have the capacity greatly to alter the familiar landscape of post-war British politics. As in New Zealand, Japan and Italy, dissatisfaction with the workings of the political system have increased demands for electoral and constitutional reform.[2] Even modest changes to the electoral rules of the game could decisively alter the familiar pattern of party competition. In this concluding chapter we need to consider the potential for electoral change produced by electoral reform.

In evaluating the electoral system the debate in Britain has produced conflict about means (concerning the effects of adopting different electoral systems) but even more fundamentally about ends (about the primary objective of the electoral system). As Iain McLean noted, 'The PR school looks at the composition of a parliament; majoritarians look at its decisions.'[3] Advocates of the Westminster model argue that responsible party government takes precedence over the inclusion of all parties in strict proportion to their share of the vote. The primary purpose of general elections in this model is to elect a House of Commons which functions as an indirect electoral college to produce an effective, stable executive. The way the system penalizes minor parties can be seen by proponents as a virtue as it thereby prevents fringe groups like the National Front or the British Communist Party from acquiring representative legitimacy.

For critics, the case for reform has been based on the 'unfairness' to minor parties which achieve a significant share of the vote, like the Liberal Democrats, but which return few members because their support is dispersed geographically. In recent years other features of the system have also generated pressures for reform, including demands for a stronger voice for Scotland and for the inclusion of more women in Parliament. The debate over electoral reform has gone through several phases. In 1975 Samuel Finer published an influential set of essays criticizing the British system.[4] The following year Lord Blake produced a report for the Hansard Society, recommending that Britain adopt the Additional Member System used in Germany.[5] The group Conservative Action for Electoral Reform (proposing STV) was established in 1974, the Conservative party seriously debated electoral reform at its 1975 conference, and in 1976 Lord Hailsham published an influential lecture expressing concern that Britain was moving towards an 'elected dictatorship', with insufficient constitutional checks on government.[6] Conservative debate died down following Mrs Thatcher's substantial majority in the 1979 election, although the subsequent growth of centre party support, and Labour's years in the opposition wilderness, heightened the salience of the issue.

The 1983 election reinforced concern about the unfairness of the system for centre parties; only 23 Liberal–SDP Alliance MPs were elected despite gaining 25.4 per cent of the vote. In contrast 209 Labour MPs were returned for 27.6 per cent of the vote. Moreover, the development of the 'north–south' divide since the mid-1950s,[7] and the revival of nationalism in Scotland, has led to increased support for an independent Scottish parliament. The Scottish Constitutional Convention was revived in 1989 to consider the most appropriate constitutional structure and electoral system for such a body. This provided an opportunity to rethink these requirements without the in-built conservatism created by the vested interests of incumbents, and the recommendations strongly influenced the constitutional debate in England and Wales.[8]

Demands from Scotland combined with demands for change generated by increasing concern about women's representation in Parliament, and the growing recognition that this is affected by the electoral system.[9] As we have seen in 1992 women were less than one in ten MPs, a level far behind female representation in most European Union countries. As discussed in chapter 8, this has produced a number of initiatives within parties, with the Labour party adopting a series of radical steps, including the use, now abandoned, of all-women shortlists for half their target seats. The Scottish Convention, concerned about this issue, considered various options including the introduction of legally binding gender quotas for party lists of candidates, dual member constituencies designated by gender, and the use of the Additional Member electoral system, combining single-member districts with party lists.

The last wave in this debate gathered momentum in the nineties, fuelled by greater concern over the imbalance of the two-party system with the return of successive Conservative administrations after 1979; continued dissatisfaction with the fairness of first-past-the-post for the centre parties; external pressures including the European Union resolution to adopt a uniform system for elections to the European Parliament; the publication of the reports of the Scottish Constitutional Convention; the rediscovery of the issue of 'citizenship' and constitutional reform by the soft left, exemplified by Charter '88; pressure from the women's movement to boost the number of women MPs; and last, but by no means least, Labour's hesitant, lukewarm and mixed conversion to the cause of electoral reform. This change in the Labour party has been within the context of a wider questioning of constitutional conventions.[10] Following their years in the electoral wilderness, under successive Conservative administrations, the Labour party has moved tentatively towards supporting electoral reform, although the party remains divided, and there is considerable disagreement among the opposition about the most appropriate alternative to first-past-the-post at different levels of government.

Different Types of Electoral Systems

There are many complex issues within 'electoral reform', including changes in the basic system of translating votes into seats for different types of contest, reforms of party financing requirements, and reform of the upper chamber. The current debate about votes into seats focuses on three main options for Britain: the Alternative Vote (AV), the Single Transferable Vote (STV), and the Additional Member System (AMS). In addition there are electoral systems based on party lists, common throughout Europe, although not on the mainstream agenda in Britain. There are many variations within these types but we can briefly outline the basic features of each system.[11]

Alternative vote

The introduction of Alternative Voting would involve least change from the present system. The system is used in elections to the Australian House of Representatives. Britain would continue to be divided into about 650 constituencies, each with one MP. Instead of a simple 'X', voters would number their preferences among candidate (1,2,3...). To win, candidates need an absolute majority of votes. Where no one gets over 50 per cent after first preferences are counted, then the person at the bottom of the pile is eliminated, and their votes redistributed amongst the other candidates. The process continues until an absolute majority is secured.

Single transferable vote

The system of Single Transferable Vote (STV) is currently favoured by the Liberal Democrats. It is used in Ireland, Malta and elections to the Australian Senate. Britain would be divided into multi-member constituencies each with about four or five MPs. Parties would put forward as many candidates as they thought could win in each constituency. Voters would number their preferences among candidates (1,2,3,4...). The total number of votes would be counted, then this total would be divided by the number of seats in the constituency to produce a quota. To be elected, candidates must reach the minimum quota. When the first preferences are counted, if no candidates reach the quota, then the person with the least votes is eliminated, and their votes redistributed according to second preferences. This process continues until all seats are filled.

Party lists systems

Electoral systems based on party lists are widespread throughout Europe. These lists may be open as in Norway, Finland, the Netherlands and Italy, in which case voters can express preferences for particular candidates within the list. Or they may be closed as in Israel, Portugal, Spain and Germany, in which case voters can only select the party, and the ranking of candidates is determined by the political party. The rank order on the party list determines which candidates are elected, for example the top ten to fifteen names. Party lists may also be national as in Israel, where all the country is one constituency divided into 120 seats. Or party lists may be regional as in Belgium, where there are seven regions each sub-divided into between 2–34 seats. Votes are allocated to seats based on the minimum quota, which can be calculated in a number of ways. In the simplest (the Hare quota) the total number of valid votes is divided by the total number of seats to be allocated.

Additional member system

The Additional Member System combines single member and party lists. This system has been recommended by the Constitutional Convention for the Scottish Parliament. It could be implemented in different ways. In Germany, for example, electors have two votes. Half the Members of Parliament would be elected in single-member constituencies. These elections could be based on first-past-the-post, as at present, or Alternative Voting. The remaining MPs would be elected from regional or national party lists. As above, party lists of candidates could be open or closed. Parties which receive less than a specified minimum threshold of votes (such as 5 per cent) would not be entitled to any seats. The total number of seats which a party receives in Germany is based on the Niemeyer method, which ensures that seats are proportional to votes. Smaller parties which received 10 per cent of the vote, but which did not win any single-member seats outright, for example, would be topped up through their party lists so that they had 10 per cent of all the seats in parliament. In recent years AMS has been adopted with variations in systems that have been reformed in New Zealand, Russia and Italy. There are a number of complex permutations within this system, for example, the proportion of parliamentary seats allocated under each method, the use of minimum vote thresholds, and the formula for redistributing votes.

First-past-the-post

Lastly, defenders of the status quo call for retaining first-past-the-post single-member constituencies with a simple plurality vote, as at present.

Each of these options would have very different consequences in terms of the election of minor parties, the proportionality of votes to seats, the exaggerative bias of the electoral system for the winning party, the nature of the choice facing the electorate, and the social representation of women and ethnic minorities.[12] After much internal debate, revolving around the Plant Report, Labour remains divided between modernizers who favour the additional (or mixed) member system, compromisers who prefer the additional (or supplementary) vote, and traditionalists who want to retain first-past-the-post for the Commons.[13] In 1996 official Labour policy proposes the additional member system for a Scottish parliament, reformed procedures for Westminster, and removing the voting rights of hereditary peers in the House of Lords. Following the New Zealand precedent, Labour has pledged to hold a referendum on reform should they be returned to power. At the time of writing it is not clear exactly what policies will become adopted in the official Labour party manifesto.[14] In contrast the Liberal Democrats continue to advocate the single transferable vote for Westminster. The Scottish National party favours a combination of the alternative vote (for two-thirds of seats) and the additional member system (for the remainder) for a Scottish parliament. Finally the Conservatives remain staunch defenders of first-past-the-post for elections at every level. In the mid-nineties the modernization of new Labour has moved the two major parties together on many of the core economic issues which formerly divided them. Nevertheless a new cleavage in party competition has developed around constitutional issues, with only the Conservatives in favour of maintaining the status quo. Public opinion remains ambiguous on this issue, in large part because most people, confronted with abstract and hypothetical choices, are strongly influenced by the framing effects of different question-wordings.[15] By the mid-nineties public opinion seems increasingly disenchanted with how the country is governed, but unclear about the most effective direction for reform.[16]

Electoral Reform and Representative Government

This book has argued that the primary function of elections in a representative democracy is to provide an essential linkage between voters and political leaders. In the Westminster model citizens have relatively few direct channels to express their concerns and priorities, and even fewer mechanisms to hold their representatives accountable. The active minority can articulate their demands through mobilizing within social movements, interest groups and community associations. Well-informed citizens participate through contacting individual officials, elected representatives or the media. People can express themselves collectively through petitions, demonstrations and protest meetings. But in Britain, civic engagement through these mechanisms remains not only a minority activity, but also one heavily dependent upon unequal resources of wealth, education and skills.[17] Political activity in Britain is sustained by a small segment of the population, with disparities in participation which are even more pronounced than in the United States. Therefore, only elections – local, European and general – let the majority of British citizens become involved in public life on a regular basis, and only elections connect the policy preferences of voters to parties which remain accountable for their actions in government. The quality of civic engagement, public participation and representative democracy in Britain, therefore, rests on how effectively elections function as a link between citizens and leaders. If there are grounds for believing that the mechanisms of responsible party government have come to rest on a cracked foundation, with increasing public disenchantment with the political system, then the demands for reforms to remedy the democratic deficit can only be expected to get louder.

Notes

1   Stephen D. Krasner, 1993. 'Approaches to the State: Alternative Conceptions and Historical Dynamics', *Comparative Politics* 16(2): 223–46.

2   See Pippa Norris (ed.), 1995. 'The Politics of Electoral Reform'. Special issue of the *International Political Science Review* 16(1).

3   Iain McLean, 1991. 'Forms of Representation and Systems of Voting', in David Held (ed.), *Political Theory Today*. Stanford, CA: Stanford.

4   Samuel Finer, 1975. *Adversary Politics and Electoral Reform*. London: Wingram.

5   Lord Blake, 1976. *Report of the Hansard Society on Electoral Reform*. London: Hansard Society.

6   Lord Hailsham, 1976. *Elective Dictatorship*. London: BBC.

7   John Curtice and Michael Steed, 1982. 'Electoral Choice and the Production of Government: The Changing Operation of the Electoral System in the United Kingdom since 1955', *British Journal of Political Science* 12: 249–98; Ron Johnston, C. J. Pattie and J. G. Alsopp, 1988. *A Nation Dividing*. London: Longman; J. Lewis and A. Townsend (eds), 1989. *The North–South Divide*. London: Paul Chapman.

8   Alice Brown, David McCrone and Lindsay Paterson, 1996. *Politics and Society in Scotland*. London: Macmillan; Scottish Constitutional Commission, 1994. *Further Steps: Towards a Scheme for Scotland's Parliament*. Edinburgh: Cosla; Scottish Constitutional Convention, 1990. *Towards Scotland's Parliament*. Edinburgh: Cosla; Alice Brown, 1995. 'Legislative Recruitment in Scotland: The Implications for Women of a New Parliament'. Paper presented at the ECPR Joint Workshops, Bordeaux.

9   Pippa Norris, 1996. 'Legislative Recruitment', in Lawrence LeDuc, Richard Niemi and Pippa Norris, *Comparing Democracies: Elections and Voting in Global Perspective*. Thousand Oaks, CA: Sage.

10   David Marquand, 1992. 'Halfway to Citizenship', in Martin Smith and Joanna Spear (eds), *The Changing Labour Party*. London: Routledge.

11   For a detailed discussion of electoral systems and their consequences see Arend Lijphart, 1994. *Electoral Systems and Party Systems*. Oxford: Oxford University Press; Giovanni Sartori, 1994. *Comparative Constitutional Engineering*. London: Macmillan; Andre Blais and Louise Massicotte, 1996. 'Electoral Systems', in Lawrence LeDuc, Richard Niemi and Pippa Norris (eds), *Comparing Democracies: Elections and Voting in Global Perspective* Thousand Oaks, CA: Sage; David Farrell, 1996. *Comparing Electoral Systems*. Herts.: Harvester Wheatsheaf.

12   Patrick Dunleavy, Helen Margetts and Stuart Weir, 1992. *Replaying the 1992 General Election: How Britain would have voted under alternative electoral*

systems. London: LSE Public Policy Paper No. 3. London; Patrick Dunleavy, Helen Margetts and Stuart Weir, 1992. 'How Britain would have voted under alternative electoral systems in 1992'. *Parliamentary Affairs* 45(4).

13 See Martin Linton and Mary Georghiou, 1993. *Labour's Road to Electoral Reform.* London: Labour Campagn for Electoral Reform.

14 For the nature of the Labour party debate see 'Plant in Retrospect', *Representation* 1995, 33(2). See also *New Labour, new life for Britain.* Labour Party, London July 1996.

15 John Curtice, 1991. 'Not such a big idea', *New Statesman & Society* 4 (167): 16–18; Patrick Dunleavy and Stuart Weir, 1991. 'Left for rights: voters are more radical than Labour thinks', *New Statesman & Society* 4 (148): 15–17; Peter Kellner, 1991. 'Do we favour reform? It depends how you ask us', *Independent*, 2 May; Peter Kellner, 1991. 'The Devil you Know Factor', *Representation* 31(113), Spring/Summer, 10-12; *The State of the Nation, 1991.* MORI, Rowntree Trust. March 1991; Stuart Weir, 1992. 'Waiting for Change: public opinion and electoral reform', *Political Quarterly* 63(2), April/June; Stuart Weir and Patrick Dunleavy, 1992. 'Terminal hubris', *New Statesman & Society* 5(198): 21–4.

16 See John Curtice and Roger Jowell, 1995. 'The Sceptical Electorate', in Roger Jowell et al. (eds), *British Social Attitudes, the 12th Report.* Hants.: Dartmouth; *The State of the Nation, 1995.* MORI. London: Joseph Rowntree Trust.

17 Geraint Parry, George Moyser and Neil Day, 1992. *Political Participation and Democracy in Britain.* Cambridge: Cambridge University Press, p. 44.

Bibliography

Abrams, Philip and Richard Brown (eds), 1984. *UK Society: Work, Urbanism and Inequality*. London: Weidenfeld and Nicolson.

Abramson, Paul and Ronald Inglehart, 1995. *Value Change in Global Perspective*. Ann Arbor, MI: University of Michigan Press.

Alderman, Geoffrey, 1989. *Britain: A One-Party State*. London: Christopher Helm.

Alford, Robert, 1964. *Party and Society*. London: Murray.

Almond, Gabriel and Sidney Verba, 1963. *The Civic Culture*. Princeton, NJ: Princeton University Press.

Amery, Leo, 1947. *Thoughts on the Constitution*. Oxford: Oxford University Press.

Amin, Kaushika and Robin Richardson, 1992. *Politics for All: Equality, Culture and the General Election of 1992*. London: Runnymede Trust.

Ansolabehere, Stephen, Roy Behr and Shanto Iyengar, 1993. *The Media Game*. New York: Macmillan.

—— and Shanto Iyengar, 1995. *Going Negative*. New York: Free Press.

Anwar, Muhammad, 1986. *Race and Politics*. London: Tavistock.

Attlee, Clement, 1954. *As it Happened*. London: William Heinemann.

Bagehot, Walter. 1964. *The English Constitution*. London: C. Watt.

Bartolini, Stefano and Peter Mair, 1990. *Identity, Competition and Electoral Availability: The Stabilization of European Electorates, 1885–1985*. Cambridge: Cambridge University Press.

Baxter, S. and M. Lansing, 1980. *Women and Politics: The Invisible Majority*. Ann Arbor, MI: University of Michigan Press.

Bealey, Frank, Jean Blondel and W. P. McCain, 1965. *Constituency Politics: A Study of Newcastle-under-Lyme*. London: Faber & Faber.

Bean, Clive and Anthony Mughan, 1989. 'Leadership Effects in Parliamentary Elections in Australia and Britain', *American Political Science Review* 83: 1165–79.

Beer, Samuel H., 1969. *Modern British Politics*. London Faber & Faber.

Bell, Daniel, 1973. *The Coming of Post-Industrial Society*. New York: Basic Books.

Berelson, B., Paul Lazarsfeld and W. N. McPhee, 1954. *Voting*. Chicago: University of Chicago Press.

Birch, Anthony Harold, 1959. *Small Town Politics*. Oxford: Oxford University Press.

——— 1964. *Representative and Responsible Government*. London: George Allen & Unwin.

——— 1993. *The Concepts and Theories of Modern Democracy*. London: Routledge.

Blackburn, Robert, 1995. *The Electoral System in Britain*. New York: St. Martin's Press.

Blake, Lord, 1976. *Report of the Hansard Society on Electoral Reform*. London: Hansard Society.

Blondel, Jean, 1963. *Votes, Parties and Leaders*. Harmondsworth: Penguin.

——— 1995. *Comparative Government*. Hemel Hempstead: Harvester Wheatsheaf.

Blumler, Jay (ed.), 1992. *Television and the Public Interest: Vulnerable Values in West European Broadcasting*. London: Sage.

——— and Denis McQuail, 1968. *Television in Politics*. London: Faber & Faber.

Bogdanor, Vernon, 1981. *The People and the Party System: The Referendum and Electoral Reform in British Politics*. Cambridge: Cambridge University Press.

——— 1983. *Multi-Party Politics and the Constitution*. Cambridge: Cambridge University Press.

——— (ed.), 1983. *Liberal Party Politics*. Oxford: Oxford University Press.

——— (ed.), 1985. *Representatives of the People? Parliamentarians and Constituents in Western Democracies*. London: Gower.

——— and David Butler, 1983. *Democracy and Elections: Electoral Systems and their Political Consequences*. Cambridge: Cambridge University Press.

——— 1992. 'The 1992 General Election and the British Party System', *Government and Opposition* 27(3).

——— and William Field, 1993. 'Lessons of History: Core and Periphery in British Electoral Behaviour, 1910–1992', *Electoral Studies* 12(3): 203–24.

Bradley, Ian, 1981. *Breaking the Mould? The Birth and Prospects of the Social Democratic Party*. Oxford: Martin Robertson.

Brand, Jack, 1978. *The Nationalist Movement in Scotland*. London: Routledge and Kegan Paul.

Brazier, Rodney, 1994. *Constitutional Practice*. Oxford: Clarendon Press.

Brook, Lindsay et al., 1992. *British Social Attitudes: Cumulative Sourcebook*. London: SCPR/Gower.

Broughton, David, 1995. *Public Opinion Polling and Politics in Britain*. Hemel Hempstead: Harvester Wheatsheaf.

——— et al. (eds), 1995. *British Elections and Parties Yearbook*. London: Frank Cass.

Brown, Alice, David McCrone and Lindsay Paterson, 1996. *Politics and Society in Scotland*. London: Macmillan.

Budge, Ian and Dennis Fairlie, 1983. *Explaining and Predicting Elections*. London: George Allen & Unwin.

—— and Hans Keman, 1990. *Parties and Democracy*. Oxford: Oxford University Press.

——, Ivor Crewe and D. Fairlie (eds), 1976. *Party Identification and Beyond*. New York: Wiley.

——, David Robertson and Derek Hearl (eds), 1987. *Ideology, Strategy and Party Change: Spatial Analysis of Post-War Election Programmes in 19 Democracies*. Cambridge: Cambridge University Press.

Burch, Martin and Michael Moran, 1985. 'The Changing Political Elite', *Parliamentary Affairs* 38(1): 1–15.

Burnham, Walter Dean, 1970. *Critical Elections and the Mainsprings of American Politics*. New York: W. W. Norton.

Butler, David, 1963. *The British Electoral System since 1918*. Oxford: Oxford University Press.

—— 1986. *Governing Without a Majority*. London: Macmillan.

—— 1989. *British General Elections since 1945*. Oxford: Blackwell.

—— and Gareth Butler, 1994. *British Political Facts, 1900–1994*. London: Macmillan.

—— and Dennis Kavanagh, 1985. *The British General Election of 1983*. London: Macmillan.

—— and Dennis Kavanagh, 1992. *The British General Election of 1992*. London: Macmillan.

—— and Austin Ranney, 1994. *Referendums Around the World: The Growing Use of Direct Democracy*. Washington, DC: AEI Press.

—— and Donald Stokes, 1974. *Political Change in Britain* (2nd edition). London: Macmillan.

—— and Austin Ranney, (eds), 1992. *Electioneering*. Oxford: Oxford University Press.

——, Austin Ranney and Howard Rae Penniman (eds), 1981. *Democracy at the Polls: A Comparative Study of Competitive National Elections*. Washington, DC: AEI Press.

Butt, Ronald, 1967. *The Power of Parliament*. London: Constable.

Cain, Bruce, John Ferejohn and Morris Fiorina, 1987. *The Personal Vote: Constituency Service and Electoral Independence*. Cambridge, MA: Harvard University Press.

Campbell, Angus, Philip Converse, Warren E. Miller and Donald E. Stokes, 1960. *The American Voter*. New York: John Wiley and Sons.

Casino, Cesar, 1995. 'Party Government: The Search for a Theory –

Introduction', *International Political Science Review* 16(2): 123–6.

Chrimes, S. B. (ed.), 1950. *The General Election in Glasgow, February 1950*. Glasgow: Jackson, Son and Company/Glasgow University Publications.

Clubb, Jerome M., William H. Flanigan and Nancy H. Zingale, 1990. *Partisan Realignment: Voters, Parties and Government in American History*. Boulder, CO: Westview Press.

Coates, David, 1980. *Labour in Power?* London: Longman.

Converse, Philip and Roy Pierce, 1986. *Political Representation in France*. Cambridge, MA: Harvard University Press.

—— and Roy Pierce, 1986. 'Measuring Partisanship', *Political Methodology* 11: 143–66.

Cook, Chris, 1993. *A Short History of the Liberal Party, 1900–92*. London: Macmillan.

Craig, F. W. S., 1989. *British Electoral Facts, 1832–1987*. Aldershot,: PRS/Dartmouth.

Crewe, Ivor (ed.), 1991. *British Elections and Parties Yearbook 1991*. Hemel Hempstead: Harvester Wheatsheaf.

——, Anthony Fox and Neil Day, 1995. *The British Electorate 1963–1992: A Compendium of Data from the British Election Studies* (2nd edition). Cambridge: Cambridge University Press.

—— and Martin Harrop, 1990. *Political Communications: The General Election Campaign of 1987*. Cambridge: Cambridge University Press.

—— and Anthony King, 1995. *The Birth, Life and Death of the Social Democratic Party*. Oxford: Oxford University Press.

—— and David Denver (eds), 1985, *Electoral Change in Western Democracies: Patterns and Sources of Electoral Volatility*. London: Croom Helm.

—— and Brian Gosschalk (eds), 1995. *Political Communications: The General Election Campaign of 1992*. Cambridge: Cambridge University Press.

—— 1984. 'The Electorate: Partisan Dealignment Ten Years On', in Hugh Berrington (ed.), *Change in British Politics*. London: Frank Cass.

—— 1985. 'Great Britain', in Ivor Crewe and David Denver (eds), *Electoral Change in Western Democracies*. London: Croom Helm.

—— 1985. 'How to Win a Landslide Without Really Trying', in Austin Ranney (ed.), *Britain at the Polls, 1983*. Washington, DC: AEI Press.

——, Pippa Norris and Robert Waller, 1992. 'The 1992 General Election: Conservative Hegemony or Labour Recovery?', in Pippa Norris et al. (eds), *British Parties and Elections Yearbook, 1992*. Hemel Hempstead: Harvester Wheatsheaf.

—— and Donald Searing, 1988. 'Mrs Thatcher's Crusade: Conservatism in Britain, 1972–1986', in B. Cooper et al. (eds), *The Resurgence of Conservatism in Anglo-American Democracies*. Durham, NC: Duke University Press.

—— 1982. 'Is Britain's Two-party System Really About to Crumble?', *Electoral Studies* 1(3): 275–313.

—— 1986. 'On the Death and Resurrection of Class Voting: Some Comments on How Britain Votes', *Political Studies* 34(4): 620–38.

——, Bo Sarlvik and Jim Alt, 1977. 'Partisan Dealignment in Britain 1964–1974', *British Journal of Political Science* 7: 129–90.

—— and Donald Searing, 1988. 'Ideological Change in the British Conservative Party', *American Political Science Review* 82(2): 361–85.

Curran, James and Jean Seaton, 1993. *Power Without Responsibility* (4th edition). London: Routledge.

Curtice, John, 1996. 'Class Dealignment Revisited'. Paper presented at the Political Studies Association Annual Conference, Glasgow.

—— 1988. 'One Nation', in Roger Jowell et al., *British Social Attitudes, the 5th Report*. Aldershot: Dartmouth.

—— 1992. 'The North–South Divide', in Roger Jowell et al., *British Social Attitudes, the 9th Report*. Aldershot: Dartmouth.

—— and Roger Jowell, 1995. 'The Sceptical Electorate', in Roger Jowell et al. (eds), *British Social Attitudes: The 12th Report*. Aldershot: Dartmouth Press.

—— and Michael Steed, 1992. 'Appendix 2: The Results Analysed', in David Butler and Dennis Kavanagh, *The British General Election of 1992*. London: Macmillan.

—— 1983. 'The Alliance's First National Test', *Electoral Studies* 2(1).

—— and Michael Steed, 1982. 'Electoral Choice and the Production of Government: The Changing Operations of the Electoral System in the United Kingdom since 1955', *British Journal of Political Science* 12: 249–98.

Daalder, Hans and Peter Mair (eds), 1985. *Western European Party Systems*. London: Sage.

Dalton, Russell, 1994. *The Green Rainbow*. New Haven, CT: Yale University Press.

—— 1996. *Citizen Politics* (2nd edition). Chatham, NJ: Chatham House.

——, Scott Flanagan and Paul Allen Beck (eds), 1984. *Electoral Change in Advanced Industrial Democracies*. Princeton, NJ: Princeton University Press.

—— 1985. 'Political Parties and Political Representation', *Comparative Political Studies* 17: 267–99.

Delli Carpini, Michael and Scott Keeter, 1996. *What Americans Know about Politics and Why it Matters*. New Haven, CT: Yale University Press.

Denver, David, 1994. *Elections and Voting Behaviour*. Hemel Hempstead: Harvester Wheatsheaf.

—— and Gordon Hands (eds), 1992. *Issues and Controversies in British Electoral Behaviour*. Hemel Hempstead.: Harvester Wheatsheaf.

—— et al. (eds) (1993). *British Elections and Parties Yearbook, 1993*. Hemel Hempstead: Harvester Wheatsheaf.

—— 1983. 'The SDP–Liberal Alliance: The End of the Two-Party System?', *West European Politics* 6(4).

Drewry, Gavin (ed.), 1989. *Commons Select Committees: Catalysts for Progress.* Oxford: Oxford University Press.

Drucker, Henry, 1989. *Multi-Party Britain.* London: Macmillan.

Duff, Andrew, John Pinder and Roy Pryce (eds), 1994. *Maastricht and Beyond.* London: Routledge.

Dunleavy, Patrick and Christopher T. Husbands, 1985. *British Democracy at the Crossroads.* London: George Allen & Unwin.

——, Helen Margetts and Stuart Weir, 1992. *Replaying the 1992 General Election.* LSE Public Policy Paper No. 3. London: LSE.

—— 1987. 'Class Dealignment in Britain Revisited', *West European Politics* 10(3).

—— 1995. 'Public Response and Constitutional Significance', *Parliamentary Affairs* 48(4): 602–16.

Durant, Henry, 1969. 'Voting Behaviour in Britain 1945–66', in Richard Rose (ed.), *Studies in British Politics* (2nd edition). London: Macmillan.

Duverger, Maurice, 1954. *Political Parties.* New York John Wiley and Sons.

—— 1955. *The Political Role of Women.* Paris: UNESCO.

Edgell, Stephen and Vic Duke, 1991. *A Measure of Thatcherism.* London: HarperCollins Academic.

Esaiasson, Peter and Søren Holmberg, 1996. *Representation from Above: Members of Parliament and Representative Democracy in Sweden.* Aldershot: Dartmouth.

Eulau, Heinz and John Wahlke, 1978. *The Politics of Representation.* London: Sage.

Evans, Geoffrey and Stephen Whitefield, 1993. 'Identifying the Bases of Party Competition in Eastern Europe', *British Journal of Political Science* 23(4): 521–48.

Finer, Samuel, 1975. *Adversary Politics and Electoral Reform.* London: Wingram.

Fiorina, Morris, 1979. *Retrospective Voting in American National Elections.* New Haven, CT: Yale University Press.

Fishkin, James, 1995. *The Voice of the People: Public Opinion and Democracy.* New Haven, CT: Yale University Press.

Franklin, Bob, 1993. *Packaging Politics.* London: Edward Arnold.

Franklin, Mark, 1985. *The Decline of Class Voting in Britain.* Oxford: Clarendon Press.

——, Tom Mackie, Henry Valen et al. (eds), 1992. *Electoral Change: Responses to Evolving Social and Attitudinal Structures in Western Countries.* Cambridge: Cambridge University Press.

Fry, Michael, 1987. *Patronage and Principle.* Aberdeen: Aberdeen University Press.

Gallagher, Michael, Michael Laver and Peter Mair (eds), 1995. *Representative Government in Modern Europe* (2nd edition). New York: McGraw Hill.

Garner, Robert and Richard Kelly, 1993. *British Political Parties Today.* Manchester: Manchester University Press.

Garrett, John, 1989. *Does Parliament Work?* London: Hamish Hamilton.

Giddens, Anthony, 1990. *The Consequences of Modernity.* Cambridge: Polity Press.

Gilbert, Martin, 1988. *Winston Churchill: Never Despair, 1945–1965.* London: Houghton Mifflin.

Goldthorpe, John, 1980. *Social Mobility and the Class Structure in Modern Britain.* Oxford: Clarendon Press.

—— and Keith More, 1974. *The Social Grading of Occupations.* Oxford: Clarendon Press.

Graham, David and Peter Clarke, 1986. *The New Enlightenment: The Rebirth of Liberalism.* London: Macmillan.

Gunter, Barrie, Jane Sancho-Aldridge and Paul Winstone, 1994. *Television: The Public's View, 1993.* London: John Libbey.

—— and Michael Svennevig, 1988. *Attitudes to Broadcasting Over the Years.* London: John Libbey.

Guttsman, W. L., 1963. *The British Political Elite.* London: MacGibbon & Kee.

Hall, Stuart, 1988. *The Hard Road to Renewal.* London: Verso.

Halsey, A. H., 1995. *Change in British Society.* Oxford: Oxford University Press.

Heath, Anthony, Roger Jowell and John Curtice, 1985. *How Britain Votes.* Oxford: Oxford University Press.

—— et al., 1991. *Understanding Political Change: The British Voter 1964–1987.* Oxford: Pergamon Press.

——, Roger Jowell and John Curtice (eds), 1994. *Labour's Last Chance? The 1992 Election and Beyond.* Aldershot: Dartmouth Press.

—— and Bridget Taylor, 1996. 'British National Sentiment'. Paper presented at the Political Studies Association Annual Conference, Glasgow.

——, Geoffrey Evans and Jean Martin, 1994. 'The Measurement of Core Beliefs and Values: The Development of Balanced Socialist/Laissez faire and Libertarian/Authoritarian Scales', *British Journal of Political Science* 24(1): 115–18.

——, Roger Jowell and John Curtice, 1987. 'Trendless Fluctuations: A Reply to Crewe', *Political Studies* 35(2): 256–77.

Hennessy, Peter, 1995. *The Hidden Wiring.* London: Victor Gollancz.

Himmelweit, Hilde, P. Humphreys and M. Jaeger, 1985. *How Voters Decide* (revised edition). Milton Keynes: Open University Books.

Hogg, Quintin, Lord Hailsham of St Marylebone, 1976. *Elective Dictatorship.* London: BBC.

Hoggart, Simon and Alistair Michie, 1978. *The Pact: The Inside Story of the Lib-Lab Government, 1977–8.* London: Quartet Books.

Houghton, Lord, 1976. *Report of the Committee on Financial Aid to Political Parties*. London: HMSO.

Huntington, Samuel, 1991. *The Third Wave: Democratization in the Late Twentieth Century*. Cambridge: Cambridge University Press.

Inglehart, Ronald, 1977. *The Silent Revolution: Changing Values and Political Styles among Western Publics*. Princeton, NJ: Princeton University Press.

—— 1990. *Culture Shift in Advanced Industrial Society*. Princeton, NJ: Princeton University Press.

Iyengar, Shanto, 1991. *Is Anyone Responsible? How Television Frames Political Issues*. Chicago: University of Chicago Press.

—— and Donald Kinder, 1987. *News that Matters*. Chicago: University of Chicago Press.

Jenkins, Peter, 1987. *Mrs Thatcher's Revolution: The Ending of the Socialist Era*. London: Jonathan Cape.

Jenning, Sir Ivor, 1962. *The British Constitution*. Cambridge: Cambridge University Press.

Jennings, M. Kent and Thomas E. Mann (eds), 1994. *Elections at Home and Abroad*. Ann Arbor, MI: University of Michigan Press.

Jessop, Bob et al., 1988. *Thatcherism*. Cambridge: Polity Press.

Johnston, Ron, 1987. *Money and Votes: Constituency Campaign Spending and Election Results*. London: Croom Helm.

Johnston, R. J., 1985. *The Geography of English Politics*. London: Croom Helm.

——, C. J. Pattie and J. G. Allsop, 1986. *A Nation Dividing? The Electoral Map of Great Britain, 1979–87*. Harlow: Longman.

Jowell, Roger et al., 1984–. *British Social Attitudes*. Aldershot: Gower/Dartmouth.

Judge, David, 1993. *The Parliamentary State*. London: Sage.

—— (ed.), 1983. *The Politics of Parliamentary Reform*. London: Heinemann.

Just, Marion et al., 1996. *Crosstalk: Citizens, Candidates and the Media in a Presidential Campaign*. Chicago: University of Chicago Press.

Kaase, Max and Kenneth Newton, 1995. *Beliefs in Government*. Oxford: Oxford University Press.

Katz, Richard, 1987. *Party Governments: European and American Experiences*. Berlin: De Gruyter.

—— and Peter Mair, 1992. *Party Organizations: A Data Handbook on Party Organizations in Western Democracies 1960–90*. London: Sage.

—— and Peter Mair (eds), 1994. *How Parties Organize: Change and Adaptation in Party Organizations in Western Democracies*. London: Sage.

—— 1997. 'Roles and Representation in the European Parliament', *European Journal of Political Research*.

Kavanagh, Dennis, 1995. *The Major Effect*. London: Macmillan.

—— 1995. *Election Campaigning*. Oxford: Blackwell.

—— (ed.), 1992. *Electoral Politics*. Oxford: Clarendon Press.

—— and Peter Morris, 1989. *Consensus Politics from Attlee to Thatcher*. Oxford: Blackwell/The Institute of Contemporary History.

—— and Anthony Seldon (eds), *The Thatcher Effect: A Decade of Change*. Oxford: Oxford University Press.

—— 1994. 'Changes in Electoral Behaviour and the Party System', *Parliamentary Affairs* 47(4): 596–612.

Keith, Bruce E. et al., 1992. *The Myth of the Independent Voter*. Berkeley: University of California Press.

Kellas, James, 1989. *The Scottish Political System*. Cambridge: Cambridge University Press.

Key, V. O., 1955. 'A Theory of Critical Elections', *Journal of Politics* 17: 3–18.

King, Anthony, 1975. 'Overload: Problems of Governing in the 1970s', *Political Studies* 23(2–3): 283–96.

Kirchheimer, Otto, 1990. 'The Catch-All Party', in Peter Mair (ed.), *The West European Party System*. Oxford: Oxford University Press.

Kitschelt, Herbert, 1994. *The Transformation of European Social Democracy*. Cambridge: Cambridge University Press.

—— 1992. 'The Formation of Party Systems in East Central Europe', *Politics and Society* 20: 7–50.

Klapper, Joseph, 1960. *The Effects of Mass Communications*. New York: Free Press.

Klingemann, Hans-Dieter and Dieter Fuchs, 1995. *Citizens and the State*. Oxford: Oxford University Press.

——, Richard I. Hofferbert and Ian Budge, 1994. *Parties, Policies and Democracy*. Boulder, CO: Westview Press.

Krasner, Stephen D., 1993. 'Approaches to the State: Alternative Conceptions and Historical Dynamics', *Comparative Politics* 16(2): 223–46.

Kumar, Krishan, 1995. *From Post-Industrial to Post-Modern Society*. Oxford: Blackwell.

Layton-Henry, Zig, 1984. *The Politics of Race in Britain*. London: George Allen & Unwin.

Lazarsfeld, Paul, B. Berelson and H. Gaudet, 1944. The *People's Choice*. New York: Columbia University Press.

Leach, Steve and John Stuart, 1992. *The Politics of Hung Authorities*. London: Macmillan.

LeDuc, Lawrence, Richard G. Niemi and Pippa Norris (eds), 1996. *Comparing Democracies: Elections and Voting in Global Perspective*. Thousand Oaks, CA: Sage.

Lewis, J. and A. Townsend (eds), 1989. *The North–South Divide: Regional Change in Britain in the 1980s*. London: Paul Chapman.

Lewis-Beck, Michael, 1991. *Economics and Election: The Major Western*

Democracies. Ann Arbor, MI: University of Michigan Press.

Lijphart, Arend, 1984. *Democracies*. New Haven, CT: Yale University Press.

—— 1994. *Electoral Systems and Party Systems*. Oxford: Oxford University Press.

—— (ed.), 1992. *Parliamentary versus Presidential Government*. Oxford: Oxford University Press.

Linton, Martin and Mary Georghiou, 1993. *Labour's Road to Electoral Reform*. London: Labour Campaign for Electoral Reform.

Lippmann, Walter, 1922. *Public Opinion*. New York: Free Press.

Lipset, Seymour Martin, 1981. *Political Man: The Social Bases of Politics*. Baltimore, MD: Johns Hopkins University Press.

—— and Stein Rokkan, 1967. *Party Systems and Voter Alignments*. New York: Free Press.

Lovenduski, Joni and Vicky Randall, 1993. *Contemporary Feminist Politics: Women and Power in Britain*. Oxford: Oxford University Press.

—— and Pippa Norris (eds), 1993. *Gender and Party Politics*. London: Sage.

—— and Pippa Norris (eds), 1996. *Women in Politics*. Oxford: Oxford University Press.

—— and Pippa Norris, 1991. 'Party Rules and Women's Representation: Reforming the Labour Party Selection Process', in Ivor Crewe et al. (eds), *British Elections and Parties Yearbook, 1991*. Hemel Hempstead: Harvester Wheatsheaf.

—— and Pippa Norris, 1994. 'Labour and the Unions: After the Brighton Conference', *Government and Opposition* 29(2): 201–17.

Mair, Peter (ed.), 1990. *The West European Party System*. Oxford: Oxford University Press.

—— 1989. 'Continuity, Change and Vulnerability of Party', *Western Political Quarterly* 12: 170–85.

March, James G. and Johan P. Olsen, 1989. *Rediscovering Institutions*. New York: Free Press.

Margetts, Helen and Gareth Smyth (eds), 1994. *Turning Japanese? Britain with a Permanent Party of Government*. London: Lawrence & Wishart.

Marr, Andrew, 1992. *The Battle for Scotland*. Harmondsworth: Penguin.

—— 1995. *Ruling Britannia*. London: Michael Joseph.

Marsh, Michael and Pippa Norris, 1997. 'Political Representation in the European Parliament', *European Journal of Political Research*.

Marshall, Gordon, David Rose, Howard Newby and Carolyn Vogler, 1989. *Social Class in Modern Britain*. London: Unwin Hyman.

McAllister, Ian and Donley Studlar, 1992. 'Region and Voting in Britain, 1979-87: Territorial Polarization or Artifact?', *American Journal of Political Science* 36(1): 168–99.

McCrone, David, 1992. *Understanding Scotland: The Sociology of a Stateless*

Nation. London: Routledge.

McCullum, R. B. and Alison Readman, 1947. *The British General Election of 1945*. London: Geoffrey Cumberlege/Oxford University Press.

McKenzie, R. T., 1955. *British Political Parties*. New York: St Martin's Press.

—— and Allen Silver, 1968. *Angels in Marble*. London: Heinemann.

McQuail, Denis, 1992. *Mass Communication Theory*. London: Sage.

Merkl, Peter H., 1980. *Western European Party Systems*. New York: Free Press.

—— and Leonard Weinberg (eds), 1993. *Encounters with the Contemporary Radical Right*. Boulder, CO: Westview Press.

Miller, Warren and Donald Stokes, 1963. 'Constituency Influence in Congress', *American Political Science Review* 57: 45–56.

Miller, William, 1981. *The End of British Politics? Scots and English Political Behaviour in the Seventies*. Oxford: Clarendon Press.

—— 1991. *Media and Voters: The Audience, Contents and Influence of Press and Television at the 1987 General Election*. Oxford: Clarendon Press.

—— et al., 1990. *How Voters Change: The 1987 British Election Campaign in Perspective*. Oxford: Clarendon Press.

——, S. Tagg and Keith Britto, 'Partisanship and Party Preference in Government and Opposition: The Mid-Term Perspective', *Electoral Studies* 5: 31–46.

Milne, R. S. and H. C. Mackenzie, 1954. *Straight Fight*. London: Hansard Society.

—— and H. C. Mackenzie, 1958. *Marginal Seat*. London: Hansard Society.

Mitchell, Austin, 1995. *Election '45*. London: Fabian Society.

Muller-Rommel, Ferdinand, 1989. *The New Politics: The Rise and Success of Green Parties and Alternative Lists*. Boulder, CO: Westview Press.

Nadeau, Richard and Matthew Mendelsohn, 1994. 'Short-term Popularity Boost following Leadership Change in Great Britain', *Electoral Studies* 13(3): 222–8.

Newton, Ken, 1991. 'Do People Believe Everything they Read in the Papers?', in Ivor Crewe et al. (eds), *British Elections and Parties Yearbook, 1991*. Hemel Hempstead: Harvester Wheatsheaf.

Nicholas, H. G., 1951. *The British General Election of 1950*. London: Macmillan.

Nie, Norman, Sidney Verba, and John Petrocik, 1979. *The Changing American Voter*. Cambridge, MA: Harvard University Press.

Nieuwbeerta, Paul, 1995. *The Democratic Class Struggle in Twenty Countries, 1945–1990*. Amsterdam: Thesis Publishers.

Nolan, Lord. *Standards in Public Life: 1st Report of the Committee on Standards in Public Life*, Vol. II. London: HMSO, Cm. 2850-II.

Nordlinger, E. A., 1967. *The Working Class Tories*. London: MacGibbon & Kee.

Norpoth, Helmut, 1992. *Confidence Regained: Economics, Mrs Thatcher, and the British Voter*. Ann Arbor, MI: University of Michigan Press.

—— 1987. 'The Falklands War and Government Popularity in Britain: Rally

Without Consequence or Surge Without Decline*', *Electoral Studies* 6(1): 3–16.

Norris, Pippa, 1990. *British By-Elections: The Volatile Electorate*. Oxford: Clarendon Press.

—— (ed.), 1997. *Routes to Power: Legislative Recruitment in Advanced Democracies*. Cambridge: Cambridge University Press.

—— (ed.), 1997. *Women, Media and Politics*. New York: Oxford University Press.

—— and Joni Lovenduski, 1995. *Political Recruitment. Gender, Race and Class in the British Parliament*. Cambridge: Cambridge University Press.

—— 1995. 'The Puzzle of Constituency Service'. Paper delivered at the American Political Science Association Annual Meeting, Chicago.

—— 1996. 'Representation in England, Scotland and Wales: Boundaries and Identities for Politicians and Voters'. Paper delivered at the Political Studies Association Annual Conference, Glasgow.

—— 1991. 'Electoral Systems and Women in Legislative Elites', in Anthony Mughan and Samuel C. Patterson (eds), *Political Leadership in Democratic Societies*. Chicago: Nelson-Hall.

—— 1994. 'Women's Quotas in the Labour Party', in David Broughton et al. (eds), *British Parties and Elections Yearbook, 1994*. London: Frank Cass.

—— 1994. 'Labour Party Factionalism and Extremism', in Anthony Heath et al. (eds), *Labour's Last Chance? The 1992 Election and Beyond*. Aldershot: Dartmouth Press.

—— 1996. 'Political Communicatons in Election Campaigns: Reconsidering Media Effects', in David Farrell et al. (eds), *British Parties and Elections Yearbook, 1995*. London: Frank Cass.

—— 1996. 'Gender Realignment in Comparative Perspective', in Marian Simms (ed.), *The Future of the Australian Party System*. Melbourne: Allen and Unwin.

—— 1990. 'Thatcher's Enterprise Society and Electoral Change', *West European Politics* 13(1): 63–78.

—— 1991. 'Traditional, Revised and Radical Models of Women's Political Participation in Britain', *Government and Opposition* 26(1): 56–74.

—— 1995. 'The Politics of Electoral Reform in Britain', *International Political Science Review* 16(1): 65–78.

—— 1995. 'The Nolan Committee: Private Gain and Public Service', *Parliamentary Brief* 3(6): 40–42.

—— 1995. 'May's Law of Curvilinearity Revisited: Leaders, Officers, Members and Voters in British Political Parties', *Party Politics* 1(1): 29–47.

—— 1996. 'The Restless Searchlight: Network News Framing of the Post Cold-War World', *Political Communication* 12(4): 357–70.

—— 1996. 'Did Television Erode Social Capital? A Reply to Putnam', *PS: Political Science and Politics*. September.

—— 1996. 'Conservatism in Disarray?', *The Brown International Journal of World Affairs* III(1): 163–9.

—— 1996. 'Mobilizing the Women's Vote: The Gender–Generation Gap in Voting Behaviour', *Parliamentary Affairs* 49(2): 333–42.

—— 1996. 'Women Politicians: Transforming Westminster?', *Parliamentary Affairs* 49(1): 89–102.

—— and Ivor Crewe, 1994. 'Did the British Marginals Vanish? Proportionality and Exaggeration in the British Electoral System Revisited', *Electoral Studies* 13(3): 201–21.

—— and Mark Franklin, 1997. 'Social Representation in the European Parliament', *European Journal of Political Research*.

—— and Joni Lovenduski, 1993. '"If only more candidates came forward . . .": Supply-side Explanations of Candidate Selection in Britain', *British Journal of Political Science* 23: 373–408

——, Elizabeth Vallance and Joni Lovenduski, 1992. 'Do Candidates Make a Difference?: Gender, Race, Ideology and Incumbency', *Parliamentary Affairs* 496–517.

Norton, Philip, 1975. *Dissension in the House of Commons, 1945–1974*. London: Macmillan.

—— 1980. *Dissension in the House of Commons, 1974–79*. Oxford: Clarendon Press.

—— 1993. *Does Parliament Matter?* Hemel Hempstead: Harvester Wheatsheaf.

—— (ed.), 1985. *Parliament in the 1980s*. Oxford: Basil Blackwell.

—— (ed.), 1990. *Legislatures*. Oxford: Oxford University Press.

—— and David Wood, 1993. *Back from Westminster: British Members of Parliament and their Constituents*. Lexington, KY: University Press of Kentucky.

Ostrogorski, Moisei, 1902. *Democracy and the Organisation of Political Parties*. London: Macmillan.

Parker, Richard, 1995. *Mixed Signals*. New York: Twentieth Century Fund.

Parry, Geraint, George Moyser and Neil Day, 1992. *Political Participation and Democracy in Britain*. Cambridge: Cambridge University Press.

Paterson, Lindsay, 1994. *The Autonomy of Modern Scotland*. Edinburgh: University of Edinburgh Press.

Paterson, Tom, 1993. *Out of Order*. New York: Vintage.

Pedersen, Morgens, 1979. 'The Dynamics of European Party Systems: Changing Patterns of Electoral Volatility', *European Journal of Political Research* 7: 1–27.

Pelling, Henry, 1958. *The British Communist Party*. New York: Macmillan.

Pempel, T. J. *Uncommon Democracies*. Ithaca, NY: Cornell University Press.

Phillips, Anne, 1993. *Democracy and Difference*. Pennsylvania, PA: University of Pennsylvania Press.

Pimlott, Ben and Chris Cook (eds), 1991. *Trade Unions in British Politics* (2nd edition). London: Longman.

Pinto-Duschinsky, Michael, 1981. *British Political Finances, 1830–1980.* Washington, DC: AEI Press.

Popkin, Samuel L., 1994. *The Reasoning Voter.* Chicago: University of Chicago Press.

Price, Robert and George Sayers Bain, 1988. 'The Labour Force', in A. H. Halsey, *British Social Trends since 1900.* London: Macmillan.

Pulzer, Peter G. J., 1967. *Political Representation and Elections in Britain.* London: George Allen & Unwin.

Punnett, Malcolm, 1968. *British Government and Politics.* London: Heinemann.

—— 1992. *Selecting the Party Leader: Britain in Comparative Perspective.* London: Harvester Wheatsheaf.

Putnam, Robert, 1995. 'Tuning In, Tuning Out: The Strange Disappearance of Social Capital in America', *PS: Political Science and Politics* 28(4): 664–83.

Pyper, Robert and Lynton Robins (eds), 1995. *Governing the UK in the 1990s.* New York: St Martin's Press.

Rae, Douglas, 1967. *The Political Consequences of Electoral Laws.* New Haven, CT: Yale University Press.

Rallings, Colin and Michael Thrasher, 1994. *Local Elections in Britain: A Statistical Digest.* Plymouth: Local Government Chronicle Elections Centre.

Ranney, Austin, 1962. *The Doctrine of Responsible Party Government.* Urbana, IL: University of Illinois Press.

Reid, Ivan, 1989. *Social Class Differences in Britain*, 3rd edition. London: Fontana Books.

Rentoul, John, 1989. *Me and Mine: The Triumph of the New Individualism?* London: Unwin Hyman.

Riddell, Peter, 1989. *The Thatcher Decade.* Oxford: Blackwell.

—— 1993. *Honest Opportunism: The Rise of the Career Politician.* London: Hamish Hamilton.

Robertson, David, 1976. *A Theory of Party Competition.* London: John Wiley and Sons.

—— 1984. *Class and the British Electorate.* Oxford: Basil Blackwell.

Robins, Lynton, Hilary Blackmore and Robert Pyper (eds), 1994. *Britain's Changing Party System.* Leicester: Leicester University Press.

Rose Richard, 1967. *Influencing Voters.* London: Faber & Faber.

—— 1969. *Studies in British Politics.* London: Macmillan.

—— 1974. *Electoral Behaviour.* New York: Free Press.

—— 1978. *The Problem of Party Government.* London: Macmillan.

—— 1980. *Politics in England.* Boston: Little Brown.

—— 1984. *Do Parties Make a Difference?* Chatham, NJ: Chatham House.

—— and Phillip L. Davies, 1994. *Inheritance in Public Policy: Change Without Choice in Britain.* New Haven, CT: Yale University Press.

—— and Ian McAllister, 1986. *Voters Begin to Choose*. London: Sage.

—— and Ian McAllister, 1990. *The Loyalties of Voters*. London: Sage.

—— and Derek Urwin, 1975. *Regional Differentiation and Political Unity in Western Nations*. Beverly Hills, CA: Sage.

—— 1995. 'A Crisis of Confidence in British Party Leaders?', *Contemporary Record* 9(2): 273–93.

—— and Derek Urwin, 1970. 'Persistence and Change in Western Party Systems since 1945', *Political Studies* 18: 287–319.

Ross, F. S., 1955. *Elections and Electors*. London: Eyre & Spottiswoode.

Runciman, W. G., 1966. *Relative Deprivation and Social Justice*. London: Routledge & Kegan Paul.

Rush, Michael (ed.), 1990. *Parliament and Pressure Politics*. Oxford: Oxford University Press.

Saggar, Shamit, 1992. *Race and Politics in Britain*. Hemel Hempstead: Harvester Wheatsheaf.

Sanders, David, 1995. 'Forecasting Political Preferences and Election Outcomes in the UK: Experiences, Problems and Prospects for the Next General Election', *Electoral Studies* 14(3): 251–72.

—— and Simon Price, 1994. 'Party Support and Economic Perceptions in the UK, 1979–87', in David Broughton et al., *British Elections and Parties Yearbook, 1994*. London: Frank Cass.

——, Hugh Ward and David Marsh, 1991. 'Macroeconomics, the Falklands War and the Popularity of the Thatcher Government: A Contrary View', in Helmut Norpoth, Michael Lewis-Beck and Jean-Dominique Lafray (eds), *Economics and Politics*. Ann Arbor, MI: University of Michigan Press.

Sarlvik, Bo and Ivor Crewe, 1983. *Decade of Dealignment: The Conservative Victory of 1979 and Electoral Trends in the 1970s*. Cambridge: Cambridge University Press.

Sartori, Giovanni, 1976. *Parties and Party Systems*. Cambridge: Cambridge University Press.

—— 1994. *Comparative Constitutional Engineering*. London: Macmillan.

Scammell, Margaret, 1995. *Designer Politics: How Elections are Won*. London: Macmillan.

Schattschneider, E. E., 1942. *Party Government*. New York: Farrar and Reinhart.

—— 1948. *The Struggle for Party Government*. College Park, MD: University of Maryland.

Schumpeter, Joseph, 1942. *Capitalism, Socialism and Democracy*. New York: Harper & Row.

Seldon, Anthony and Stuart Ball (eds), 1996. *Conservative Century: The Conservative Party since 1900*. Oxford: Oxford University Press.

Sepstrep, Preben, 1990. *Transnationalization of Television in Western Europe*.

London: Academic Research Monographs.

Sewell, Terri, 1993. *Black Tribunes: Black Political Participation in Britain.* London: Lawrence and Wishart.

Seyd, Patrick, 1987. *The Rise and Fall of the Labour Left.* London: Macmillan.

—— and Paul Whiteley, 1992. *Labour's Grass Roots: The Politics of Party Membership.* Oxford: Clarendon Press.

Seymour-Ure, Colin, 1996. *The British Press and Broadcasting since 1945* (2nd edition). Oxford: Blackwell.

Shaw, Eric, 1988. *Discipline and Discord in the Labour Party.* Manchester: Manchester University Press.

—— 1994. *The Labour Party since 1979.* London: Routledge.

—— 1996. *The Labour Party since 1945.* Oxford: Blackwell/The Institute of Contemporary British History.

Shell, Donald and D. Beamish (eds), 1993. *The House of Lords at Work.* Oxford: Oxford University Press.

Silj, Alessandro, 1992. *The New Television in Europe.* London: John Libby.

Silk, Paul, and Rhodri Walters, 1995. *How Parliament Works.* London: Longman.

Shafer, Byron (ed.), 1991. *The End of Realignment.* Wisconsin: The University of Wisconsin Press.

Smith, David, 1989. *North and South.* Harmondsworth: Penguin.

Smith, Eric, R.A.N., 1989. *The Unchanging American Voter.* Berkeley, CA: University of California Press.

Smith, Martin J. and Joanna Spear, 1992. *The Changing Labour Party.* London: Routledge.

Social Trends, 1995. London: HMSO.

Solomos, John, 1989. *Race and Racism in Contemporary Britain.* London: Macmillan.

Steel, David, 1979. *A House Divided: The Lib–Lab Pact and the Future of British Politics.* London: Weidenfeld and Nicolson.

Steinmo, Sven et al. (eds), 1994. *Structuring Politics.* New York: Cambridge University Press.

Stevenson, John, 1993. *Third Party Politics since 1945.* Oxford: Blackwell/Institute for Contemporary British History.

Strom, Kaare, 1990. *Minority Government and Majority Rule.* New York: Cambridge University Press.

Studlar, Donley, 1996. *Great Britain: Decline or Renewal?* Boulder, CO: Westview Press.

—— and Ian McAllister, 1987. 'Protest and Survive? Alliance Support in the 1983 British General Election', *Political Studies.*

Swanson, David L. and Paolo Mancini, 1996. *Politics, Media and Modern Democracy.* New York: Praeger.

Thayer, G., 1965. *The British Political Fringe*. London: A. Blonde.

Thomas, J. A., 1939. *The House of Commons, 1832–1901*. Wales: University of Wales Press.

Thomas, Sue, 1994. *How Women Legislate*. New York: Oxford University Press.

Thomassen, Jacques and Hermann Schmitt, 1997. 'Political Representation in the European Parliament', *European Journal of Political Research*.

Touraine, Alain, 1969. *La Société Post-Industrielle*. Paris: Denoel.

Trenaman, Joseph and Denis McQuail, 1961. *Television and the Political Image*. London: Methuen.

Vicker, Ray, 1962. *How an Election Was Won*. Chicago: Henry Regnery.

Vickers, J. and G. Yarrow, 1988. *Privatisation: An Economic Aspect*. Cambridge, MA: MIT Press.

Vowles, Jack, 1995. 'The Politics of Electoral Reform in New Zealand', *International Political Science Review* 16(1): 95–116.

Wald, Kenneth D., 1983. *Crosses on the Ballot: Patterns of British Voter Alignments since 1885*. Princeton, NJ: Princeton University Press.

Ware, Alan, 1996. *Political Parties and Party Systems*. Oxford: Oxford University Press.

Weakliem, David L., 1995. 'Two Models of Class Voting', *British Journal of Political Science* 25(2): 254–70.

Whiteley, Paul, Patrick Seyd and Jeremy Richardson, 1994. *True Blues*. Oxford: Oxford University Press.

Wright, Erik Olin et al., 1989. *The Debate on Classes*. London: Verso.

Zaller, John, 1993. *The Nature and Origins of Mass Opinion*. Cambridge: Cambridge University Press.

Index